JAPAN'S ECONOMIC EXPANSION

Japan's Economic Expansion

G. C. ALLEN

Professor of Political Economy in the
University of London

Issued under the auspices of the
Royal Institute of International Affairs

OXFORD UNIVERSITY PRESS
LONDON   NEW YORK   TORONTO
1965

Oxford University Press, Amen House, London, E.C.4

GLASGOW NEW YORK TORONTO MELBOURNE WELLINGTON
BOMBAY CALCUTTA MADRAS KARACHI LAHORE DACCA
CAPE TOWN SALISBURY NAIROBI IBADAN ACCRA
KUALA LUMPUR HONG KONG

To

MY FORMER COLLEAGUES AND PUPILS

at the

NAGOYA KOTO SHOGYO GAKKO
(*now the Department of Economics, Nagoya University*)

Contents

Abbreviations*

EPA:	Economic Planning Agency.
IPR:	Institute of Pacific Relations.
Japan Statist. Yb.:	Prime Minister's Office, *Japan Statistical Yearbook*.
Orient. Econ.:	*Oriental Economist*.

---

* Excluding those which are either self-evident or are in common usage (e.g. *J.* for *Journal*, *B.* for *Bulletin*, etc).

Preface

CONTEMPORARY Japan stands before the world as the classic model of a rapidly growing economy, and her success has earned for her the admiration or envy of advanced and underdeveloped countries alike. In this book I seek to describe and explain the process of development in agriculture, industry, finance, and trade since the time when the economy lay in ruins at the end of the Second World War. I discuss economic policy, planning, labour problems, and education. I attempt to analyse the factors mainly responsible for what is generally recognized as an extraordinary achievement, and I consider whether the rate of growth is likely to be maintained.

My purpose is to carry further the task that I began in *Japan's Economic Recovery*, published in 1958. When that book was being written the economy had already recovered from the effects of war and defeat, but the great expansion still lay ahead. During the last eight years Japan has moved to a new plane of accomplishment, and some of the most familiar features of her economic life have been transformed. In preparing a new edition, therefore, I could not content myself merely with supplementing my earlier description of events nor with modifying my interpretation of them. A reassessment of the facts and a much more detailed analysis of causes were required. For this reason, although the present book preserves the same general structure as its predecessor, a great part of it, outside the sections that provide the historical background or the narrative of early post-war events, is entirely new. In *Japan's Economic Recovery* I was much concerned with the differences (and identities) in the organization and functioning of the economy between pre-war and post-war times. Such comparisons and contrasts are still illuminating, for it is difficult to understand the changes of the last decade without knowledge of what went before. But in the present book my attention is directed particularly towards the new phase of economic development upon which Japan now seems to be entering, and towards the unfamiliar problems which are beginning to perplex her.

During a visit to Japan in the spring of 1963 I was able, as on previous visits, to gather documentary material, to inspect industrial establishments, and to discuss policies and problems with civil servants, economists, and businessmen. I am grateful to those who so readily helped me. If I cannot name them all here, this must be blamed on the number of my benefactors and not on any failure on my part to recognize their kindness. There are some to whom I am especially indebted. Mr S. Okita, now Executive Director of the Japan Economic Research Centre, not merely gave me the benefit of his own wide knowledge of recent economic developments, but also went to much trouble to ensure that I should meet civil servants, bankers, industrialists, economists, and others who were well informed about Japan's affairs. I must also express my deep obligation to Mr Y. Kawashima, who, on this as on a previous visit, helped me to draw up my programme of inquiry and accompanied me at many interviews. Another old friend, Mr A. Morikawa, brought to my notice a number of significant economic changes, and both he and Mr S. Kawamura of Teijin greatly contributed to the success of my visit.

Among civil servants, the Director and staff of the Economic Planning Agency were very helpful, and I remember particularly several stimulating conversations with Mr T. Shishido. I must also thank Dr Shimomura of the Prime Minister's Office, Mr J. Okabe and Mr Omiya of the Ministry of Labour, Mr Matsumura and Mr N. Maeda of the Ministry of International Trade and Industry, Mr Yamashita of the Ministry of Agriculture, and Mr Sakane of the Fair Trade Commission. Mr T. Yoshino and Mr K. Suzuki of the Bank of Japan explained to me the present-day monetary policy, and Mr Miyashita and Mr J. Kano of the Japan Development Bank, Mr K. Sano of the Mitsui Bank, Mr S. Kurebayashi of the Fuji Bank, and Mr T. Ihara of the Bank of Yokohama, informed me about other financial problems. The officials and members of the Japan Economic Research Institute and of the Japan Institute of Labour were also helpful, and I benefited from discussions with the economists of the Hitotsubashi University.

Professor S. Sakai, Professor T. Shionoya, and my former colleagues and pupils at what is now Nagoya University arranged some instructive visits to industrial establishments in Aichi Prefecture. In this connexion I am particularly indebted to Mr S.

Nass, the indefatigable secretary of the *Kitankai* (the Old Students' Association of the former Nagoya Koto Shogyo Gakko) for his part in these arrangements, and also to the President, the Senior Managing Director, and other officials of the Tokai Bank for their generous hospitality during my visit to Nagoya. At Kobe Professor S. Fujii and his colleagues guided me on a tour of factories in their neighbourhood, as did Professor R. Ichihara of Kwansai University. I am heavily indebted to the industrialists and members of their staff who spent their time so generously in discussion or in showing me round their plants. I cannot name them all and it would be invidious to select a few. I am also grateful to Mr S. Matsumoto, the Director of The International House of Japan and to his staff for the invaluable help which they gave me during the whole period of my stay in Tokyo. Finally, I must express my thanks to the Trustees of the Houblon-Norman Fund for a contribution towards the expenses of my visit to Japan.

My wife has helped me at every stage in preparing this book for publication.

University College London G. C. A.
September 1964

CORRIGENDA

...e 20. *For* familiar *read* unfamiliar.

...able 1 line 2 of the first footnote. *For* 1963 *read* 1...

275. Table 17 (b). The last date in column 1 should ...
1962.

I

Economic Development in the 1930s

BETWEEN the World Depression of 1929–31 and the outbreak of the Sino-Japanese War in 1937, Japan passed through a period of exceptionally rapid economic growth. In manufacturing industry her progress was especially remarkable. She demonstrated her command of new skills and technologies. She made extensive additions to her capital equipment at home and she invested heavily in regions beyond her own shores. At a time when international trade as a whole was stagnating, her exports flourished. In a wide range of products and in a diversity of markets she became a formidable competitor of the older industrial countries of the West, while to the countries of Asia she made available a variety of consumption goods at prices which their impoverished inhabitants could afford to pay. These remarkable achievements were not, of course, fortuitous. The ground had been prepared for many previous decades. Those who presided over economic policy at critical moments had been bold and far-sighted, and in the middle 1930s Japan at last began to gather the harvest of her enterprise.

We are not concerned here to trace the course of the country's economic history during the modern era nor to describe in detail the work of preparation;[1] but we must at least refer briefly to the outstanding economic events of the years which immediately preceded the period of industrial expansion. These years gave little promise of the prosperity to come. From 1927, when there was a serious financial crisis, until the end of 1931 Japan passed through a period of economic stress. In the first part of that period she was engaged in a struggle to eliminate inflationary forces from her economy in preparation for her return to the gold standard at pre-war parity to the pound and dollar. In January 1930 she effected this return even though her prices had not fallen sufficiently to justify it. The moment was particularly ill

---

[1] For a comprehensive study of Japan's economic development see W. W. Lockwood, *The Economic Development of Japan* (1954); for a briefer review see G. C. Allen, *A Short Economic History of Modern Japan* (1962).

chosen, for the World Depression had just begun. The yen would probably have been overvalued on the exchanges even if world prices had not collapsed by that time. As it was, the Japanese government felt itself obliged to resort to a still more rigorous deflationary policy in an attempt to follow world prices on their downward course and so make possible continued adherence to the gold standard. Consequently the economy suffered from an intense depression. The decline in industrial production and in the volume of manufactured exports was comparatively slight, although in value the fall was steep.[2] It was in agriculture that the deterioration was most conspicuous. The peasants of modern Japan had come to depend increasingly for their well-being on the export trade in raw silk, from the production of which they derived much of their cash income, and they had been among the chief beneficiaries of 'American prosperity'. The depression brought a sudden fall in the American demand, with the result that silk prices collapsed. While the cash incomes of the silk raisers were diminished, the indirect effect on family incomes was also serious. Many members of the peasant families, having lost their employment in the silk-reeling mills or in other textile establishments, returned to the farms only to contribute to the mounting distress.

These domestic difficulties were accompanied by tensions in international economic relations. The decline in the value of raw-silk exports, which accounted for two-fifths of the total exports to foreign countries in 1929, upset the balance of payments and led to a shrinkage in the monetary reserves. International troubles in turn reacted on the domestic economy, for every effort on the part of Finance Minister Inouye to restore equilibrium by the dogged pursuit of an orthodox deflationary policy intensified the industrial depression and the social *malaise*. The crisis arrived when in September 1931 the United Kingdom and other Western countries abandoned the gold standard. The competitive position of Japan was at once weakened and any possibility of maintaining the yen on gold was removed.

The period ended in a political upheaval—provoked in part by the economic troubles—and the government which took office towards the end of 1931 hastened to throw over the gold

[2] The index of industrial production for Japan fell from 100 in 1929, to 95 in 1930, and to 92 in 1931. The corresponding figures for the US were 100, 83, and 68.

standard. The yen was allowed to decline to its equilibrium level, a considerable fall even in terms of depreciated sterling. At the same time the deflationary policy was abandoned in favour of reflation. Government expenditure, financed to a large extent by borrowing, was much increased, and easy credit conditions were instituted by the monetary authorities. The direction of the new government expenditure and the character of the additional investment were determined largely by the military clique, who were intent upon large-scale rearmament and the development of strategic industries in Manchuria. But Takahashi, the Finance Minister who succeeded Inouye, was by no means a cat's-paw of the militarists. His policy of reflation and theirs of rearmament were in general alignment up to a point; but while he aimed at increasing effective demand to the extent needed to restore 'full employment' (as we should now say), he was not prepared to allow loan-financed government expenditure to rise beyond the point at which inflation would set in. Consequently, a conflict between him and the military cliques was bound to arise sooner or later, for when the unemployed resources of Japan had been called into use (at any rate to the point at which bottle-necks were encountered), Takahashi would hold that reflation had been pressed far enough, whereas the military, who were concerned only with securing the resources necessary for their strategic designs, recognized no such limit. The crisis came in February 1936 when the military revolted against the government and assassinated Takahashi, by then the arch-opponent of their policy.

The year of Takahashi's assassination was the year of the publication of *The General Theory of Employment, Interest and Money*. For the previous four years Takahashi had successfully practised, without benefit of Keynes, a policy in full accord with what was soon to become the new economic orthodoxy. In the light of the new theory as well as of practical experience the deflationary policy of Takahashi's predecessors may seem wrong-headed and even pernicious. Yet such downright condemnation would scarcely be justified. There are reasons for thinking that no small part of the economic progress achieved during Takahashi's régime can be attributed to foundations laid in the years immediately before 1932. During the harsh conditions of that period, inefficiencies were weeded out, improved methods were widely adopted, and productivity in the manufacturing trades rose steeply. The discipline of the deflationary years was a necessary prelude to the progress achieved under the 'full-employment' policy.

A complete assessment of Takahashi's and Inouye's work cannot, of course, ignore the political and social consequences of economic policy; but neither side in this financial controversy can draw much comfort from Japan's experience. The social pressures exerted by deflation helped to produce a successful revolt against parliamentary government and to strengthen the political influence of the military cliques. The 'full-employment' policy meant lavish provision for the militarists' appetite, and this ultimately could have only one result. The Japanese term used to describe the economy of the Takahashi period, *junsenji keizai*, means literally 'quasi wartime economy'; this, says a recent writer on the period—perhaps not without irony—is the 'equivalent in modern economic terminology . . . of full employment induced by deficit financing'.[3] In other words, if deflation ended in political reaction, reflation ended in war.

There is room for controversy over the leading causes of Japan's economic expansion, but there can be no doubt about the facts. With these this chapter is mainly concerned, and it is convenient to begin with a description in outline of the industrial growth. The most striking fact of all is the rise in the quantity of output. All the estimates agree that this rise was very considerable. The index of industrial production given in the *Statistical Year Book* of the League of Nations shows a fall from 100 in 1929 to 92 in 1931 and then a rapid and uninterrupted rise to 151 in 1936 and 171 in 1937. This immense increase in output took place during a period in which production in the United States failed to regain the level of 1929; in the United Kingdom it increased, between 1929 and 1937, by less than 25 per cent.

Nearly all Japanese industries shared in this general advance, but it was the capital-goods industries that grew most rapidly. The result was a striking change in the composition of industry. Textiles, to which Japan had been very highly specialized during the 1920s, diminished in importance. On the other hand, there was a marked relative growth in the metal, engineering, and chemical industries, which had previously played a minor role

[3] J. B. Cohen, *Japan's Economy in War and Reconstruction* (1949), p. 9.

in Japan's economy. The *Factory Statistics*, which cover an important part, though by no means the whole, of Japan's manufacturing industry, show that in 1929 textiles accounted for over 55 per cent of total factory employment, and metals, engineering goods, and chemicals for just under 25 per cent. In 1937 the respective proportions were 37 and 43 per cent.[4] The various indices of industrial production point to the same conclusion. Between 1930 and 1937, while the index for consumption goods rose from 100 to 154, that for investment goods rose from 100 to 264. The increase in the output of the latter class was accompanied by a wide extension in the range of products turned out by the metal, engineering, and chemical industries. Whereas in the 1920s Japan had relied heavily upon imports of machinery to equip her manufacturing industries, by 1937 she was able herself to construct most of the plants that she required, including textile machinery, many kinds of machine tools, scientific instruments, and electrical appliances. By then she was capable of meeting her needs for complete power-station plants. She had become largely self-sufficient in the chief chemical products.[5]

This advance in the capital-goods industries was achieved without any absolute contraction in textiles. It is true that in the middle 1930s both output and employment in silk reeling were still less than in the late 1920s. But raw silk was the only large industry that suffered an absolute decline. Among other textiles there was not only a substantial rise in output but also a widening of the range of products. The cotton industry secured a steadily increasing proportion of world trade. The woollen and worsted industry, which was small before 1929, expanded and new branches of the trade, such as the manufacture of woollen cloth and worsted fabrics for Western-style dress, grew especially fast. The rayon industry was in a very early stage of development in 1929. By 1937 Japan was the leading producer of continuous filament in the world and she also had a large output of staple fibre. Other branches of manufacture, such as the well-established pottery trade, and a number of miscellaneous-goods industries engaged in the production of toys, rubber shoes, hosiery, and

---

[4] These figures cover operatives and clerical staff employed in factories with five or more employees. They are for private industry only.

[5] For a detailed study of industrial developments during the 1930s see E. B. Schumpeter, ed., *The Industrialization of Japan and Manchukuo* (1941).

metal smallwares made a notable expansion. The fuel and power trades also grew. The output of coal rose by nearly one-third between 1930 and 1937 and electricity generating capacity by about two-thirds. By the end of 1936 there were probably about 8 million persons engaged in the mining and manufacturing industries, compared with under 6 millions in 1930.[6] In spite of the large rural population, the contribution of manufacturing industry to the national income in 1937 was more than twice that of agriculture.[7] In other words, by that time Japan could claim to be an industrialized State. This gave her a unique position in Asia. The industrial production of Japan in 1936–7 was probably nearly twice that of the whole of the rest of Asia (excluding the Soviet Union).

All these estimates apply to Japan Proper (that is, the four main islands of Honshu, Kyushu, Shikoku, and Hokkaido, together with the adjacent small islands and Southern Saghalien). On the continent of Asia, especially in Korea and in the newly constituted state of Manchukuo, and also in Formosa, Japan had other achievements to her credit. In Formosa the industrial development was almost entirely limited to the food-processing industries, especially sugar refining. In Korea plants for the production of electrical goods, paper, cement, vegetable oils, iron and steel, and non-ferrous metals were operated by Japanese concerns. In that colony mineral resources were widely exploited and there was a large production of hydro-electric power. The major developments on the continent, however, occurred in Manchuria.

Before the Japanese seized control of that country in 1931 agriculture had been the predominant activity, and mining and manufacturing were mostly confined to the South Manchuria Railway zone, and to the Kwantung Leased Territory. With the foundation of Manchukuo, Japan poured capital into the country and set going a process of rapid industrial development. By the outbreak of the Sino-Japanese War in 1937, a number of heavy industries—coal- and ore-mining, iron and steel production, chemical manufacturing, and electricity generating—were firmly established, and the foundations had been laid for

---

[6] *Statist. Yb. Japan. Emp.* (various issues), and Orient. Econ., *Japan in 1938*, p. 19. Includes about 1 m. in building.

[7] Cohen, *Japan's Economy*, p. 6.

the great expansion that occurred during the next few years. Most of the semi-products were sent to finishing factories in Japan, and the Manchurian industries thus formed an integral part of Japan's economy.[8]

Even outside the territories under her political administration, Japan owned and operated many important industrial undertakings. In the development of the Chinese cotton industry, her capital and entrepreneurship took the lead after the First World War and by 1937 nearly half the spindleage was under her control.[9] She had interests in many other manufacturing establishments in China Proper as well as in coal- and iron-mining. Her enterprise was also found much farther afield, for example, in Indonesia and Malaya, where she had mining properties.

The enlargement of Japan's economic activities both at home and overseas was accompanied by continuous improvements in industrial methods. In the older industries (cotton and silk textiles and pottery) productivity increased most rapidly between 1927 and 1931 when costs were under pressure. In the newer trades (rayon, chemicals, metals, and engineering) the chief advances occurred after 1931, during the period of reflation. The progress came about partly through additions to capital equipment and partly through the more efficient organization of plants and processes.

The agricultural sector of Japan's economy was very differently affected. For the farmers there was no complete recovery from the conditions of the early 1930s. The prices of rice and of most other agricultural products remained low. The failure of silk prices to regain their pre-depression levels meant that cash incomes from the sale of cocoons were comparatively small and fewer opportunities than hitherto were available for employment in the reeling mills. The depressed conditions in the countryside compelled members of farming families to seek employment outside agriculture, some in large factories but the majority in the service trades or in the small workshops which still accounted for a high proportion of the output of most industrial goods. This large supply of labour in search of employment enabled manufacturing industry in general to increase its

[8] Cf. F. C. Jones, *Manchuria since 1931* (1941), pp. 10, 154–5, and *passim*.
[9] G. C. Allen and A. G. Donnithorne, *Western Enterprise in Far Eastern Economic Development: China and Japan* (1954), pp. 175–7.

manpower without raising wages. Indeed, the flow of recruits
from the countryside into manufacture is the key not only to the
growth of industrial employment during the 1930s, but also to
the movement of wages and prices during that time. Although
real wages increased in the heavy industries during the period of
recovery after 1932, they actually fell in the textile industry and
in many other consumption-goods trades. Over industry as a
whole they were probably rather lower in 1936 than they had
been in 1929.[10]

Japan's experience was not, of course, unique. In all countries
with large agricultural interests the catastrophic fall in the prices
of primary products during the World Depression brought grave
hardships, and in all of them attempts were made to divert resources to the production of those types of manufactured goods
which the people could no longer afford to import. But Japan
was one of the few countries that achieved an outstanding success
in the pursuit of this policy. Her achievement is to be explained
partly by the fact that she had already laid the foundations for
extensive industrial developments and partly because she deliberately pursued a monetary policy favourable to such a redistribution of her resources. It is true that in the period now
under review the policy did not succeed in relieving the farmers
from their economic distress, but it certainly mitigated the effects
of the rural depression.

The industrialization of the 1930s was achieved without
leading to significantly greater dependence on overseas supplies
of food. The fisheries furnished most of the animal foodstuffs
consumed in Japan as well as large exports. Four-fifths of the
total consumption of rice was still home-produced, and most of
the rest came from Korea and Formosa. These colonies, together
with Manchuria which was the source of soya-bean imports,
also supplied the greater part of such other foodstuffs as were
not produced by Japanese farms and fisheries. The net import
of food from foreign countries was very small.[11] This condition
of imperial self-sufficiency in foodstuffs had not been disturbed
by the immense growth in the population of Japan Proper from
60 millions in 1925 to 69 millions in 1935. But it was otherwise
with the industrial raw materials which the expanding industries

[10] Cf. T. Uyeda, *The Small Industries of Japan* (1938), pp. 297 ff.; see also p. 10 below.
[11] There was a large import of wheat but this was balanced by exports of flour.

required in ever-growing quantities. Most of these materials had to be imported for, apart from fuel and power, timber, and materials for raw silk, Japan possessed only small domestic resources. Practically all the cotton, wool, mineral oil, iron ore, and most non-ferrous ores had to be obtained from abroad, and domestic supplies even of wood pulp, chemical raw materials, and coal were insufficient for the needs of industry.

The empire's contribution to Japan's need for minerals and textile raw materials was comparatively small. It is true that the countries which afterwards comprised the 'yen bloc' (namely China and Manchuria, together with the colonies) supplied Japan in 1936 with more than a third of her total imports, and that the relative importance of the area as a source of imports steadily increased throughout the 1930s, largely as the result of deliberate policy.[12] But the imports were mainly foodstuffs. Even at the end of the decade Japan still remained dependent on distant foreign sources of supply for the greater part of her industrial raw materials. This reliance upon areas outside her political control might have strategic disadvantages, but it could hardly be regarded as a serious economic weakness during a period in which the conditions for multilateral trading were still reasonably well satisfied. So long as the world remained at peace, the only danger lay in the deliberate creation of obstacles to Japan's enterprise in the export markets. During the 1930s a number of countries tried to weaken her competition by raising tariffs or imposing quota restrictions on her goods. These obstacles no doubt worsened Japan's terms of trade, but during that decade they certainly did not arrest the expansion of her exports, for while the import trade increased in volume between 1929 and 1937 by only about one-third, the volume of exports grew by about three-quarters.[13] This was a remarkable expansion in a period in which international trade in general was stagnant, and it explains why Japanese competition was so greatly feared by foreign producers. Moreover, whereas before the World Depression about two-fifths of Japan's exports consisted of a commodity which did not compete with the products of her chief commercial rivals, in 1936 this commodity (raw silk) accounted for only 15 per cent of the exports. Its place had been

[12] Cf. S. Okita, *Japan's Trade with Asia* (1954), p. 2.
[13] League of Nations, *Review of World Trade, 1937*, p. 41. Excludes colonial trade.

taken by manufactured goods. The detailed changes in the composition of the export trade and in the chief markets between 1929 and 1937 will be considered in Chapter XII.

The fact that exports during these years grew much faster than imports requires an explanation. Briefly it is as follows. Japan's balance of payments was adverse in 1929, and from then until 1932 large exports of gold were needed to meet the deficit on current trading. The fall in the yen during 1932 helped to produce an equilibrium, but it worsened the terms of trade. A similar influence was subsequently exerted by the discriminatory restrictions imposed by foreign governments on Japanese goods. By 1936 the terms of trade had deteriorated by about 30 per cent as compared with the pre-depression period.[14] Although the fact that the Japanese were obliged to exchange more manufactures for a given quantity of raw materials does not mean that they were to that extent worse off (since productivity in manufactures had greatly increased in the interval), these circumstances nevertheless account for a considerable part of the discrepancy noted above. Further, it must be remembered that Japan was investing heavily abroad, mainly in Manchuria. Part of her export surplus on her current trading was required to implement this investment.

The worsened terms of trade and the industrial investment programme, together with the rise in population and heavy armament expenditure, explain the failure of the standard of life to improve during a period in which output substantially increased.[15] That the standard of life of the masses in fact failed to rise is borne out both by statistical data and by the observation of contemporaries. The cost of living seems to have risen faster than money earnings during the years of recovery, with the result that the index of real earnings in the first half of 1937 was about 10 per cent below the index for 1931 and was scarcely equal to that for 1929. Although the significance of this statistical measure is affected by the fact that there was a large increase in the number of new recruits to industry during this time, it was

[14] Allen, *Short Economic History*, p. 140.
[15] It has been argued that, despite this deterioration in the terms of trade, the continued rise in exports, through its multiplier effect, substantially increased employment and output and so helped to accelerate domestic economic growth (see M. Shinohara, 'Economic Development and Foreign Trade in Pre-War Japan', in C. D. Cowan, ed., *The Economic Development of China and Japan* (1964), p. 244).

concluded by a Japanese economist, highly regarded for his sound judgement, that the unsatisfactory tendency disclosed by these figures must be accepted.[16]

Averages obscure divergent movements in particular trades, and they are liable to give a misleading view of economic trends unless they are supplemented by detailed figures. During this period there is no doubt that experienced and skilled men in the engineering and shipbuilding industries greatly improved their real earnings. But the female textile operatives were worse off in 1936 and 1937 than they had been in 1929, except perhaps those who worked in large mills where substantial semi-annual bonuses were paid during the recovery period. The real earnings of men in the rubber, wood, pottery, and food and drink trades also declined. On the farms it is certain that standards fell. This was especially true in the northern parts of Japan. One may indeed sum up the changes in the period by stating that the increased real national income generated by the rise of productivity in particular trades, by the diversion of labour from low-productivity to high-productivity industries, and by calling into use the unemployed resources that existed in 1930–1, was applied mainly to investment (largely of a strategic kind), to providing for a greater population, and to countering the adverse movement in the terms of trade. Very little was left over to provide for increased civilian consumption a head.

The organization of Japan's economy during the 1930s was full of apparent inconsistencies. On the one hand, a considerable part of industry, trade, and finance was concentrated in the great concerns known as the *Zaibatsu*, which will be the subject of a later chapter. Each of these houses had interests in many branches of industry, commerce, and finance. They were not only prominent in large-scale highly-capitalized enterprises, but also, through their banks and merchanting companies, they penetrated into that part of the economy composed of numerous small and medium-sized producers. The latter were characteristic of the trades that produced goods of a traditional type: Japanese-style clothing, footwear, furniture, pottery, prepared foodstuffs, narrow-width textiles, and papier-maché wares. Some of these trades were widely distributed; others were strongly localized. Nearly all depended heavily on manual processes and

[16] Uyeda, pp. 305–8.

many of them, notably the *meibutsu*[17] trades at Kyoto, employed
highly skilled craftsmen. Small and medium-sized firms were
also numerous in industries of a modern type, including some
that served the export markets. For instance, very small weaving-
sheds were typical of the new worsted-weaving trade as well as of
the older silk weaving. Part of the pottery exports came from
small producers. In the metal and miscellaneous goods trades
there were many small establishments engaged in the manufacture of castings, bicycle parts, cheap electric lamps, rubber footwear, and toys. Almost every large engineering factory was surrounded by numerous subcontracting workshops which supplied
it with parts or performed processes to its orders. Some of these
small-scale industries were elaborately organized. The producers
often specialized on particular components and supplied them
to merchants or factory owners who co-ordinated their activities.
If in general their workshops were poorly constructed and their
machinery inferior to that used in the factories, there were exceptions. For instance, the worsted weavers of Ichinomiya
possessed well-built mills equipped with modern looms, and
many of the small machine-shops used power-driven machine-
tools adequate to their purposes.

The quantitative importance of the small and medium-sized
units may be measured with reasonable accuracy. In 1930,
4,760,000 persons were recorded by the Census as being engaged
in private manufacturing industry as their principal occupation.
Of these, 58 per cent worked in establishments with under 5
operatives, and only 21 per cent in establishments with 100 or
more operatives.[18] These figures exaggerate the importance of
the small producers, since many of their employees were part-
time workers, and for this and other reasons labour productivity
was much lower in them than in the large factories. Nevertheless,
this qualification does not disturb the fact that in 1930 small
producers played a most significant role in Japanese industry.
Their position changed but little up to the outbreak of the
Second World War.

The small unit which flourished not only in the traditional
industries but also in newer branches of manufacture was to be
regarded not as a survival but rather as a type of undertaking
well suited to the economic conditions of Japan at that time.

---

[17] 'Speciality'.   [18] Lockwood, pp. 112, 204; see also p. 112 below.

While there were some industries in which technique prescribed that production could take place economically only in large, highly capitalized plants, there were many others where organization could be adapted to the country's factor-endowment. In that sector, the relative scarcity of capital and the relative abundance of skilled labour exerted an influence in favour of processes that could be efficiently conducted in small establishments. Since the great merchant and manufacturing firms interested themselves in the small-scale sector, providing finance, technical knowledge, and access to markets, it was often possible to combine the advantages of large-scale financial and commercial organization with those of small-scale manufacturing.

The dichotomy in Japanese industry was influenced during the 1930s by changes in the government's economic policy. The State had been active in introducing Western industrial methods during the early Meiji era, and in later times it had taken the lead in promoting the development of industries of strategic importance, often in conjunction with the *Zaibatsu*. Yet in the early 1930s the enterprises actually owned by the State were limited to special fields, such as the main-line railway system and part of the iron and steel industry.[19] Similarly, governmental intervention in economic affairs was mainly concerned with supplying the deficiencies of private enterprise (as in the official supervision over certain processes in the raw-silk industry), or in assisting the farmers and fishermen to handle their price and marketing problems. In manufacturing industry there was comparatively little official supervision or regulation.

The political and economic crises of the 1930s were responsible for fundamental changes in policy. During the years when the economy was suffering from the effects of the World Depression, the government introduced schemes designed to bring about co-operation among producers and traders with the object both of raising efficiency and also of mitigating what were then regarded as the excesses of competition. Measures were devised for encouraging rationalization in the large-scale industries, and for strengthening or establishing guilds or associations (*kumiai*) of small producers and traders.

After 1932 economic policy was affected not merely by the im-

[19] In 1931-3 about 8 per cent of the total number of 'factory' workers (as defined on p. 5) were employed in State-owned establishments.

provement in economic circumstances but also by the political and social changes of the time. The military cliques, now in the ascendant, were antagonistic to the *Zaibatsu* and were intent upon weakening their power. Both in Manchuria and in Japan Proper they turned to new capital groups (*Shinko-Zaibatsu*) to serve as the economic instruments of their strategic purposes. They also used their influence to strengthen the associations of small manufacturers and traders with the object of freeing those enterprises from the domination of the merchant companies owned by the old *Zaibatsu*. The associations received additional support for other reasons. For instance, the government tried to meet the outcry against Japan's 'social dumping' by requiring the export guilds to control sales to foreign markets in the hope of forestalling restrictions. These measures had only moderate success. Of far greater significance was the assumption by the State of control over certain basic industries for strategic reasons. An early example was the establishment of the Japan Iron and Steel Company by the amalgamation in 1934 of six private firms and the government's Yawata Works. Control was also extended over the operations of the oil-distributing companies, Japanese and foreign alike.[20]

After the outbreak of the Sino-Japanese War, State intervention was carried much further. The producers' guilds came to be used as efficient instruments for fixing prices and rationing supplies of raw materials. The electric-power industry was nationalized in 1938 and in the same year the National General Mobilization Law conferred on the government far-reaching powers of economic control. By 1940 a considerable number of strategic industries had been brought under centralized administration, and several 'national policy companies' had been established to develop particular manufactures under official guidance. Thus, under the influence of war, economic power was increasingly concentrated in the State and in the organs of control that it created or adapted to its purposes.

[20] The changes in economic policy are examined in detail in Schumpeter, chs. xxi, xxii, and Conclusion.

II

The Course of Recovery and Expansion

AT the end of the Second World War, Japan's economy was in ruins. Her great centres of population had been laid waste. In the sixty-six cities subjected to air attack about half the dwelling-places had been burnt down; these represented about a quarter of the total housing accommodation of the country.[1] A high proportion of the industrial and commercial buildings together with the equipment they contained had been destroyed, and much plant and machinery formerly used in production for the civilian market had been scrapped to provide metal for munitions. The amount of physical destruction is estimated to have been equivalent to about twice the national income of the fiscal year 1948–9.[2] What is more, the economy had been seriously disorganized even before the surrender, for the scarcity of materials and of transport equipment together with the confusion caused by the evacuation of the larger cities had produced a breakdown of production and distribution. The once massive export trade no longer existed, and the mercantile marine, in pre-war days the third largest in the world, had been reduced to a few coasting vessels. In 1945 the people were short of food, clothing, fuel, housing, and all other necessaries of life.

In Europe it was at first confidently expected that Japan's emergence from these confusions would not be long delayed, and her former competitors, particularly those in the textile trades, awaited with anxiety her early return to world markets. These expectations proved to be erroneous, and recovery, especially in international trade, was very slow. The overestimate of Japan's recuperative capacity can be attributed in part simply to a failure to realize the extent of the physical damage sustained by the economy. Furthermore, foreign observers made insufficient allowance for the effects of defeat and Occupation upon the

[1] Cohen, *Japan's Economy*, pp. 406–8.
[2] Estimate of Econ. Stabilization Board, see Orient. Econ., *Japan Econ. Yb., 1954*, pp. 20–1.

spirit of enterprise among the Japanese people. For nearly seven years, from August 1945 until March 1952 when the Peace Treaty took effect, the government's economic policy was profoundly influenced, if not entirely determined, by directives from SCAP,[3] while Japanese businessmen and officials fumbled with situations which they were powerless to control.

Some uncertainties were inevitable in the immediate post-war years when Allied policy towards Japan was being worked out. The Japanese could make some estimate of the damaging effects of the loss of their empire and of their great overseas assets upon their country's international trade and its food and raw-material supplies. But the Allied Powers at that time were actively concerned with exacting reparations and with ensuring that Japan's freedom to reconstruct industries of strategic importance should be strictly limited. Some of the reparations were in fact supplied by the distribution of the country's foreign assets. But others, so it was thought, might take the form of plant and machinery wrenched from the factories.[4] Until this question had been resolved by the victorious Powers, the Japanese moved in a penumbra of uncertainty. This was not all. In the early post-war years SCAP was indifferent to economic recovery and was committed to ambitious measures of social and political reform. Its aim was to destroy completely the material basis of Japan's imperialism and at the same time to foster institutions and forms of organization believed to be favourable to democratic modes of life. With the object of preventing the re-creation of an industrial war potential, proposals were put forward for restricting the capacity of the metal, chemical, and engineering industries and for limiting the size and speed of ships. The policy also expressed itself in various reforms calculated to diffuse wealth and economic initiative more widely. The dissolution of the *Zaibatsu*, the purging of many business leaders, the enactment of an anti-trust law, the Land Reform designed to transform tenants into peasant proprietors, the introduction of labour laws and measures for the promotion of social welfare—all these are major examples of the reformist policy in the economic sphere. An estimate of their

---

[3] SCAP stands for Supreme Commander of the Allied Powers, and was used to designate both a person and the Occupation Administration in general.

[4] Some machine tools and other types of equipment were transferred to China and other Far Eastern countries.

effects will be given in some detail in later chapters. Here it is sufficient to assert that, whatever the political and social merits of these measures, they certainly made no immediate contribution to economic recovery. Most of them actually impeded it. 'Punishment and Reform' is indeed an apt description of this first phase of American policy.[5]

Such statistical indices as are available demonstrate the deplorably low levels of economic activity in the early post-war years. In 1946 the volume of industrial production (manufacturing and mining) was little more than 30 per cent of that of the pre-war period (1934–6), and in the next year it reached only 37 per cent. In the cities consumption a head was then very low, perhaps only half the pre-war consumption. An export trade scarcely existed, and the destruction of the mercantile marine and the loss of foreign assets meant that there were no earnings of foreign exchange from those sources. The value of the currency had been virtually destroyed by a violent inflation. Agriculture, which had suffered least from wartime destruction and post-war dislocation, was the only sector of the economy to show some improvement. Even there, however, output in 1946 and 1947 was still well below the pre-war level.[6]

Before the end of 1947 the catastrophic conditions in Japanese industry and the deepening financial crisis persuaded the Americans that their policies must be revised. The widespread economic distress provided an uncongenial environment for the growth of new democratic institutions and its relief imposed heavy burdens on the American taxpayer. In 1947 alone aid amounted to over $400 million. At the same time the deterioration in relations between the Western world and Russia, together with the growing recognition that Nationalist China was unlikely to serve as a stabilizing force in East Asia or an apt vehicle for American policy, caused a change in strategic plans. SCAP was, therefore, compelled to abandon its indulgence in reformist zeal and to concern itself increasingly with the promotion of economic recovery. Reparations were halted. Imports of raw materials and foodstuffs under the aid programme were enlarged. Private trade with the outside world was permitted under certain

[5] Columbia Univ., Amer. Assembly Grad. Sch. of Business, *The United States and the Far East* (1956), p. 36.
[6] For detailed statistics and sources thereof see Statist. App., pp. 263 ff. below.

safeguards. The militant labour movement, which had grown up under the wing of the Occupation authorities was sharply discouraged, and the policy of destroying the *Zaibatsu* was pursued with a more moderate enthusiasm. 'Recovery' was now the watchword, and by the end of 1948 it had been decided that an essential preliminary was the restoration of monetary stability. This policy was announced under the form of a Nine-Point Stabilization Programme which provided *inter alia* for a balanced budget, credit restrictions, and the expansion of trade and production. Early in 1949 Mr Joseph Dodge arrived and proceeded to bend Japanese policy to this new aim.

The measures which he caused to be executed enjoyed an immediate success. The rise in prices was checked. The government and the business world were now able to grapple with the tasks of reconstruction in the consciousness that among the Occupation authorities anxiety for a rapid economic recovery had almost completely supplanted the earlier preoccupation with social and political reform. By the spring of 1950, although manufacturing production was still less than before the war, industry had already gone far towards adapting itself to the new financial situation. The crippling shortages of fuel and basic materials had been largely overcome and agricultural output had regained its pre-war level.

In June 1950 the outbreak of the Korean War swept the economy on to a new plane. Heavy 'special procurement' expenditure on account of the United Nations forces brought about a sharp increase in the output of manufactures, and orders flowed into the factories from abroad. Boom conditions prevailed throughout the economy and the short period of relative price stability came to an abrupt end. Yet since the boom was brought about by a great expansion in what were in effect foreign demands for Japanese goods and services, a rise in prices of more than 50 per cent between June 1950 and June 1951 proved to be quite consistent with the appearance of a very favourable balance of payments. In 1951 the growth in output was such that the index of industrial production exceeded the pre-war annual average for the first time since 1944.[7]

The Korean War not merely promoted Japan's economic

---

[7] By 'pre-war' in this context is meant the average of 1934–6; a comparison with 1937 (when Japan's war with China began) is much less favourable.

recovery, it also exerted a powerful influence upon Occupation policy. If Japan had not been under American control, South Korea could hardly have been defended, and it was realized that even when the war was over, Japan would remain an essential base for the deployment of American power. A strong Japan closely allied to the United States became, therefore, the key to Far Eastern strategy. The facts of the international situation left no place either for vindictiveness or political idealism. These were the circumstances that determined the character of the Peace Treaty and the Security Treaty which were signed in September 1951 and came into effect in the spring of 1952. The treaties returned full sovereignty to Japan (although they also confirmed the loss of her empire), restored to her the right of rearming, and permitted the Allies to maintain bases and troops in the country. They were silent about the economic reforms, and while they recognized the obligation of Japan to make reparations, they also conceded her present inability to do so. One result of the Peace Treaty was that even after the conclusion of the Korean War, Japan continued to receive large dollar payments for 'special procurement' chiefly in respect of the American military establishments. Between 1952 and 1956 these payments amounted to $3,380 million, ranging between $824 million and $557 million annually. In 1955 they were equivalent to 27 per cent of the value of the export trade.[8] It is scarcely possible to exaggerate the importance of these payments to Japan's economic recovery during the critical years after 1951. At a time when the revival of the export trade was in an early stage, they provided her with a large and fairly steady dollar income which greatly assisted in the re-equipment of her industries and the restoration of pre-war levels of consumption.

Even when the Korean War boom broke, Japan's industrial production continued to expand and her earnings of foreign exchange remained sufficient to enable her to build up large dollar reserves. It is true that under the influence of the continu-

---

[8] This general account of economic changes in the early post-war period is based largely on Economic Counsel (Planning) Board (now Economic Planning Agency) *Economic Survey of Japan* (various issues), referred to as EPA, *Econ. Survey;* see also S. Tsuru, 'Business Cycles in Post-War Japan', in Internat. Econ. Assoc., *The Business Cyele in the Post-War World* (1955). For complete figures of 'special procurement' expenditure see Statist. App., p. 278 below.

ing boom Japanese prices moved out of line with world prices and that by 1953 she was again in balance-of-payments difficulties. Nevertheless, in that year her industrial production was 55 per cent greater than in the base period (1934–6) and her real national income probably 30 per cent greater. In spite of the steep rise in the population (from 69 millions in 1935 to 87 millions in 1953) income a head had risen above the pre-war level. The period 1951–3 thus saw Japan at last set on the road to economic recovery.

The industrial investments of these years, while they were largely responsible for the critical turn in the balance of payments, laid the foundations for future progress. For after the Japanese government had administered, during 1954, a sharp corrective to the inflationary movement, not only was equilibrium in the balance of payments restored, but industrial expansion was resumed at an enhanced rate. By this time prosperity had become widely diffused throughout the economy. Whereas in the early 1950s the larger firms had been the chief beneficiaries both of 'special procurement' demand and of new investment, after 1955 the small and medium-sized firms began to share in the prosperity. This was a period in which the export trade, hitherto most resistant to the forces of recovery, went ahead with extraordinary speed.

By the fiscal year 1955–6 Japan could be said to have completed her economic recovery. Her gross national product (in real terms) was 44 per cent higher than in the middle 1930s and income a head over 10 per cent higher. For several years her international accounts had shown a favourable balance and she had accumulated substantial foreign-exchange reserves. She had carried through the re-equipment of her major industries and productivity had risen well above the pre-war level and was rapidly increasing. She had brought inflation under control and her people had begun to save again. Even if full account is taken of the American contribution to recovery, first in aid and then in 'special procurement', these achievements were impressive for a country which had sustained such heavy physical damage during the war and had permanently lost vast overseas assets. Throughout 1956 and during the early months of 1957 the economy continued to move forward at an undiminished rate. The export trade, though still less in volume than before the war, maintained the pace of its advance, stimulated towards the end of 1956 by the Suez crisis.

The pace of the industrial advance led as before to difficulties with the balance of payments, and in the course of 1957 it was necessary for the authorities again to impose severe restrictions on credit. Prices fell steeply as stocks were liquidated; fixed investment was reduced; and in 1958 industrial production ceased to expand. This hesitancy, however, was only a prelude to further rapid growth which carried Japan far beyond the stage of mere 'recovery'. Industrial production rose exceptionally fast during 1959 and 1960, and in 1961 it was nearly 80 per cent greater than in 1958. This boom, like the previous one, was generated by very heavy investment in industrial equipment, but it was also carried forward by a 'consumption revolution' that may be said to have started in 1958. This was marked by a large increase in the demand for consumers' capital goods and for higher-quality clothing. The latter part of the period also witnessed a rise in the demand for services, especially those associated with travel and entertainment; hence the so-called 'leisure boom'. Japan was entering an era of affluence.

During this period the export trade at last (in 1959) surpassed the pre-war level in volume, and soon went far beyond it. But the familiar pattern of 'boom and bust' was repeated. A balance-of-payments crisis accompanied by restrictive monetary measures, again checked expansion and in 1962 the growth in the economy was only moderate. On this occasion, however, the fall in prices and costs was less violent than in the previous recessions. The explanation is to be sought in the behaviour of certain constituents of national expenditure. During the down-turn of 1958 the decline in investment (chiefly investment in stocks) was not offset by any substantial rise in other types of expenditure. In 1962, on the other hand, the decline in investment was accompanied by a considerable increase in spending by consumers and the government, and it would seem that the disequilibrium in the economy was not fully corrected. In the early months of 1963, under the stimulus of easy credit conditions, the country emerged from the recession and another phase of rapid growth followed. But this period of expansion was very short. In the early months of 1964 the condition of the balance of payments again caused anxiety, and the government was obliged to impose restraints.

C

The significance of this latest phase of the trade cycle will be considered later on. Here it is sufficient to emphasize that in 1963 the gross national product (real) was probably about three times that of 1950–1 (and also of the middle 1930s) and that industrial production was four or five times greater.

Several features of this remarkable growth must be stressed. First, let us consider the movement of prices. Wholesale prices tended to fall during the 1950s, and even in 1963, after this tendency had been reversed, they stood at about the same level as ten years earlier.[9] The retail prices of *commodities* (in Tokyo) rose by under 4 per cent between 1952 and 1960, but the consumer price index (for all cities) increased by about 20 per cent during this period. The reasons for the contrasting movements in wholesale and consumer prices help to illuminate some of the chief trends in the economy. Wholesale prices fell partly because of cheaper imports but mainly because of the rise in industrial productivity which much exceeded the rise in wages. This fact also explains the relatively small increase in the retail prices of *goods* up to 1960. The faster rise in the consumer price index is attributable chiefly to increases in the cost of services, rents, and certain public utility charges. Here the rise in wages played an important part, and it was this that led to the sharp upward turn in the index after 1960. The current problem of prices and costs will be discussed later, but it is worth emphasizing at this point that the Japanese economic expansion of the 1950s was accomplished without inflation.

Yet the period was by no means one of steady or stable growth. The pace of the advance, as we have seen, varied widely within short periods and there were violent oscillations of prices. As in the past, so in the post-war era, economic development was associated with phases of rapid expansion punctuated by short periods of ruthless deflation. It has been argued elsewhere that the growth of the economy might have been smaller in the absence of these fluctuations, distasteful as this conclusion may seem from the standpoint of social welfare.[10]

The high rate of growth can be ascribed to a number of factors which, since they are to be examined in subsequent chapters, will

---

[7] Price statistics are conveniently presented in Bank of Japan, *Econ. Statist.*, *1963*, pp. 283–303. See below Statist. App., Table 18, p. 276.

[10] Allen, 'Factors in Japan's Economic Growth', in Cowan, pp. 196–204.

here receive only brief mention. In the early post-war period (that is to say, the period of recovery up to 1953–4), American aid and 'special procurement' expenditure were of outstanding importance not only because they provided foreign exchange for imports, but also because of their indirect effects on investment.[11] The pace of the recovery at that time was assisted by the presence of ample supplies of technicians and skilled workers and of large quantities of under-used fixed assets, the legacy of the war. The capital-output ratio was consequently low and this was of considerable advantage at a moment when investment resources were scanty. From the early 1950s onwards innovations in manufacturing methods and forms of production played a leading role. Japan found herself after the war far behind Western countries in technical efficiency, but by the early 1960s the gap had been closed largely by the import of foreign techniques. The application of these new techniques would have been impossible without an exceptionally high rate of investment, especially after 1956 when several capital-intensive industries began to develop fast. The huge absolute increase in industrial investment depended closely on the high rate of saving, both institutional and personal, and on the efficiency of the financial machinery in directing these savings into productive use. Personal savings are believed to have amounted to over 10 per cent of the distributed national income during the 1950s. As a proportion of disposable personal income they have risen steeply in recent years. In F.Y. 1955 the ratio was 14 per cent and in F.Y. 1961 over 22 per cent, far higher than in any other country.[12]

The reasons for the high rate of saving are well known. The profits of companies have been high because of the full-capacity working of most of the plants (except in textiles), the low effective rate of tax on company earnings, and the lagging of wages behind productivity. The propensity to save a high proportion of personal incomes was associated partly with the steep rise in incomes at a time when the Japanese tradition of austerity still remained powerful, and partly with the still modest public pro-

[11] Cf. M. Shinohara, 'Factors in Japan's Economic Growth', *Hitotsubashi J. Econ.*, Feb. 1964, p. 30.
[12] The ratio was 7 per cent for the USA and 8 per cent for the UK in 1961. It should be remarked, however, that because of the large number of self-employed persons in Japan, personal savings in that country include a great amount of business savings.

vision against illness, unemployment, and old age. The system of wage payment itself may also exert an influence. A substantial part of total earnings takes the form of biannual bonuses. The result is that the workers' current consumption is related to the monthly wage, and the bonuses are commonly regarded as windfalls and are put by as savings.

We now come to what in the view of many economists was the chief factor in Japan's economic growth, namely the abundant supply of high-quality labour available for industrial employment. This is a large question which will be approached by way of the statistics of population. Between 1920 and 1940 the population of Japan Proper had increased from 55·5 millions to 71·4 millions.[13] Although during the 1930s the size of the average family began to fall, a large absolute annual increase was then forecast for the next few decades because of the high proportion of the population in the fertile age-groups. Between 1935 and 1939 the crude birth-rate averaged 29·2 per thousand, the crude death-rate 17·4, and the rate of natural increase 11·8.[14] The birth- and death-rates, though high by Western European standards, were low by Asian standards.

Immediately after the war the population began to expand very rapidly. The number of Japanese (soldiers and civilians) who were repatriated from overseas territories far exceeded the number of foreigners (chiefly Chinese and Koreans) who left Japan. On the demobilization of the armed forces the pre-war downward trend in the birth-rate was for a time reversed, and between October 1946 and September 1950 the natural increase amounted to 1,630,000 a year. The Census of 1950 put the population at 83 millions. Then a remarkable change began. By 1956 the crude birth-rate had fallen to 18·4 and the crude death-rate to 8·0, and by 1961 to 16·8 and 7·4 respectively. Japan thus passed into the class of countries with low birth-rates, although her rate of increase remained high because of the steep fall in the death-rate. It seems probable, however, that the rate of increase will diminish, since the death-rate is unlikely to fall much further and the downward trend in the birth-rate will probably continue. Even so, the population, which reached 90 millions in 1956 and 97 millions in 1964, is likely to exceed 102 millions by

[13] Excluding military personnel overseas, estimated at over 1 m.
[14] *Japan Statist. Yb.*, *1962*, and earlier years, for these and other figures of population.

1970.[15] After that the increase may be comparatively small.[16] Long-term forecasts of population can, however, be disregarded, for experience shows that they are seldom fulfilled, and it is to the changes of the recent past and of the next few years that attention can be usefully directed.

Since 1940 Japan has added 24 millions to her numbers, an increase of about a third. During this period the age structure of the population has changed profoundly. In 1940 36 per cent of the total was under 15 years of age and 56 per cent was in the 'productive' age-group (15–59). In 1960 the proportion in the first group had fallen to 30 per cent and that in the second group had risen to 61 per cent. This trend is expected to continue. Between 1961 and 1970, a period in which the population is expected to rise by $8\frac{1}{4}$ millions, numbers in the 0–14 age-group are expected to diminish by $4 \cdot 8$ millions, while those in the 'productive' age-group are expected to grow by $10 \cdot 7$ millions. From an economic standpoint the importance of this structural change can be seen in its effect on the labour supply. Between 1956 and 1959 the 'productive' age-group increased on an average by over a million a year; the increment fell to 600,000 in 1960 (when the effects of the war on births were felt in this age-group); it is expected to rise to $1\frac{1}{2}$ millions in 1963 and then to decline steadily as the post-war fall in the birth-rate exerts its effects. By 1970 the increment is likely to be little more than 600,000.[17]

During the early post-war years the chief problem appeared to be that of finding employment, in work of high productivity, for the additional numbers likely to enter the labour market. What seemed disquieting to contemporaries was that between 1945 and 1955 the bulk of the increase in the occupied population had gone into occupations where productivity was low. This applied not only to primary industries and to certain classes of services, but also to small-scale manufacturing industry. The expansion in the numbers engaged in the large factories was comparatively small.

Yet events soon dispelled these misgivings. Between 1955 and 1961, when the total occupied population grew by about 4

[15] EPA, *New Long-Range Econ. Plan, 1961–70* (1961), p. 4.
[16] However, the Institute of Population Problems of the Ministry of Health has recently estimated that the population will exceed 108 m. by 1975.
[17] Cf. *Orient. Econ.*, Feb. 1962, p. 90.

millions, employment in the primary industries declined by nearly $2\frac{1}{2}$ millions, while in manufacturing industry and construction it rose by more than $3\frac{1}{2}$ millions. In the service industries there was not only a growth in employment but also a shift to the more highly paid work. It was this transference from low- to high-productivity occupations which was largely responsible for the growth in GNP and in the standard of life. The tendency has persisted. The modern and efficient sectors of Japan's economy have continued to absorb the entire annual increment in the labour force and have also drawn extensively on the other sectors for the workers they have required. Until recently, however, the manpower reserves in the low-productivity occupations were sufficient to make possible the rapid expansion of manufacturing industry without inducing a cost inflation. Thus the presence of a great mass of underemployed labour at the beginning of the period now under discussion clearly made a leading contribution to the economic expansion. In addition, it helped to preserve highly competitive conditions in the Japanese economy and these in themselves were instrumental in keeping prices down. Whether these conditions are likely to be present in the future will be discussed in later chapters.

In considering the increasingly effective use of resources, including manpower, we must not neglect the important fact that Japan after the war was restrained from any indulgence in lavish expenditure on the armed forces. Formerly the burden of defence and armament was extremely heavy. In the middle 1930s military and naval expenditure came to over two-fifths of the central government's outlay, and the proportion increased after 1937. The San Francisco Treaties required Japan to re-establish a limited defence force, but most of the cost was provided by the United States, and in the fiscal year 1955–6 defence expenditure amounted only to about 13 per cent of the central government's outlay and in the fiscal year 1962–3 to 9 per cent, or about 1·5 per cent of the national income. Another saving was effected in the servicing of the public debt, which required only 3 per cent of public expenditure in 1962–3 compared with about 17 per cent a quarter of a century earlier.[18]

---

[18] The saving on interest payments on the domestically held debt did not yield any economies in real resources, since these payments were merely transfers. But it had an influence on fiscal policy.

The large savings on defence and the servicing of debt permitted the government to enlarge its subventions for the promotion of agriculture and industry and its expenditure on social welfare (including grants to local authorities for these purposes), without increasing the proportion of its own outlay to the national income. In 1955–6 social welfare payments including expenditure on education, pensions, and the social services, accounted for 35 per cent of total public expenditure and development grants to nearly 20 per cent.[19] These two items together maintained their share in the total public expenditure (which doubled in real terms in the next seven years), although their relative importance changed. In F.Y. 1962 the share of social welfare amounted to about 30 per cent and development grants to nearly 25 per cent.[20] Since part of the grants to local authorities were in respect of public enterprises and relief, it follows that most of Japan's public expenditure is now of a kind characteristic of a Welfare State. This is symptomatic of a profound change in Japanese society.

Government expenditure as a whole, however, has formed since the war a much smaller part of the Japanese national income than has been the case for the United Kingdom or for most Western countries. In F.Y. 1956 the ratio of the government's expenditure on goods and services to gross national expenditure was only 17 per cent and in F.Y. 1961 18 per cent. This was not very different from before the war, but, as we have explained, the expenditure was of a more productive kind. The above analysis refers to the General Account of the government and does not, of course, provide an accurate index of the importance of the public sector as a whole. It excludes, for instance, the accounts of the Monopoly Corporations, the National Railways, and other large public corporations, and the State-owned banks.

The sources of revenue have changed as profoundly as the form of the public expenditure. During the middle 1930s about a third of the public revenue (central government) was raised by bond issues. This was the era of reflationary finance, when the ratio of the tax revenue (national and local) to the national income was only 13 per cent compared with 23 per cent in the

[19] EPA, *Econ. Survey, 1955–6*, pp. 117–36, Annex Tables, pp. 45–51.
[20] Ibid. *1961–2*, p. 149; *1962–3*, p. 133.

United Kingdom at that time. Since the war most of the revenue has been raised by taxation, and for the last ten years the ratio of the tax revenue to the national income has ranged between 20 and 23 per cent,[21] far lower than in most Western countries. The rapid growth in the national income enabled the Japanese authorities to enlarge their revenue without imposing heavier taxation, and in recent crises they relied on monetary measures rather than on fiscal measures to curb expenditure. The adverse effects on incentive of high taxation have thus been avoided, and the buoyancy of the Japanese economy can be ascribed in some degree to that fact. At the same time the method of raising taxation has also changed. In the middle 1930s 65 per cent of national tax revenue and 45 per cent of the national and local tax revenue combined were obtained from taxes on commodities. In the early 1960s the proportions were 45 and 39 per cent respectively. It follows that a much larger share of the revenue is raised now by taxes on personal and corporate incomes.[22] This is symptomatic of another change in Japanese society. In the past the taxation system was very regressive and pressed lightly on the rich and the profit-earner. It was calculated to preserve a very unequal distribution of incomes and to stimulate the accumulation of private capital. The reforms of the early post-war years which destroyed many private fortunes, together with the changes in the incidence of taxation, have produced a more equal distribution of income.[23] But the change has not required the imposition of penal rates of taxes on high business incomes and the accumulation of capital so essential for industrial progress has not been frustrated. Indeed, the rise in direct taxation, so far as the major companies are concerned, has been largely offset by lavish depreciation and investment allowances, which have actively encouraged the modernization of equipment, as well as by a generous interpretation of expenses that can be set against profits.

Some of the gravest problems faced by Japan in the post-war world were those that affected her international economic rela-

---

[21] EPA, *Econ. Survey, 1961–2*, p. 413. For F.Y. 1963 the ratio was 21·5 per cent (15·0 per cent national and 6·5 per cent local).

[22] Ibid. p. 413.

[23] The reform of the Japanese taxation system after the war is associated with the name of Dr Shoup, who put forward his recommendations in 1949 (see S. Shiomi, *Japan's Finance and Taxation, 1940–56* (1957)).

tions. The steep decline in her former sources of foreign income as a result of the destruction of her mercantile marine, the loss of overseas investments and of areas of trading privilege in East Asia, and finally technical changes which almost destroyed her chief export to the United States, gave rise to recurrent anxieties in regard to her balance of payments. She showed resilience in finding substitutes for former markets and imports, but ten years after the war the volume of her exports was a quarter less than in the middle 1930s, and it was not until 1959 that it rose above the pre-war level. Even if 'special procurement' expenditure is added to export values the achievement in this field remains modest.[24] By resort to various expedients she has been able to reduce her reliance upon imports needed for her industrial development, but it is now realized that a very rapid growth of foreign trade during the remainder of this decade is a necessary condition for achieving the rate of growth postulated in the Income Doubling Plan.[25] Japan is now dismantling the elaborate system of controls imposed since the war on foreign trade and exchange dealings, because she hopes to share in the benefits of trade liberalization in the outside world, benefits which were withheld from her for most of the post-war period by discrimination against her goods. The next few years will show whether she can reconcile rapid economic growth and a favourable balance of payments in conditions of commercial freedom, and the continued buoyancy of international trade as a whole will become for her a matter of lively concern.

With the recovery of her trade during the late 1950s the flow of Japan's resources to the outside world was resumed. This flow is now variously composed. In the first place, there are reparations payments to countries that were victims of Japan's aggression during the Second World War. Difficulties in coming to terms about these delayed the restoration of unrestricted commercial intercourse with some Asian countries, and it was not until 1960 that the last agreement was concluded. All the agreements provide for settlements to be made by the delivery of goods, chiefly capital goods, to the claimants. The total bill came to

---

[24] Her balance of invisible items has been generally unfavourable, largely because of her large payments in respect of shipping services and of royalties owed to foreigners.

[25] See chs iii and xii below.

over US $1,000 million, and at the end of 1962 about three-fifths of this sum was still outstanding.[26] Although the payment of reparations is a heavy burden for Japan, she can reasonably hope that it will open the way for ever-increasing trade with the countries concerned. Secondly, there are grants and long- and short-term loans made by the Japanese government, chiefly to underdeveloped countries, together with contributions to multilateral agencies. The latter include the International Development Agency and the United Nations Technical Assistance and Relief Agencies which deal *inter alia* with the training of technicians in South East Asia and Africa. Japan's contribution of aid, at any rate as this is defined by OECD, is regarded as meagre. She has been reproached on the ground that such grants and loans as she has made to underdeveloped countries have been related to her own interests rather than to the recipients' needs, and she has lately been under pressure to show greater generosity.

Finally, there is the flow of private capital. Foreign investment was resumed six years after the end of the war when one of the iron and steel firms acquired interests in ore mines in Goa. For some years Japan's capacity for foreign investment was narrowly limited and by 1956 the total investment amounted to only about £12 million, excluding expenditure incurred in connexion with arrangements for technical assistance to South East Asia. In the later 1950s, however, foreign investment greatly expanded, spreading to a wide variety of industries all over the world from Ireland to South America. Some of the most important Japanese properties overseas comprise textile mills, steel plants, and shipyards in Brazil, oil installations in the Persian Gulf and Sumatra, sugar refining mills in Thailand, and a wire factory in India. In December 1963 the total value of Japan's overseas investments, including long-term credits given on exports, amounted to about £560 million.[27] The annual flow of official and private financial resources (excluding short-term credits) to underdeveloped countries is set out below. The total disbursement in 1961 came to just under 1 per cent of the national income, but the

[26] This is the amount recognized as reparations by the Japanese government itself.

[27] *Japan Trade Guide, 1964* (Jiji Press), p. 39; and *B. of Anglo-Japan. Econ. Inst.* (London), Apr. 1964, p. 7.

amount in that year was exceptionally high and in 1960 the
ratio was only 0·77 per cent and 1962 0·65 per cent.[28]

Disbursements to Underdeveloped Countries
(Annual ave.; in $ million)

	1950–5	1956–9	1960	1961	1962
Official					
Reparations . . .	2	52	64	65	67
Grants	—	45	3	3	8
Loans (net) for over 1 year	7	48	48	142	86
Multilateral contributions	1	11	30	11	7
Total official . . .	10	156	145	221	168
Total *private* (net) . .	5	32	101	160	118
Total official & private .	15	188	246	381	286

Source: Based on figures in OECD, *The Flow of Financial Resources to the Less Developed
Countries, 1956–62.*

Foreign investment in Japan, like Japan's investment overseas,
was of little significance until the late 1950s. In the early post-
war period foreigners doubted the viability of the Japanese
economy. They were, therefore, reluctant to commit their resources, even though they then enjoyed tax concessions, later
removed because of protests from Japanese business firms. Even
by June 1955 outstanding foreign investment amounted to only
about £50 million of which about 65 per cent was held by
Americans. Much of this was provided in connexion with
arrangements for technical collaboration, as in the oil-refining
and distribution, the chemical and the electrical industries.
Subsequently the remarkable expansion of the economy transformed the standing of Japan in the world's capital markets, and
the recent abolition of her own onerous exchange restrictions
gave further encouragement to foreign investors. Some very
large loans were obtained during the 1950s from the World
Bank for various projects, including steel works and railway construction, and in spite of Japanese suspicion of large American

[28] J. White, *Japanese Aid* (Overseas Develop. Inst., 1964), p. 45. Japan's obligations
to the US are in a different category and do not enter into these estimates. She is
required to repay part of the American aid received between 1945 and 1952. The
amount has been scaled down to $490 m. from the original $2,000 m., and re-
payment (it was agreed in Jan. 1962) is to be made over sixteen years.

participation in their industries, the amount of direct investment by foreigners in joint enterprises has been rising. The American commercial banks have provided many short loans, and during periods of monetary stringency the Japanese banks have been large borrowers of Euro-dollars. Recently Japanese manufacturing and merchant firms have been turning to the European capital markets, and investment by Europeans in Japanese securities has much increased. After 1960 foreign investment in Japan was exceptionally heavy. In the fiscal years 1961 and 1962, it is estimated to have been £425 million. For the whole period from 1950 to 1962 the capital induction is put at about £800 million.[29] This is, of course, a very small proportion of total Japanese industrial investment, but for certain concerns and, indeed, industries, the amount provided from abroad has been substantial. As the Economic Planning Agency has stated: 'No one will dispute the fact now that foreign capital made an impressive contribution to Japan's capital accumulation in the very thick of its economic expansion.'[30]

Trends in the general organization of the economy have been consistent with those in public finance. Some of the immense changes in organization that occurred during the period of the Occupation were imposed deliberately by the Americans. Others were the result of internal factors—the economic dislocation after the war, the long-continued inflation, and the shift in political power within the country. Some of these influences were subsequently removed or weakened. After the end of the Occupation, Japan became actively engaged in establishing, or re-creating, forms of organization considered appropriate to her economic situation. By 1955 her banking and financial system, which was in disorder for many years after the war, had been reconstructed, and displayed many of its former features. Her commercial and industrial organization, which at one time appeared to have disintegrated, had regained some of its former cohesion. Many of the institutional arrangements introduced during the reform period had been modified. Yet in treading this 'reverse course' (*Gyaku-kosu*), Japan was by no means returning to a type of economy and society identical with that of pre-war days. Some sections of the old ruling class had gone or had been

---

[29] *Sumitomo Bank R.*, May 1962, p. 6; and EPA, *Econ. Survey, 1962–3*, p. 216.
[30] Ibid. p. 218. In 1963 foreign investment made a further increase.

thrust into sullen obscurity. The working people were less pliable and docile than in the past, and the peasantry, secure in the enjoyment of the fruits of the Land Reform, was in no mood to accept a return to its former inferior economic status. A redistribution of income in its favour had occurred on a considerable scale. It was not until 1954 that the average urban standard of living regained its pre-war level, whereas the rural standard was then more than a quarter above it. At that time the middle classes and some of the very wealthy families had suffered an absolute decline in their standards of life. Since then the surge forward of the economy has created new sources of private wealth and has lifted all classes to what a few years ago would have been regarded as affluence. The average standard of life is probably about twice that of pre-war days. In this new environment many of the economic institutions of the past, though they may often have served as a basis for new constructions, have usually proved unsuitable in precisely their old form for handling the issues of the present day, and some of them have been profoundly modified. To trace the development of new patterns of organization and new systems of economic relations in finance, trade, industry, agriculture, and labour will be among the leading tasks undertaken in subsequent chapters.

III
Planning for Economic Growth

DURING the post-war period Japan, like other countries with a mixed economy, experienced oscillations both in the degree of central control exercised over economic processes and also in the emphasis placed by policy on the public and private sectors respectively.[1] In the years of confusion immediately after the war, government supervision necessarily extended over a wide area. An official organ known as the Economic Stabilization Board, established at the instance of SCAP in the autumn of 1946, was made responsible for working out plans for reconstruction which had a considerable influence on what was actually done. One of its chief tasks was to draw up comprehensive reports, such as the Economic Rehabilitation Plan of 1949–53, and these provided information used in connexion with claims for United States aid and for loans from the World Bank.

With the end of the Occupation and the completion of the first stage of recovery, planning and centralized control fell into disfavour, and in 1953 the conversion of the Economic Stabilization Board into the Economic Counsel Board, with diminished functions, signified a trend towards a *laisser-faire* policy. This trend, however, was soon reversed. Public investment had been cut back sharply as a remedy for the balance-of-payments crisis of 1953–4, and when expansion was resumed bottle-necks were quickly encountered in the supply of electricity and steel, with the result that continued recovery was jeopardized. Furthermore, it then seemed probable that American 'special procurement' expenditure, which at that time financed a high proportion of imports, would soon decline sharply. Opinion, therefore, veered round to the view that there was advantage in preparing systematic forecasts of economic trends and long-term plans for public investment. In 1955 the Economic Counsel Board was renamed the Economic Planning Board and was given new func-

[1] Information about planning is based on data papers supplied by the EPA and on discussions with officials. See also EPA, *New Long-Range Econ. Plan, 1958–62* (1957) and *New Long-Range Econ. Plan, 1961–70* (1961).

tions. It prepared a five-year plan in 1955 which envisaged a rate of growth of the gross national product of 5 per cent per annum, and it looked to the achievement of a viable economy, independent of any special dollar revenue, by the end of the period. The forecast of output was arrived at simply by multiplying the estimated active labour force by the estimated labour productivity for the years covered, a method that had obvious defects for a country in which productivity was liable to change profoundly because of large-scale movements between the different sectors of the economy. In fact, the gross national product in the first two years of the plan grew twice as fast as had been planned, and in the preparation of subsequent plans a more sophisticated procedure, better attuned to the economic conditions of Japan, was followed.

The first result was the Long-Range Plan for 1958–62 which provided targets of investment, saving, employment, and production for the public and private sectors and also of foreign trade. It envisaged an overall rate of growth of GNP of 6·5 per cent per annum.[2] For the execution of the plan a distinction, similar to that once suggested by Professor D. H. Macgregor, was drawn between the part of the economy subject to 'planning' and the part subject to 'policy'. For the former sector accord with the plan could be ensured by government decisions in regard to the share of the national investment that lay within official control. This included investment in the infrastructure (e.g. roads, ports, sewage, water, publicly-provided housing) and was referred to as 'administrative investment'. For the sector subject to 'policy' the plan provided simply a guide for private entrepreneurs. Even here the government was in fact able to exert an influence not only by its fiscal and monetary measures but also by its control over such investment resources as were in the hands of official financial agencies like the Japan Development Bank and by various other means less easily identified and defined about which something will be said presently.

In the event, the actual growth was far greater than that planned. Between 1958 and 1960 GNP increased by about 10 per cent per annum and the target for 1962 was hit two years earlier. The underestimation can be attributed to several causes

[2] The years referred to in this chapter are fiscal years; e.g. F.Y. 1961 covers the period from 1 Apr. 1961 to 31 Mar. 1962.

—an unexpected improvement in the terms of trade, an exceptionally steep rise in the rate of gross capital formation (35 per cent of GNP in 1959 and 1960 compared with 28·5 in the plan), and rapid technical innovation in the machinery trades. During this period the relation between planning and execution remained tenuous. It is doubtful if the plan had any substantial effect on events, except to the extent that it may have influenced the government to go forward with its own investment projects during the balance-of-payments crisis of 1957–8 instead of cutting them back as in the previous crisis.

In the light of these experiences a new long-range plan was worked out in 1960 to cover economic development for the period 1961–70. This Plan for Doubling the National Income was prepared by the Economic Planning Agency[3] assisted by an Advisory Council with committees and sub-committees composed of industrialists, bankers, civil servants, and economists. The procedure used in preparing the previous plan was elaborated, and while the estimates for the private sector, as before, were to be considered as 'guides' or forecasts, arrangements for securing a coincidence between the plan and its execution in the public sector were much improved. For example, the allocation of funds for several types of public works over the decade was determined and to this extent the planned investment could be accommodated within the national budget.

The new relationship between planning and execution was important, for the plan aimed at greatly increasing the share of 'administrative' investment (that is, investment by the central government and the local authorities in the infrastructure). The ratio of such investment to 'enterprise' investment was to rise from 1:3 in 1958 to 1:2 in 1970. It should be observed that 'enterprise' investment refers not only to the investment of private undertakings but also to that of certain public corporations, including the Japanese National Railways, the Japanese Telegraph and Telephone Corporation, and the nationalized part of the electricity-supply industry. For all these much new investment was also planned. To obtain a just impression of the increased importance of social capital in the plan, it is reasonable to add investment in private housing to 'administrative' investment. In 1958 the ratio of these two types of investment com-

[3] The Economic Planning Board became the Economic Planning Agency in 1957.

bined to other investment was 1:2, in 1970 it is expected to be 9:11.

Distribution of Investment
(*at 1958 prices*)

	F.Y. 1958		F.Y. 1970	
	'000 m. yen	%	'000 m. yen	%
Gross capital formation .	2,947	100·0	8,283	100·0
Government enterprise .	254	8·6	754	9·1
Public investments . .	551	18·7	2,059	24·9
Private housing . . .	206	7·0	993	12·0
Private equipment investment	1,529	51·9	3,621	43·7
Inventory investment . .	407	13·8	857	10·3

Source: EPA, *New Long-Range Econ. Plan, 1961–70*, p. 19. This plan is commonly referred to as the Income Doubling Plan.

The doubling of the national income between 1961 and 1970 requires an annual average rate of growth of 7·2 per cent. As it was estimated that the rise in the first three years of the plan would be faster than the average (about 9 per cent), it follows that for the remainder of the decade the rate would be about 6·4 per cent. The chief reason for deceleration is to be found in the probable shortage of labour. Between 1960 and 1965 the population of working age was expected to increase by 2·2 per cent a year, compared with 1·5 per cent in the next five years. Furthermore, it seemed probable that the rise in productivity brought about by the redistribution of labour would be greater in the first part of the decade than in the latter. In the decade as a whole, this redistribution will certainly exert a major influence in securing the necessary increases in productivity. Agriculture including forestry and fishing, is expected to lose 30 per cent of its labour force, a decline from about 15 millions in the late 1950s to under 11 millions in 1970, although agricultural production is to rise substantially. If these results are achieved, an important step will have been taken towards removing the striking contrasts that still exist in income a head and productivity between the large-scale and the small-scale sectors of the economy.

The disappearance of the 'dual structure' will also be assisted by the migration of workers from small to large manufacturing concerns and by improvements in the efficiency of the former.

D

These improvements will be achieved partly by the pressure of market forces in a situation in which labour becomes increasingly scarce and expensive, and partly by the direction of capital into the small- and medium-scale sectors. Here the government's own financial agencies will have a part to play. Even the tertiary trades will be affected. It is expected that the forces that are already operating to raise the costs of small retailers and to transfer business from them to large stores, including the new supermarkets, will gather strength. In sum, while part of the increase in national income will result from a growth in the size of the labour force, a much greater part will be achieved by an increase in productivity.

Industrial production will have to expand very fast if the target is to be hit. The index of mining and manufacturing production is expected to rise from 100 in 1956–8 to 432 in 1970. The metal and engineering industries, as in the immediate past, will be called on to make a very large contribution to this growth. The output of machinery should rise four and a half times and that of steel should double. The plan provides for an increase in the output of private motor cars from 165,000 in 1960 to 1 million in 1970. In order to reach these production targets, imports will have to grow faster than income, and it is estimated that the ratio of imports to the national income will rise from 14·2 per cent in 1959 to 16·7 per cent in 1970. This disproportionate increase will be the consequence of the liberalization of trade and of restrictions on the use of import-saving devices. Exports also must grow faster than income; for them a rate of growth of 9 per cent a year is forecast. The greater part of this increase will take the form of heavier sales to the advanced countries of the world, since the import propensities of the less developed countries are unlikely to grow fast. Should the plan succeed, income a head in 1970 will amount to $580, well above Italy's in 1958 and rather lower than Germany's.

The statistical estimates are illuminating in that they reveal what is involved in doubling the national income. But the actual figures may be regarded with considerable scepticism, for if one thing is certain in this world it is that long-term quantitative predictions always turn out wrong. Indeed the practical importance of the plan lies rather in its influence on the decisions of private entrepreneurs and in its prescriptions for long-term economic policy in the public sector. These may be considered in turn. The announcement of the plan was followed by an upsurge of private investment and production which in 1961 brought about a rate of economic growth far in excess not only of the average rate for the decade but also of the higher rates expected in the first two or three years. In consequence, the economy became, as was said, 'overheated', and a balance-of-payments crisis occurred. According to official opinion, the reason was that the private industrialists misunderstood the nature of the plan. They regarded the targets as minima in some sense guaranteed by the government, and each entrepreneur in the highly competitive Japanese economy sought to ensure that his own business obtained a disproportionate advantage from the prosperity to come. Since the previous plans had grossly underestimated Japan's capacity for growth, there was some justification for such a response. Of this interpretation the plan provided an additional stimulus to entrepreneurs already inclined towards optimism. While it contributed to faster development, it failed in its aim of promoting the stable growth on which great emphasis had been laid. On the other hand, some of the leading manufacturers in central and western Japan, in response to inquiries by the present writer, denied that they took any notice of the plan in formulating their projects which, they declared, were based (and would continue to be based) solely on their own judgement of market prospects. This affirmation, however, is not without ambiguity, for market prospects themselves were presumably not unaffected by the announcement of the plan, especially by that part of it concerned with the government's own projected investment.

So far as policy for the public sector is concerned, the plan certainly marks a significant turning-point in Japanese experience. Hitherto a disproportionately large share of new investment has gone into manufacturing industry and power generation. The infrastructure and social investment have been neglected. The main significance of the plan, therefore, is to be found in the change in the ratio of public to private investment that has already been referred to, and this change can be controlled. Support for this conclusion is to be found in the fact that apart from its quantitative estimates of public investment, the plan has also much to say about economic and social policy in general. Its statements in this context relate not merely to the fiscal and monetary measures needed to provide a congenial environment for stable growth and full employment. Much greater attention than hitherto is paid to social welfare, including national insurance. The proposals for the further development of the educational system are considered later on.

Japan's advance towards affluence, it is now realized, has carried her to a point at which it is expedient to devote more of her resources than in the past to fostering the amenities of life of the ordinary people and to removing the wide discrepancies between sectoral incomes. In another sense, a rise in social investment has been accepted as a necessary condition for further advances in the national income. The state of part of the infrastructure is such that it can hardly support further increases in industrial production, while the approaching exhaustion of labour reserves means that for future increases in productivity Japan will have to rely on improvements in the quality of labour and on her own ingenuity in devising innovations in industrial techniques. It is significant that expenditure on scientific research is to be raised from 0·9 per cent of national income in 1958 to 2 per cent in 1970.[4] The ambitious plans for technical education and training are discussed in Chapter XI.

One aspect of the increased preoccupation with the infrastructure is to be found in the new projects for regional economic development, projects which have some affinity with the British location of industry policy.[5] Industrial growth has resulted in a strong concentration of manufacturing activity and of population in three great areas, Tokyo–Yokohama, Nagoya, and Kyoto–Osaka–Kobe. In 1961 the three great regions of which these towns are the centres were responsible for 75 per cent of the total industrial output and together they held nearly half (47 per cent) of the total population. The concentration was increasing, chiefly because of the growth in the Tokyo area: in 1955 the three regions accounted for only 70 per cent of the total industrial output and for only 45 per cent of the population. Some of the prefectures remote from the great industrial belt suffered an absolute decline in population during this period and

---

[4] The proportion has been estimated at 0·5 per cent in 1950 and 1·5 per cent in the early 1960s. Source: OECD, *Science, Economic Growth and Government Policy* (1963).

[5] EPA, *Outline of Regional Development Programmes in Japan* (July 1961) is the source of much useful information about regional development projects.

in them the rise in income a head lagged far behind that in the developing areas. One of the objects of the Plan for Doubling the National Income was to reduce regional as well as sectoral differences in income a head and the present Regional Development Programme was designed as a means to that end. It aimed at mitigating the extreme congestion in the neighbourhood of Tokyo and at diverting new industries to areas where labour, land, and water supplies were less scarce.

The concept of regional development planning goes back a long way. In early Meiji times the government had drawn up a development plan for Hokkaido and had made budgetary appropriations for land reclamation and the improvement in communications. Then in 1935 when Tohoku[6] became a depressed area because of crop failures and the fall in agricultural prices, government agencies were set up to promote the development of local resources. Shortly after the Second World War the State addressed itself again to the problem of these areas and provided funds chiefly for the encouragement of higher food production. In the late 1950s other backward regions, including South Kyushu and Shikoku, received official attention. In addition to these special measures, a certain number of areas were specified under the Compensation Land Development Law 1950 as places where public expenditure was authorized for improvements in public utilities and communications, land conservation, and urban redevelopment. Works were in fact undertaken.

The latest policy aims at co-ordinating the regional development projects as a whole in the light of the Plan for Doubling the National Income. The country has been divided into eleven regions with the object of achieving what the Barlow Commission in England called 'a balanced distribution of industry and population'. From the standpoint of the policies to be applied, three groups of regions were distinguished:

(a) the congested areas, which consist of the Tokyo–Yokohama area (Kanto) and the Kyoto–Osaka–Kobe area (Kinki);

(b) the hinterland areas of the two above centres together with the Nagoya area (Tokai);

(c) the development areas, which include Hokkaido, Tohoku, Shikoku, and Chugoku–Kyushu.

[6] Tohoku is the northern part of the main island.

The policy aims at limiting expansion in the first group of areas by restricting the establishment of new factories there and by assisting firms to move elsewhere. Further growth in the hinterland areas will be 'regulated'. For the rest a number of points of growth have been selected in the underdeveloped regions. Efforts will be made by public investment in their infrastructure and by various financial inducements to entrepreneurs (including tax concessions and loans from government banks) to build up large industrial cores round which other industrial zones will cluster. In 1963 thirteen such places were selected for new industrial centres.[7] The plan is intended to produce by 1970 the changes in the regional distribution of industry shown in the following table. The most striking of them are the substantial reductions planned for the Kinki and Kanto regions, although even this relative decline would be consistent with a considerable absolute expansion.

Estimated Value of Industrial Production by Regions
(*as percentages of total value*)

	F.Y. 1961	F.Y. 1970
Hokkaido	2·5	3
Tohoku	3·9	6
Hokuriku	2·3	3
Shikoku	2·3	3
Kyushu	6·6	8
Chugoku	6·9	9
Tokai	15·8	19
Kinki	25·2	20
Kanto	34·5	29
	100·0	100

Source: EPA.

Whether these results can be achieved is doubtful, since the policy will be working against hitherto powerful trends. British experience testifies to the difficulty of checking tendencies towards increased concentration and of fostering development in areas previously unattractive to modern industry. Yet the con-

---

[7] An investment of £150 m. will be required, it is supposed, for each centre. The government and its agencies will contribute about one-third in the form of grants, loans, and investments.

ditions in the two countries are different and the policies themselves not identical. In Great Britain the chief aim of the develop-
ment-area policy was to encourage new activities in regions
where the older industries had decayed, in order to prevent the
reappearance of heavy localized unemployment. But Japan has
not been troubled like Great Britain by the local effects of the
decay of great established industries. In that country the object
of policy is rather to effect a transference of local resources from
low-productivity to high-productivity occupations in the interests of the projected rate of growth in the economy as a whole.
The regions favoured by the programme are those which up to
the present have been mainly agricultural. It is not unemployment which gives concern but rather the existence of large numbers of workers with incomes far lower than those in the prosperous areas.

There is, however, one exception. The nearest analogy to the
British situation in this respect is to be found in the coal-mining
industry. Because of the successful competition of other sources
of power, Japanese coal-mining, like British coal-mining in the
inter-war period, has lately constituted a depressed sector of the
economy. The fall in demand together with the mechanization
of the pits has left many thousands of miners redundant, and their
condition has obliged the government to introduce retraining and
resettlement schemes which have not up to the present been very
successful. In the coal-mining regions, therefore, the policy is to
encourage new industries that may absorb the displaced miners.

A description of Japanese planning procedures would be
incomplete without some reference to the complex relations
between government and private industry, for these affect
economic planning and its execution. On this question the
evidence is doubtful and conclusions must be tentative. The
difficulty of discovering where authority in any sphere resides
in Japan has often been asserted. It is not only foreign observers
who are baffled; even Japanese, who are naturally less inclined
than foreigners to pose the question, can seldom provide a con-
vincing answer, especially in the context of the rapidly changing
post-war conditions. In the end one is left with paradoxes that
are not easily explained. The fact that differences of view or
conflicts of opinion are commonly resolved by informal discussions and bargains among organized interests rather than by

parliamentary procedures is the least troublesome part of the problem. The main difficulty arises when we seek to discover the means by which new policies are initiated and disseminated and the way in which power is deployed.

The influence of the bureaucracy was undoubtedly enhanced as a result of the economic confusion of early post-war years and, despite the revival of the great aggregates of private economic power, it has retained much of its importance. But the bureaucracy does not speak with one voice. It is composed of factions whose conflicts are on a different plane from the departmental rivalries in the British Civil Service. These conflicts are found not only in the chief departments of State but also in official or semi-official bodies to which the government has delegated tasks of economic administration. An instance is afforded by the well-known rivalry between the Ministry of Finance and the Bank of Japan which will be referred to in Chapter IV. Yet, despite these conflicts, the administration of the economy has usually been conducted with vigour and efficiency.

As in most other countries, political influence in favour of sectional interests is constantly being exerted and the content and the execution of the economic plans are subject in some degree to that influence. For example, it would be disingenuous to suggest that the selection of the points of growth in the Regional Development Plan was determined solely or mainly by a rational appraisal of the relative merits of the alternative localities. There was, in fact, a struggle between the civil servants who based their recommendations on economic calculation, and the rival factions of politicians who were concerned with satisfying their constituents or backers. It appears that the actual choice of the 13 places (out of some 44 competitors) was the result of political bargaining. Yet we cannot judge at this stage how seriously the aims of the plan have been compromised by this jobbery. The advantage of developing new industrial districts in North Japan may be so overwhelming as to permit many mistaken choices as to actual locations. In other words, the distortion may not be fatal to the success of the plan. On the other hand, the manufacturer who declared that his firm was not interested in the Regional Development Plan because it was simply a politicians' 'fiddle', may be representative of a considerable section of industrial opinion. The demand by the

Ministry of International Trade and Industry for wider powers of control over the siting of factories in congested areas has also given rise to dissension. So far the Ministry has failed to over-come the opposition of industry, expressed both through poli-ticians and its own representative bodies, to the granting of these powers which the civil servants consider essential to the success of the location of industry policy. Again, the proposal to increase substantially the government's investment in and responsibility for long-range industrial and scientific research has been bitterly disputed. The civil servants concerned with economic develop-ment have advocated the proposal because they believe that Japan can no longer be content with importing the results of foreign technical and scientific discoveries and that the govern-ment alone can foster the fundamental research required. The policy has encountered strong political opposition based on the ground that it involves an undesirable and unnecessary enlarge-ment of the State's functions. Here, of course, the politicians are speaking for their industrial backers.

When we come to examine the direct relations between the bureaucracy and private business we meet much obscurity and complexity. The economic administrator finds his task of policy-making simplified in some ways by the concentration of economic power in a few large, diversified groups and by the presence in all sections of the economy of numerous business associations. Channels of communication are easily available to the bureau-crat, and Japanese social arrangements provide ample oppor-tunities for persuasion at other than formal meetings. Further, there is an inter-penetration of personnel which goes far beyond what we are accustomed to in Great Britain. Japanese civil servants in the administrative grade are promoted by seniority up to a certain point in their careers, but this has the result that by the time they reach the middle or late forties many of them cannot expect further advancement. It is usual, therefore, for such persons to retire from the service at that age and to enter other callings. Those from the economic departments, especially the Ministry of International Trade and Industry, find jobs in private industry and trade and those from the Ministry of Finance in banking.[8] The presence of so many ex-civil servants

[8] On inquiring whether officials of the Ministry of Agriculture took up farming on retirement, I was told: 'No, they go into politics'!

in the higher ranks of industrial and financial management has probably been of value to the bureaucracy in disseminating ideas and in enlisting support for policies, but, of course, the traffic in influence is by no means only one way. In the past, as we shall see in Chapter X, the government used the great business houses as agents of its economic policy, but this relationship did not prevent the business houses from bringing pressure on the government. The same is true today, although from time to time there have been changes in attitudes and circumstances. In the early post-war period the government was obliged to take the lead in many economic activities previously left to private enterprise, and industry on the whole welcomed this initiative. During the last decade industry has begun to demand greater independence, but many firms who assert this claim are among the first to call for government help when they encounter an unfamiliar situation. On the other hand, some great firms (e.g. Hitachi, Matsushita, and Toyota) consistently repudiate official interference and are far from responsive to leads from the government. Thus, as is to be expected in a period of rapid growth, the relations between industry and officialdom are by no means of a uniform pattern.

There are certain respects in which Japanese industrialists show definitely less docility than their British counterparts when they are called upon to co-operate in the execution of official policy. In the ordering of the British economy, the government depends heavily on extra-legal measures, on informal understandings between government departments and industrial groups, and on what Sir Dennis Robertson called 'jockeying along'. For example, in putting into effect the recommendations of the Monopolies Commission the government has seldom used its compulsory powers but has been content to rely upon undertakings by industries to abandon condemned practices. In the determination of policy for the nationalized industries ministers have often preferred to persuade or to cajole the controlling boards rather than to use their legal powers of issuing directives. For many years the division of the output of cars between home and foreign markets was regulated simply by an understanding between the motor manufacturers and the Board of Trade. To take another example, the Post Office, in buying telephone cable, at one time followed the policy of placing bulk orders with the manufacturers' association and of relying on the association to distribute the business among the several firms.

Now in Japan, as already indicated, the government also makes use of non-statutory means of exerting pressure, but there are circumstances and occasions when it finds greater difficulty than the British government in obtaining the co-operation of business. In regard to economic planning, as we have seen, the attitude of industry is ambiguous, but in some fields it is quite clearly defined. The officials of the Fair Trade Commission declare that few results in the sphere of anti-monopoly policy would be achieved by extra-legal cajolement or understandings between the government and industry. A distinguished administrator, with much experience of the area where government and private industry confront each other, had no doubt that it was impossible in Japan to delegate to the cable-makers' association the task of allocating orders, as happened in Britain; the Ministry had to assume full and detailed responsibility for the placing of the orders.

The explanation is to be found not so much in hostility to government leadership as in the fierce rivalries among different industrial groups which are themselves bound together by strong ties of loyalty. Independent firms often co-operate effectively with one another in matters of clearly recognized common concern, but outside that range of interests their rivalries oblige the government to keep in its own hands functions which in Britain are often shared with industry. Where executive duties are farmed out, as in the *Yushutsu Kumiai* (Export Associations), which allocate quotas of exports subject to foreign restrictions, the procedure is governed by fixed rules laid down by the Ministry. In these circumstances, it is not surprising to find that co-operative research, such as that undertaken by the various research associations organized in Britain by the Department of Scientific and Industrial Research, is difficult to arrange in Japan. There competition in research as in much else is the rule. Who can say with confidence that the Japanese way is not to be preferred?

IV

The Financial System and
Monetary Policy

FINANCIAL TRENDS

JAPAN's finances during several periods of her modern history
have been gravely disordered and her traditional expansionist
policy has brought recurrent anxieties about the balance of
payments. At the close of the Second World War her finances
entered upon the most chaotic period in her modern history and
a long struggle was needed before even a modest degree of
stability was restored. By the middle 1950s, however, Japan's
financial position was reasonably stable and her banking and
monetary system was ready to make its contribution to the economic progress that lay ahead. In this chapter we shall trace in
outline the course of financial events after 1945, and against that
background we shall examine the banking system as it emerged
from the confusions of war and inflation. We shall then discuss
the outstanding issues of financial policy that have lately been the
subject of vigorous debate. In this sector of the economy, as in
others, reconstruction in its early stages was powerfully influenced by the ideological promptings of the Occupation authorities. It will be necessary, therefore, to pose the question: to what
extent did Occupation policy exercise an enduring effect on the
institutional pattern?

The collapse of the Japanese economy in the summer of 1945
was accompanied by a violent inflation which owed its initial
impulse to the lavish distribution of funds by the government in
settlement of war-expenditure accounts and to the withdrawal
of bank deposits. By the beginning of 1946 the index of wholesale
prices (1934–6=100) had risen to about 800, and prices in the
black market had increased even more. In February and March
of that year the government made its first attempt to arrest the
movement. The outstanding notes of the Bank of Japan were
compulsorily exchanged for a new issue, withdrawals from
deposit accounts were drastically restricted, and a capital levy

was carried out. These measures temporarily checked the rise of prices. But the inflation had been a symptom of a fundamental disequilibrium. Industrial production was at a very low level, and stocks of materials left over from the war were almost exhausted. Meanwhile demand was being increased by the release of purchasing power previously dammed up by wartime controls and by the heavy budgetary deficits which the government, faced by enormous claims for reconstruction finance, could not avoid. The currency reform and the capital levy wiped out past obligations but could not touch the causes of the current *malaise*. So the inflationary trend was soon resumed. By September 1946 the note issue outstanding again rose above its pre-reform peak. It continued to grow rapidly throughout the remainder of 1946 and during the next year. In the course of 1948 the expansion was at a somewhat slower rate. By this time industrial production had achieved some measure of recovery, and American aid made possible the import of large quantities of food and raw materials without taxing domestic resources. Yet the inflation was by no means under control and the note issue and prices still continued their upward course. In March 1949 the amount of bank-notes outstanding was twenty times greater than immediately after the currency reform of March 1946. The index of wholesale prices (1934–6 = 1) increased from 15 in April 1946 to 197 in March 1949, and the rise in retail prices corresponded.[1]

During this first post-war period the government and the central financial authorities supplied funds lavishly to industry both indirectly through the purchase of bank bonds and directly through subsidies. Subsidies paid to producers of basic materials came to 22,500 million yen in 1947, 62,500 million yen in 1948, and 97,900 million yen in 1949.[2] Up to the end of 1946 the Central Bank, which granted credit liberally to the other banks for financing industrial reconstruction, was the chief agent of the inflation. Thereafter the role was assumed by the Reconstruction Finance Bank. This concern was founded in February 1947 to furnish loans for the reconstruction of the 'essential' or 'basic' industries and to say that it made an important contribution to industrial recovery would be an understatement. In 1947 it

[1] Tsuru, in Internat. Econ. Assoc., *The Business Cycle*, pp. 178 ff., where an outline of these developments is given.
[2] *Fuji Bank B.*, Sept. 1956, p. 5.

furnished no less than 72 per cent and in 1948 69 per cent of the total funds applied to corporate fixed investment.[3] The coal-mining, electric power, and shipping industries obtained nearly all their new capital from this bank. Yet, since the funds it required were obtained by selling its debentures to the Bank of Japan, its operations contributed powerfully to the inflationary pressure of the time. This is not necessarily a condemnation. It may be argued that in the desperate condition of the economy after the end of the war, a transference of real resources to those who would apply them to rebuilding the country's industries was an overriding necessity and that the method used for this purpose was the only means to hand.

Throughout the period from 1945 to the beginning of 1949 the Japanese economy was insulated from the rest of the world. Foreign trade was strictly controlled, under the supervision of SCAP, and was conducted for the most part by official trade bodies. A multiple-exchange system came into being for these transactions, so that for every commodity dealt in a specific rate was constructed which represented the ratio between the Japanese price and the world price for that commodity. The rates ranged between 100 and 900 yen to the dollar. What the equilibrium rate stood at during this period is a question of only theoretical interest, for Japan's heavy debit balance on current account was met by American aid on a lavish scale. In 1947 and 1948 this aid amounted to $404 million and $461 million, equivalent to 77 per cent and 68 per cent respectively of the c.i.f. value of the total commodity imports. Without the aid it would have been impossible for Japan to finance sufficient imports to avoid starvation among her urban population or to restart many of her industries. The disinflationary effect of these aid imports was offset by the disbursement of counterpart funds by the government, chiefly in its subsidies to producers and traders.

The post-war inflation was brought to a sudden end by the effective intervention of the Occupation authorities, who became convinced that financial stability was a prerequisite of industrial recovery. In February 1949 Mr Joseph Dodge came to Japan as economic adviser to SCAP and, on his advice, a rigorous deflationary policy was imposed on the Japanese government. The measures included the discontinuance of lending by the Recon-

[3] Shinohara, in *Hitotsubashi J. Econ.*, Feb. 1964, p. 29.

struction Finance Bank, the reduction of subsidies and of public expenditure as a whole with the object of producing a large budgetary surplus for the financial year 1949–50, and the establishment of a single exchange rate (360 yen to the dollar). This policy met with some considerable success, but it is evident that the Dodge deflation was less ruthless in practice than in original intention. The Japanese government at this time feared that the deflationary measures advocated by Mr Dodge were likely to be so severe as to frustrate industrial recovery. So they took steps to mitigate the impact of the deflation on industry. Various means were introduced for this purpose, including the reduction of interest rates, the abolition of excess profits tax on companies, and a legal provision for the revaluation of assets which had the effect of reducing the burden of income tax on business.[4] The government also sought to alleviate the difficulties caused by the winding up of the Reconstruction Finance Bank by granting loans from the United States Aid Counterpart Fund which was credited with the proceeds of the sale of American 'aid' materials. In 1949 about 19 per cent and in 1950 about 17 per cent of private fixed investment was supplied from this source.[5] Meanwhile industry, deprived of its chief source of loans, turned increasingly to the commercial banks for accommodation, with the result that loans refused at the front door were generously provided at the back. The outcome of these inconsistent policies was that between March 1949 and June 1950 the note issue remained virtually unchanged, wholesale prices rose slightly, and retail prices actually fell.

The end of the disinflationary period was as sudden as its beginning. Although the budget for 1950–1 again provided for a surplus, the outbreak of the Korean War in June 1950 subjected the economy to the pressure of large new demands. Apart from the 'special procurement' requirements of the United Nations forces, a substantial foreign demand arose for Japanese manufactures. Since imports were strictly controlled, the result was a marked improvement in Japan's balance of payments and at the same time a renewal of the inflation. The Central Bank gave heavy advances to the Foreign Exchange Control Board for the purchase of the incoming foreign exchange and it also

[4] Industr. Bank, *Survey Fin. & Ind.*, Mar.–Apr. 1955, p. 2.
[5] Shinohara, in *Hitotsubashi J. Econ.*, Feb. 1964, p. 30.

increased its credits to the commercial banks which were being
called upon to finance the growing volume of trade and production.[6] Towards the end of 1950 the government and the Bank tried
to check the inflationary pressure by introducing measures to encourage imports. Then, early in 1951, the Bank raised interest
rates and extended its use of selective credit controls. These re-
straining measures, however, were insufficient to prevent a rise
in prices that was very steep even by the standards of the period,
and Japanese wholesale prices moved seriously out of line with
world prices in the course of the Korean boom.[7] Retail prices
and money-wage rates also moved upwards, while profits soared.

The collapse of the war boom in the spring of 1951 led to a
decline in the foreign demand for Japanese goods, and later the
restrictions imposed on imports into the sterling area brought
about a further contraction in exports. 'Special procurement'
expenditure, however, still remained at a high level, and for
some time industrialists continued to invest heavily in new
buildings and equipment. In this policy they were encouraged
by the government, which made investment funds available
through a number of new financial institutions set up at this
time, namely the Japan Development Bank and the Japan Export–Import Bank. The first-mentioned of these in effect took
over the business hitherto conducted by the United States Aid
Counterpart Fund, and it was this bank that was subsequently
responsible for most of the State loans made for private fixed
investment; these in 1952 accounted for about a quarter of all
corporate fixed investment. Meanwhile heavy borrowing from
the commercial banks continued. The result was that the disparity between Japanese and world prices which had appeared
during the Korean boom persisted into the subsequent recession.
These sudden changes in economic conditions were reflected in
the state of Japan's financial reserves. In the period before 1949
United States' aid had been sufficient to enable Japan not only
to pay for her imports but also to permit some investment in
foreign exchange. The aid came to an end in 1951, but by then
'special procurement', including expenditure by United States'

[6] E. E. Ehrlich and F. M. Tamagna, 'Japan', in B. H. Beckhart, ed., *Banking Systems*
    (1954), p. 530.
[7] Between June 1950 and Apr. 1951 Japan's wholesale prices rose by 52 per cent,
    American prices by 17 per cent, and British prices by 22 per cent.

soldiers in Japan, had taken its place as a source of dollars.[8] By the use of these resources Japan was able not only to raise substantially her imports during 1951 and 1952, but also to make large additions to her holdings of foreign currencies. These rose from $260 million in March 1950 to $1,178 million in May 1952.

After the middle of 1952 the financial situation seriously deteriorated. Whereas inflation abroad had been brought under control by resort to dear-money policies, in Japan credit was still extended on easy terms. Private industry continued to invest heavily in re-equipment, and in this it was financed by the commercial banks, which in turn were provided with ample credit by the Bank of Japan. An even more important factor was the rise in loans from government agencies and in government spending, especially on equipment for hydro-electric power-stations and other public utilities. Thus another boom was set going by bank-financed industrial investment and by increased government expenditure. Money wages, which had not kept pace with prices or production during 1950 and 1951, now rose faster than either, and domestic consumption expanded accordingly, to the detriment of the export trade. In 1953 these trends persisted, and the divergence between Japanese and world prices grew wider. Although 'special procurement' expenditure continued at a high level, the export trade stagnated and an enormous rise in imports led to a large deficit on current trading. A balance-of-payments crisis seemed to be approaching. Between May 1952 and May 1953 the foreign-exchange reserves fell from $1,178 million to $852 million.[9]

The crisis persuaded the government, during the later months of 1953, to introduce a retrenchment policy to correct the imbalance. Its main instrument was not fiscal (although the austerity budget of 1954–5 played its part), but rather monetary policy. Rates of interest were raised in the autumn of 1953 and again in the early months of the next year. In the execution of its lending policy the Bank of Japan henceforward made increasing use of a device that discriminated sharply against large borrowing. It allowed each of its customer banks a basic amount of credit, and varied its rates according to the extent to which the borrowings approached, attained, or exceeded that amount.

---

[8] For a definition of 'special procurement', see Statist. App., p. 278 n. below.
[9] EPA., *Econ. Survey, 1953–4*, pp. 1–26 and *passim*.

E

Since the commercial banks depended on the Central Bank for their resources, and since industry at this time relied mainly on bank loans to finance development, these measures were extremely effective. Equipment investment diminished and stocks were liquidated. In March 1954 wholesale prices, which then stood at 60 per cent above the level of June 1950, turned downwards. By September they had fallen by 8 per cent, and by the end of the year the disparities between foreign and domestic prices had narrowed. As Japan was becoming more competitive at a moment when international trade as a whole was expanding she was able to increase her exports very substantially and to end the year with a small surplus on her balance of payments. During the next two years her financial achievements were even more impressive. The enlargement of the export trade gave Japan a payments surplus in the fiscal year 1955–6 of $535 million, about equivalent to her revenue from 'special procurement'. For the first time since the war Japan had succeeded in balancing her accounts out of the proceeds of her current trading. Her exchange reserves now reached $1,400 million, a gain of 30 per cent in the course of the year.

The expansion in 1955 occurred without any rise in prices; indeed, both wholesale and retail prices were lower at the end of the year than at the beginning. This contrast with the conditions of the boom in 1950–1 requires explanation, for, although the improvement started in the export trade, it might have been expected that domestic demand also would have risen as money incomes increased. Several reasons may be suggested. First, Japan entered upon this period with a surplus of industrial capacity, so that there was no immediate need for new domestic fixed investment to enable her to meet the increased home and foreign demand. Secondly, wage rates remained stable, largely because of the existence of many underemployed persons who could be absorbed at the existing levels of money wages. Thirdly, there was an exceptionally good harvest. Finally, domestic demand was damped down by a large increase in savings, both by companies and by individuals, so that it was possible to finance the expansion without resort to bank credit.[10] These conditions were not seriously disturbed in 1956, although, under the impact of the continuing boom, prices moved upwards, bank

[10] EPA, *Econ. Survey, 1955–6*, pp. 1–23.

credit expanded, and the balance of payments deteriorated in the later months of the year.

The reconstruction period was now over and a new era in Japan's economic development was at hand. In 1956 economic expansion was so rapid as to earn the appellation 'the Jimmu Boom'.[11] A steep rise in exports, for which the Suez crisis was partly responsible, enlarged the foreign-exchange reserves, and the inflow of funds increased the liquidity of the commercial banks. Despite the revival of demand on the part of industry for fresh funds for capital investment, the banks found themselves able to dispense with advances from the Bank of Japan and these fell to their lowest level since the end of the war.

In the early months of 1957, however, symptoms of inflation again appeared. Prices rose, imports increased very fast, the balance of international payments deteriorated, and by June the reserves had fallen to $879 million compared with $1,484 million in December 1956. The authorities were again impelled to introduce deflationary measures. The Bank of Japan raised its interest rates in several stages and put other pressure on the commercial banks to curtail their advances. This pressure was effective since by that time the boom had exhausted the banks' liquidity and had brought them once more into dependence on loans from the Central Bank. In addition, the government's investment projects were postponed and various emergency measures (such as a tightening of controls over foreign exchange) were introduced. As in 1953–4 the deflationary policy had an almost immediate effect on the economy which seemed to have lost none of its flexibility. Stocks were quickly sold, prices fell sharply, and fixed capital investment declined. By the summer of 1958 equilibrium was restored and the rise of industrial production was resumed. In 1959 trade and industry again boomed. Investment in stocks increased rapidly in the first half of that year and this was soon followed by a rise in fixed capital investment. Industrial production expanded by about a quarter in both 1959 and 1960, and exports achieved a record. At the end of 1960 the foreign-exchange reserves were more than double those of 1958.[12]

---

[11] i.e. The biggest boom since Jimmu, the legendary first Emperor of Japan.

[12] See Fuji Bank, *Banking in Modern Japan* (1961), pp. 232 ff.; EPA, *Econ. Survey, 1961–2*, ch. i, and *1962–3*, ch. i, for information about monetary developments and policy.

The monetary authorities were anxious on this occasion to prevent the boom from getting out of hand, and in 1959 they tried to restrain the commercial banks not merely by raising interest rates but also by introducing a special-deposit system which obliged the commercial banks to maintain with the Central Bank reserves equivalent to about 1 per cent of their deposits. The authorities were persuaded that the effect of this policy was such as to warrant their easing the controls during the summer of 1960. The Bank of Japan not merely reduced its rates of discount but also purchased securities in order to increase banking liquidity. Japan had now entered, so it was believed, a period of 'sustainable growth', and stability seemed so assured as to induce the authorities to encourage a further expansion of credit early in 1961. But the optimism was short-lived. By the summer of that year inflationary symptoms appeared and the balance of payments deteriorated. The economy, it was said, had become 'over-heated'. It was again necessary, therefore, for the authorities to impose restraints. The government was averse from increasing taxes, especially as its accounts were in surplus, and the solution was left entirely to monetary policy. Interest rates were raised in stages, the compulsory deposit-reserve rate was increased, the Bank tightened its 'window' controls, and various items of government expenditure were postponed.

It is significant that on this occasion the response of the economy to the restrictions was much slower than in 1957 or in 1954. It is true that wholesale prices fell as stocks were liquidated, but for a time investment as a whole was hardly checked and retail prices continued to rise. Since in the opinion of some economists the limited response on this occasion may well foreshadow a decline in the flexibility of the Japanese economy, it is necessary to offer an explanation in some detail. In the first place, it appears that the mood of the business world remained optimistic despite the restrictions. The mounting prosperity of the previous decade and the generous long-run forecasts of growth set out in the Income Doubling Plan persuaded manufacturers and bankers that it was safe to regard the setback as temporary and unimportant. The preceding boom in its later stages, moreover, was primarily a boom in fixed capital investment, and it was difficult to cut back projects quickly and, in the light of the optimistic forecasts, it seemed unnecessary to do so. Further, industry had found new sources of borrowing. The volume of savings had risen fast with the forward surge of incomes and part of these savings were absorbed by a number of new investment trusts. Firms were therefore able to command additional resources by selling their securities to the trusts. At the same time inter-firm credit was extended on a much larger scale than before, a point that British readers of the Radcliffe Report will note with interest. This was not all. Japanese growth had at last been recognized in the outside world. There was a substantial increase in foreign investment in Japan, while Japanese financial houses acquired a large supply of Euro-dollars which escaped the net of foreign-exchange controls. Finally, the government was becoming more sensitive to the effects of deflationary measures on small firms which in the past had been ruthlessly exposed to them, and it took various steps to mitigate the damage that the restriction of credit inflicted on such firms. Thus the availability of sources of credit outside the banking system, combined with a somewhat ambivalent policy on the part of the government, delayed the effectiveness of the restrictions.

For these reasons about twelve months elapsed before equilibrium was restored. By the summer of 1962, however, the visible trade balance had improved and foreign-exchange reserves were again rising. The monetary authorities relaxed their controls by stages after October 1962; wholesale prices began to increase before the end of the year; and in the early months of 1963 production turned upwards. Another move forward then seemed imminent. But conditions differed in certain important respects from those that had attended the first stages of previous booms. Japan was now far more closely linked with the international capital and money markets than in the past. Her authorities were no longer operating in a closed system, and the liberalization of trade was striking formerly effective weapons of control from their hands. Further, because of the changed conditions in the labour market presently to be described, the upward trend of wages had persisted during the period in which production was stagnating. The effect was particularly evident in the mounting cost of services. This was the main cause of the rise in consumer prices by 6·7 per cent in 1962, in marked contrast to what had happened during previous periods of credit restriction. In these circumstances it is natural that the monetary

authorities should subject the financial system to a critical examination and that those responsible for economic policy as a whole
should refuse to allow the magnitude of past achievements to
lure them into complacency. The problem which they faced,
however, cannot be fully understood without further analysis of
the structure and functioning of the financial system as a whole.

THE STRUCTURE OF BANKING

An understanding of the post-war changes in Japan's banking
system requires a brief reference to the evolution of that system
during the modern era. As in other branches of her national life,
Japan built up her financial institutions by the skilful adaptation
of Western models to her own needs, an adaptation that called
for experiments over many years. In the 1870s she introduced a
national banking system on the American pattern, and vestiges
of this were long to be found in the names of certain of the banks.
Early in the next decade she abandoned the American system
in favour of a central banking system of the European type. This
occurred with the foundation of the Bank of Japan in 1882, an
institution subject to strict control by the Minister of Finance.
From then onwards a large number of commercial and savings
banks were founded by private interests and these conducted
business similar to that of their counterparts overseas. But the
government's economic policy required the establishment of
other banks with special functions, and before the end of the
nineteenth century several banks of this type were created on
official initiative. They included the Yokohama Specie Bank,
which throughout its career conducted most of the foreign-
exchange business of the country, the Industrial Bank of Japan
formed for the purpose of making long-term loans to industry,
the Hypothec Bank, which (together with numerous prefectural
Agricultural and Industrial Banks) was intended to provide long-
term loans to agriculture, and the Hokkaido Development Bank.
Various colonial banks for operating in Korea and Formosa were
also established. These Special Banks became important instruments of national policy both in Japan Proper and overseas.[13]

---

[13] A useful account of the development and operation of the banking system in the
Meiji period is given in US Monetary Commission (1910), *Reports*, vol. xviii;
see also US Dept of Commerce, *Japanese Banking*, by H. M. Bratter (1931), and
Allen, *Short Economic History*, chs. iii, vi, and ix.

In the commercial banking centres the leading institutions were developed as constituents of the *Zaibatsu*, and neither those banks nor the numerous small banks that served local needs had close relations with the Central Bank. The system, therefore, presented some contradictory features. On the one hand, the existence of a group of Special Banks, over which the government exercised control, pointed to a highly centralized system. On the other hand, the commercial banks were unco-ordinated and far from responsive in their credit policy to leads given by the Central Bank.

The number of ordinary banks continued to increase until the end of the First World War and in the early months of 1920 there were nearly 2,000 of them. During the inter-war period a process of consolidation set in. A succession of financial crises, notably those of 1920 and 1927, led to the disappearance of many independent local banks by bankruptcy or absorption. The government actively encouraged amalgamations, especially during the 1930s, in the interests of financial stability and in order to secure a more highly centralized control over the creation of credit. By 1929 the number of separate banks had fallen to 874 and by 1937 to 377. Seven of them were of outstanding importance. By the end of the 1930s they were together responsible for nearly three-fifths of the deposits and for nearly two-thirds of the loans, discounts, and advances of all the ordinary banks.[14] With one exception, these great banks were controlled by the *Zaibatsu*. The same interests dominated the trust companies which held substantial deposits, and also the chief insurance companies. There were also many savings banks. Like the ordinary banks, these were reduced in number as the result of amalgamations during the inter-war years—from 648 in 1913 to 72 in 1937. The needs of small producers and traders were served by various types of co-operative credit banks which were co-ordinated by a central institution. Mutual loan companies of a type traditional to Japan also flourished. Finally, the Deposits Bureau of the Ministry of Finance and Post Office Insurance Authority occupied an important place in the financial system. They collected savings and premiums from the people and invested mainly in government securities and in the debentures issued by the Special Banks.[15]

[14] Ehrlich and Tamagna, in Beckhart, *Banking Systems*, p. 538.   [15] Ibid. p. 545.

The movement towards consolidation had created a more stable financial structure, but it had failed to bring about fundamental changes in the character of the banking system, which was still composed of distinct groups of banks with slender links between them. The Bank of Japan's position remained much weaker than that of central banks in the chief Western countries. It grew up as an institution for issuing currency, for the conduct of the government's financial business, and for providing cheap finance to the Special Banks, notably the Yokohama Specie Bank. Yet, although it was called upon to lend lavishly to the commercial banks in times of emergency, its control over their credit policy remained weak. The Bank did not hold the reserves of the ordinary banks and its rate was not a determining one. Indeed, the leading commercial banks were members of great economic empires and their ample resources permitted them to maintain their independence of the Central Bank's policy.

Throughout its history the Bank of Japan had been expected to lend financial help to the government in times of difficulty, and when Takahashi's reflation policy began in 1932, it was required to issue and later to absorb large quantities of government bonds. This, as a Japanese banker declared, marked 'the beginning of the role of the Bank of Japan as a supplier of unlimited credit to the government'.[16] Nevertheless, in the Takahashi period, although the government was bent on reflation, the ordinary banks preferred to pursue a different policy and were sufficiently independent to do so. They refrained from creating private credit to match that of the government and its institutions. In fact, they reduced their loans to industry and trade. This damped down the inflationary effect of the deficit financing of the period.

Many of the peculiar features of Japan's banking system are to be explained by the absence of well developed capital and money markets. No large class of private investor in industrial securities existed in Japan. Personal savings normally went into fixed-deposit accounts in the commercial banks or, via Post Office savings, into the Deposits Bureau of the Ministry of Finance. The city banks belonging to the *Zaibatsu* held a key position in the several groups and through them the *Zaibatsu* were freed from dependence upon sources of capital supply

[16] S. Horie, *Banking System and Bank Liquidity in Japan* (1952), p. 5.

external to their own organizations. The smaller banks still financed local traders and producers, although by the middle 1930s this function was being increasingly assumed by the *Zaibatsu* trading companies.

In both classes of ordinary banks the resources provided to industry took the form of advances on promissory notes and the purchase of debentures. The *Zaibatsu* banks were accustomed to make large advances to the holding companies at the centre of each *Zaibatsu* empire to enable them to acquire shares in subsidiary or affiliated companies. All the Japanese commercial banks differed from those of England in regard to the structure both of their assets and of their liabilities. A high proportion of their deposits (normally about 60 per cent) consisted of time deposits, and they furnished long-term as well as short-term loans to industry. The Special Banks, for their part, operated in a number of distinct fields. The Yokohama Specie Bank had the right of borrowing from the Central Bank on favourable terms, but it established only slender links with the commercial banks concerned primarily with domestic finance. The Industrial and the Hypothec Banks raised resources for long-term loans to industry, agriculture, and public utilities by issuing debentures which were largely taken up by other financial institutions closely connected with the government. The government itself relied to a considerable extent for long- and short-term financing on the Treasury Deposits Bureau and the savings banks as well as on the Bank of Japan.[17] In the absence of a well organized discount market to serve as a link between the operations of the various types of banks, authority over the system remained diffused.

The necessities of wartime finance caused fundamental changes in the banking structure and a more highly centralized control over the operation of the whole system was imposed. After 1937 vast quantitities of government bonds were issued to cover budgetary deficits and the Central Bank itself invested heavily in them. At the same time its influence over the policy of the other banks was extended. During the first few years of the war the main instrument for industrial financing was the Industrial Bank of Japan. The government guaranteed this Bank against losses that might arise from advances to the munitions

[17] Bank of Japan, *Outline of the Financial System in Japan* (1953), pp. 2–4.

industries and raised the upper limit on its debenture issues. Then, in 1942 the government set up a new institution, the War-time Finance Bank, with the special function of financing the worst risks in the munitions trades. Like the Industrial Bank this institution obtained its funds by issuing debentures guaranteed by the government. These were taken up mainly by the ordinary banks. Other official organs were founded for financing enterprises in territories overseas. During this period the commercial banks were subjected to strict official control, and their business was governed largely by the provision of government guarantees on their advances to the 'essential' industries. As the various *Zaibatsu* played a leading part in the expansion of war production, their banks became especially heavily committed in that field.

The government's influence was used in promoting further bank amalgamations, for it was realized that with a more highly concentrated system, central control could be the more easily exercised. The result was that by the end of the war the number of commercial banks had been reduced to sixty-one. Savings banks as distinct institutions almost disappeared. This occurred because the government, in order to increase savings, authorized the ordinary banks to establish savings departments. Thereupon savings banks were merged with the other banks and by the end of the war only four survived. Shortly afterwards even these were turned into ordinary banks. The largest of them became the Kyowa Bank, one of the major post-war banks. In the same way and for similar reasons the various trust companies were absorbed during the war by the *Zaibatsu* banks to which they were related. What in effect had happened was that the enforcement by the government of a cheap-money policy and the overwhelming predominance of government bonds and officially guaranteed advances in the assets of the banking system as a whole destroyed the previous distinctions between the commercial banks, savings banks, and trust companies. The post-war inflation, which made the collection of savings deposits impossible for several years, confirmed the change brought about by the war.[18] It also left the

[18] Data for early post-war financial developments from Horie, *passim*; Bank of Japan, *Outline of Financial System*, pp. 4–23; Industr. Bank, *Survey Fin. & Ind.*, Mar.–Apr. 1955, pp. 1–9; Ehrlich and Tamagna, in Beckhart, *Banking Systems*; and personal inquiries.

commercial banks without sufficient liquid resources to finance reconstruction.

Conditions in the years immediately after the war were affected not only by the continuing inflation but also by the policy of the Occupation authorities. These authorities, at any rate during the early period of reform, were intent at once upon destroying the economic power concentrated in the *Zaibatsu* and also upon loosening State control over economic processes. In the pursuit of their first aim they insisted upon the separation of the *Zaibatsu* banks from other undertakings within the same group. Their determination to put an end to the former integration of finance and industry showed itself in their requirement that even the names of the banks should be changed so as to evoke no echo of the past. The Special Banks, which could be regarded as the financial instruments of Japan's imperialist policy, underwent an equally impressive transformation. Those which had operated in the colonies or overseas, including the Bank of Chosen and the Bank of Taiwan, were immediately closed, and the Yokohama Specie Bank came to an end in 1946. In their policy towards the three debenture-issuing Special Banks[19] the Occupation authorities were moved not only by a desire to democratize Japanese institutions, but also by a respect for orthodox banking principles. These had been offended because, just as the ordinary banks had appeared to be all too ready to sacrifice liquidity to profitability, the banks designed for long-term lending operations had attempted to increase their resources by accepting deposits on a large scale. The Special Banks, therefore, were presented with a choice which required them to confine their activities either to deposit banking, thereby surrendering their rights of issuing debentures, or to long-term financing with strict limits on the amount of deposits that they might accept. The Hypothec Bank and the Hokkaido Development Bank chose the former career, the Industrial Bank the latter.

This, however, was by no means the end of the story. The privilege of issuing debentures was of little value during the years of violent inflation when the provision of long-term loans for reconstruction was taken over by the Reconstruction Finance

[19] Namely, the Industrial Bank of Japan, the Hypothec Bank, and the Hokkaido Development Bank.

Bank, which obtained its resources from the Bank of Japan. With the introduction of the Dodge deflation and the abolition of the Reconstruction Finance Bank in 1949, opportunities for the operation of the debenture-issuing banks again appeared. It is true that the legal distinction between those banks and the ordinary banks was destroyed in 1950 when all banks were given the right of issuing debentures within certain limits. In practice, however, the privilege was exercised only by three of the former Special Banks, and by them only because the government subscribed to their stocks and debentures from the United States Aid Counterpart Fund and from the Treasury Deposits Bureau. Finally, by a law of 1952, the debenture-issuing privilege was withdrawn from the ordinary banks. The Hypothec Bank and the Hokkaido Development Bank remained as deposit banks, while the Industrial Bank and a new institution called the Long-Term Credit Bank of Japan became specialized debenture-issuing banks for supplying industry with long-term loans. In the middle 1950s, of the outstanding debentures issued by these two banks, about 25 per cent were held by the city banks, 13 per cent by the local banks, 7 per cent by various co-operatives and savings institutions, and nearly 30 per cent by the Trust Fund Bureau.[20] By such devious courses Japan returned to a position which had been characteristic of this section of her finances for many decades.

The same train of events can be perceived in the field of foreign exchange. The abolition of the Yokohama Specie Bank in 1946 transferred most of the responsibility for foreign-exchange transactions to the government and the Bank of Japan, although a number of leading commercial banks together with branches of foreign banks were authorized, as before the war, to engage in exchange business. Among these banks was the Bank of Tokyo, which had inherited the properties of the Yokohama Specie Bank and carried on business as an ordinary bank with a foreign-exchange department. As long as foreign financial transactions other than official transactions were few and were subject to close government regulation, the risks attendant upon foreign-exchange business were inconsiderable. But as Japan's international business recovered and as controls were lifted, the banking system felt the lack of the former specialized exchange insti-

[20] In 1951 the Treasury Deposits Bureau was renamed the Trust Fund Bureau.

tution. The ordinary commercial banks were preoccupied with
domestic trade and could command neither the liquid resources
nor the expertise and overseas organization adequate for the
foreign-exchange business. A specialized bank, it was believed,
would alone be able to operate on a sufficient scale for efficiency
and to win confidence in foreign financial centres. Such a bank,
as in the past, might be expected to play a part in bringing in
short funds for financing foreign trade by borrowing in markets
where rates of interest were low. In April 1954, therefore, the
Bank of Tokyo was transformed into a specialist foreign-exchange
bank by a law passed for that purpose.[21] Since then the Bank has
operated under a licence granted by the Minister of Finance and
has acted, like its predecessor the Yokohama Specie Bank, as an
agent for the government and the Bank of Japan; in this capacity
it has held part of the foreign-exchange reserves. In legal form
the Bank of Tokyo is rather more independent of government
control than its predecessor and it has not inherited all the
privileges of the old bank. Yet its actual operations are not significantly different, although its share of the foreign-exchange
business remains much lower than before the war. Here also
policy, and the pressure of economic circumstances, restored,
with some modifications, a feature of the pre-war banking system
which the Occupation had destroyed.

The exceptional circumstances of the post-war years compelled the State to undertake new financial functions beyond the
diminished sphere of the Special Banks, and a number of institutions, owned and directly operated by the government, were
established for this purpose. They included the Japan Export–
Import Bank for extending loans in connexion with the export
trade, the Japan Development Bank for lending long term at low
rates of interest to the basic industries, the Agricultural, Forestry,
and Fisheries Finance Corporation for similar operations in the
industries described in its title, the Small Business Finance Corporation for long-term lending to small- and medium-sized
firms, and several others. These banks differed from one another
in practical importance. For example, the Export–Import Bank
for many years played a modest role, although it has lately increased its business through becoming the channel for the long-

[21] *Announcement* by Bank of Tokyo, 1 July 1954, and *Semi-Annual Reps.*; also *Orient. Econ.*, July 1954, pp. 342–3.

term credits and aid to underdeveloped countries. On the other hand, from its foundation, the Japan Development Bank played an important part in the long-term financing of the basic industries after the winding up of the Reconstruction Finance Bank.[22] Its funds have been supplied mainly from government sources, originally from the United States Aid Counterpart Fund and the Reconstruction Finance Bank and later from the Trust Fund Bureau and other government accounts. In recent years it has also acted as the channel for the government's borrowings from the World Bank. Its loans have been made to those sectors of the economy which the government has been especially concerned to promote, and in 1962 48 per cent of its outstanding loans were to the electric-power industry, 25 per cent to shipping, and 10 per cent to the steel industry. The pattern of its lending is now changing and its loans to the export industries and for new projects in the less developed areas of Japan have been growing. The business once conducted by the Development Bank with small enterprises was taken over by the Small Business Finance Corporation established in 1953. Thus the old semi-official or Special Banks for long-term lending were supplemented by a number of purely official banks with similar functions. It is evident that SCAP's policy of fostering the decentralization of financial control and of developing a securities market to promote a wide diffusion of industrial capital foundered. The reasons are clear. The shape of Japan's pre-war financial structure was determined by her policy of accelerating industrial growth in an economy where capital was scarce. These conditions were present in an exaggerated degree after the war, and the justification of the former structure was at least as firmly established as in earlier times. Subsequently the active policy of economic development pursued by the government reinforced the need for financial agencies through which its investment decisions could be carried out.

The succession of changes among the ordinary or commercial banks supports this view. Immediately after the war those banks found themselves gravely weakened. A high proportion of their assets consisted of wartime advances to industry which had been guaranteed by the government. The collapse of production in

[22] Japan Develop. Bank, *Activities and Functions* (1960), and other reports of the Bank (1960–2).

1945 and the cancellation of the government's guarantees left them with meagre resources. The *Zaibatsu* banks which had been especially deeply committed were in an even weaker position than the provincial banks. The dissolution policy dealt them a further blow. Thus it was that in the financing of reconstruction in the early post-war years the main responsibilities were assumed by the government and its financial agencies. After the application of the Dodge policy the commercial banks were called upon to assume the main burden of financing reconstruction. Yet since their resources were exiguous, they could meet the demand for loans only by borrowing heavily from the Central Bank. A Japanese banker himself declared that 'the commercial banks in the early 1950s became merely a channel through which the Central Bank fed industry with investment funds'.[23] The extent to which industry relied upon the banking system for new capital in this period can be illustrated by a few figures. It is estimated that before the war about 45 per cent of new industrial investment by companies was provided by self-financing, while about 30 per cent came from share and bond issues. In 1950–2 the proportion of investment funds provided by self-financing (retained profits and provision for depreciation) was in the neighbourhood of 20–25 per cent, while share and bond issues accounted for only 10 or 12 per cent and direct loans from the government for 7 or 8 per cent.[24] So the major part of the capital required (about 60 per cent) came from bank advances.

This condition did not alter significantly during the rest of the decade, for the rapid growth of production created demands for both long- and short-term capital which only the banks could provide. As a result they found themselves continually in an extremely illiquid state and the ratio of loans to deposits has normally been over 100 per cent.[25] This is commonly described as the 'over-loan' position which, though a source of misgivings to the Central Bank, has merely reproduced in an exaggerated form a condition for long familiar in this section of the banking

[23] Horie, p. 36.
[24] Data from Industr. Bank of Japan; see also, EPA, *Econ. Survey, 1953–4*, p. 184; Min. Fin., *Gen. Survey Japan. Econ.* (1953), Attached Tables, p. 34.
[25] Cf. A. Koizumi, 'The Overloan Problem', in *Hitotsubashi J. Comm. & Management*, Nov. 1962, p. 53; T. Yoshino, *Excessive Dependence of Commercial Banks on Central Bank Loans* (1960).

system. Close links were again forged between particular banks and particular industrial enterprises, even though the association has not been as exclusive as in the old days. A Mitsubishi manufacturing firm still relies on the Mitsubishi Bank for the greater part of its borrowings. Even new concerns which have arisen outside the old *Zaibatsu* have entered into close, though not exclusive, relationships with particular banks; for example, Matsushita with the Sumitomo Bank and the denationalized Yawata Steel Company with the Fuji Bank. As in the past, the bulk of the banks' resources comes from fixed deposits. The contrast between these banks and the deposit banks of the United Kingdom is still as sharp as ever.

There are, however, signs of change. The public is now becoming inclined to invest more of its savings by direct subscription to industrial issues, and the new investment trust companies have attracted an increasing proportion of investment funds. As this tendency gathers strength, the banks may be forced to modify their function as providers of long-term capital for industry. Already they are concerning themselves with alternative lines of business. They have taken an interest in consumer finance especially in the hire-purchase business, and with the growth in the demand for consumer-durables this business is likely to expand.[26] The commercial banks have also participated to a far greater extent than before the war in the foreign-exchange market, another rapidly growing field of activity.

These generalizations apply mainly to the group of banks known as the city banks. In 1963 there were 13 such banks[27] with about 1,900 branches. Together they were responsible for over 60 per cent of the total deposits of the private banks.[28] Besides the city banks, there were 65 local banks with 3,750 branches. These have in some respects taken the place of the *Zaibatsu* trading companies in the financing of small and medium firms. Together with certain financial institutions that operate in rural areas (e.g. mutual loan and agricultural-credit associations) they have also played an increasingly important part in supplying the city banks with call loans, a business which in periods of tight money has been very profitable. The local banks are,

---

[26] *Fuji Bank B.*, June 1961, p. 8.   [27] Including the Bank of Tokyo.
[28] 'Private banks' include city banks, local banks, trust banks, and long-term credit banks.

therefore, clearly more liquid than the city banks, a condition largely attributable to the fact that government payments are normally in excess of government receipts in rural areas. The city banks have been unable to move into those areas because of restrictions placed by the Ministry of Finance on the opening of new branches.[29]

FINANCIAL OPERATIONS AND POLICIES

The illiquid condition of the commercial banks and their dependence upon the Bank of Japan for advances naturally buttressed the power of the central monetary authorities. This was vividly demonstrated upon the introduction of the deflationary policy in 1954. Industrial companies then found themselves at the mercy of their creditor banks to whose recommendations for retrenchment or reorganization they had perforce to conform. The creditor banks for their part found their policy dictated by the Central Bank. Despite the efforts of SCAP to decentralize authority, by that time financial control had become more highly concentrated than ever before.

Subsequently there were wide oscillations in the Central Bank's power. Deflation and austerity in 1954 removed the bad risks, promoted efficiency in industry, and prepared the way for the rapid expansion of the next two years. As industrial profits rose, dependence upon bank loans decreased, especially since the expansion in production was accomplished without much new investment. The commercial banks in turn became less dependent upon the Bank of Japan. Indeed, they were able greatly to reduce their outstanding indebtedness. A result of this change was to bring down the loans of the Central Bank from nearly 300,000 million yen in December 1953 to 27,000 million yen in March 1956.[30] The Bank's note issue also fell substantially. At the same time, the old *Zaibatsu* banks drew closer to their former associates in industry and trade, and as the pattern of economic organization was restored, the practice of self-financing by each of the groups tended to return. The lessened dependence of the commercial banks upon the Bank of Japan put an end to the

[29] See Bank of Japan, *Money and Banking in Japan* (Mar. 1961), and H. F. Schiffer, *The Modern Japanese Banking System* (1962) for data on recent developments in the banking system.

[30] Bank of Japan, *Econ. Statist. Monthly*; also *Fuji Bank B.*, Sept. 1956, pp. 51–52, 63.

F

latter's financial ascendancy and a banking situation in many respects comparable with that before the war was re-established. As a Japanese commentator remarked: 'the redemption of Bank of Japan loans by almost all city banks resulted in the fact that the Bank of Japan lost its power of regulating finance as a central bank'.[31]

That it had temporarily lost its power over the credit operations of the commercial banks is clear, for despite its efforts to reduce the liquidity of the system, the loans of the commercial banks began to rise during 1955 and when in the following year they again began to borrow heavily from the Central Bank, the latter was obliged to meet their demands. It was only when the expansion of credit had produced a crisis in the balance of payments that the Bank of Japan found itself able to exert effective pressure on its clients. This situation was repeated in the course of the subsequent boom of 1960–1.

How far these oscillations of power are to be regarded as a serious weakness in the Japanese financial system is open to debate. There are those who consider that the Japanese system, under which the Bank of Japan by the ruthless exercise of its power when the economy is over-extended can quickly restore equilibrium, has considerable advantages over, say, the British system, in which effective deflationary pressures in times of emergency are more difficult to exert without retarding effects on development. They argue that instability is a small price to pay for rapid secular growth. Some, indeed, go so far as to suggest that fluctuations of considerable amplitude have been an inevitable concomitant of Japan's growth. Throughout the modern era, Japan's development has depended both on her determined pursuit of a vigorously expansionist policy and also on her readiness to impose ruthless restrictive measures at times when that policy has placed the economy in jeopardy. If these measures had not been available, Japan could hardly have pressed on with such eager confidence. There is force in these arguments, but something must be said on the other side. Many Japanese bankers and economists are certainly less complacent. The critics admit that monetary policy has achieved a considerable success so far, but they are inclined to attribute it

---

[31] 'Economic Conditions in Japan', *Sumitomo Bank R.*, July 1956, p. 7. Cf. also IMF, *Ann. Rep., 1956*, p. 77.

mainly to the fundamental characteristics of the economy rather than solely to the technique of financial control. Such a technique, they say, can be effective only when costs are very flexible, and flexibility has hitherto depended on the existence of a large sector in which intensely competitive conditions prevail in both the product and the labour market. Should these conditions change, and there are signs that they are changing, the balance of the economy once lost might be difficult to restore unless new methods of credit control were introduced.

The problem can scarcely be understood without further analysis of fundamental processes in the banking system and without some consideration of the methods of money supply and the structure of interest rates. In the United Kingdom the increase in the money supply (bank deposits and notes) is matched by a corresponding increase in the Bank of England's holdings of government securities, and the Bank tries to control that supply by the use of Bank Rate and by 'open-market' operations. In Japan the money supply, which in the absence of a highly developed cheque currency consists mainly of Bank of Japan notes, is controlled by other means.[32] Since the government's indebtedness incurred before 1945 was wiped out by inflation, and since during the greater part of the postwar period there has been a budgetary surplus, the volume of government securities is small. At the same time many official operations, including advances to private industry through such agencies as the Development Bank, are financed by calling on official resources, chiefly those in the Trust Fund Bureau. Hence the only way in which the money supply can be increased is by advances by the Bank of Japan to the commercial banks and by the purchase of gold and foreign exchange from exporters.

In its credit operations the Bank of Japan is *normally* a passive agent, for it lacks instruments of control that can be applied continuously. This deficiency can be attributed not only to the shortage of government securities but also to the virtual absence of a money market in the British sense. Practically all the government's short-dated bills (corresponding to the British

---

[32] For details, see Bank of Japan, *The Bank of Japan: Its Function and Organization* (Mar. 1962).

Treasury bills) are taken up by official agencies such as the Trust Fund Bureau and by the Bank of Japan. Commercial banks have no inducement to hold them because the bill rate is pegged by the government well below the level of market rates for call money, and because they pay little or no attention to their own liquidity ratios in regulating their own lending policy. Thus Bank Rate cannot exert what is regarded in the West as its traditional role in governing the liquidity of the commercial banks. As will be explained presently, 'open-market' operations are of little importance and are employed mainly to offset such fluctuations in liquidity as are caused by seasonal variations in the government's receipts and disbursements. The recently introduced requirement for the compulsory reserve can also have only a moderate effect in view of the commercial banks' dependence on the Bank of Japan for advances in normal times. So none of the conventional instruments of monetary policy is very effective, and the Bank of Japan must depend on administrative controls. The most effective of these are associated with its function as a supplier of loans to the commercial banks. For each of its clients its sets a limit on the amount that it is prepared to lend at the lowest rate of interest. For loans above this limit it imposes higher or penalty rates, and it is by raising or lowering this ceiling and by modifying the penalty rates that the Bank seeks to exercise its control over the supply of credit. This method is reinforced by what is called 'window' regulation, that is by moral suasion.[33] Obviously when the commercial banks are finding business prosperous and are being pressed for loans by industrial customers, they are not easily brought into line with the Bank's policy. For the Bank bluntly to refuse advances, or to push up penalty rates before an emergency has appeared, is to expose itself to the charge of hampering growth and provoking a crisis. It can hardly take such drastic steps until inflation has in fact endangered the balance of payments. Thus although the Bank commands very powerful instruments of control, these can be employed only in emergencies.

Until recently these weaknesses, if weaknesses they are, have not seriously perturbed the authorities, and the Bank of Japan's present anxiety to find methods of credit control that would enable it to exercise continuous regulation is probably associated

[33] Bank of Japan, *The Bank of Japan*, pp. 22–31.

mainly with modifications of the country's commercial policy.[34] The effectiveness of the Bank's instruments has hitherto depended in part on the existence of a network of regulations affecting foreign trade and the movements of funds across the exchanges. These conditions, however, are being profoundly modified by the liberalization of trade and exchange dealings. The change was emphasized during the last few years when the commercial banks sought with some success to overcome the restrictions of the central monetary authorities by borrowing abroad. In co-operation with the Ministry of Finance the Bank of Japan is now considering how it can make more effective use of 'open-market' operations, although for reasons already considered the path to reform is not likely to be easy to tread. It will not be made smoother by the conflict, at present unresolved, over the relations between the Bank of Japan and the Ministry of Finance. But an examination of this problem must be deferred until we have glanced at the structure of interest rates. This, when regarded from a Western standpoint, presents several peculiar features.

As in other countries, movements of Bank Rate are taken as signals of changes in monetary policy and the rates of commercial banks are expected to move in accord. But the Japanese Bank Rate is not a single rate of discount. It consists of no less than seven different rates which vary according to the type of bill and the collateral provided. Export bills, for instance, are always discounted at a relatively low rate. As we have seen, the complication in the Bank Rate structure is increased by the Bank's practice of setting, for each of its customers, a ceiling for loans beyond which penalty rates are charged and of moving that ceiling according to changing financial circumstances. The effect of this device is to make the penalty rates, rather than the basic rates, the real cost of borrowing. It is these that exert the major influence on market rates for loans. Even the effect of the penalty rates varies from customer to customer and from time to time according to the incidence of the Bank's 'window' policy. The commercial banks' own rates for advances and their investments

---

[34] Another motive is the desire of the Bank of Japan to free itself from political pressures. The present system, expecially the 'window' regulation, being personal in its operation, opens the way for political interference with credit-granting decisions.

in industrial securities are influenced by the close connexions
between particular banks and particular enterprises; in other
words, they are not primarily concerned with yields in their
purchase and holdings of securities. At the same time the fact
that they possess hardly any government securities, either short-
term or long-term, and are indifferent to liquidity ratios in
regulating their own lending, explains why 'open-market'
operations on the part of the Central Bank are usually ineffective
as instruments of monetary policy. On the other hand, the fact
that the liabilities of industrial concerns are so heavily weighted
on the side of bank loans means that any increase in the interest
rate on advances has at once a drastic effect on their costs and
results in a rapid liquidation of stocks and usually a curtailment
of fixed investments. The rates of interest paid by the commercial
banks for deposits are fairly stable, and competition between the
banks for these deposits has at times been mitigated by agreements.

Perhaps the most remarkable feature of the rate structure is
the fact that short-money rates in the market normally stand well
above long rates. This peculiarity is not difficult to explain.
Since the government pegs its rates for short loans, the commercial banks have no cushion of Treasury Bills and they are forced
to rely heavily, whenever money is tight, on the call market supplied largely by the local banks, the trust banks, and the Central
Co-operative Bank. Because of their lack of liquid resources in a
situation in which they encounter heavy pressure from their
customers for advances, call market rates are naturally liable to
rise to very high levels.[35] On the other hand, many long-term
transactions are carried out at relatively low rates by official or
semi-official institutions.

It is evident that the relation of the government sector to the
money market is a key to many of the paradoxes found in the
operation of the Japanese financial system. An outstanding
feature of that system is the clear-cut institutional separation
between the two sectors. This separation can be inferred from
the absence of government securities in the private sector and
from the practice of official banks, such as the Japan Develop-

---

[35] The amount of call money among the city banks' borrowings has risen very
steeply during the last ten years; the rate of increase has usually been in inverse
proportion to the rate of increase in loans from the Bank of Japan.

ment Bank, in obtaining most of their resources on favourable terms from various government agencies, especially the Trust Fund Bureau. It is inevitable that this division between the government sector and the private money and capital markets should be reflected in the whole structure of interest rates. At the same time transfers of funds between the two sectors are on occasion very large, although the amount fluctuates wildly in the short period. These fluctuations lead to corresponding oscillations in bank liquidity and increase the commercial banks' dependence on the Bank of Japan. In summary, what is noteworthy about the financial situation is not that interest rates are very high, for this is what can be expected in a country where capital is still scarce, but rather the lack of uniformity or consistency in the rate structure and especially the peculiar relations of long and short rates. In these circumstances it is not surprising that the monetary authorities should be compelled to use what to Western eyes appear to be unconventional methods of credit control. These, it must be admitted, they have so far applied with exceptional skill.

Post-war reforms were accompanied by changes in the legal status of the several banks and in the disposition of authority in the system as a whole.[36] Before the war the ordinary banks were regulated by an Act of 1927 which gave the Ministry of Finance certain powers of supervision. The Special Banks, which had been established by *ad hoc* legislation, were subject to official control and their chief officers were appointed by the government. The Act of 1882, which created the Bank of Japan and defined its powers and objects, was still in force, together with the Convertible Bank Notes Act of 1884, which governed its note-issuing authority. The majority of the Bank's shares were held by the government which appointed its chief executives. During the war, when the Ministry of Finance assumed strict control over the banking system as a whole, its powers over the Central Bank were redefined by an Act of 1942. After the war the commercial banks reverted to their previous legal position in regard to official supervision, and government control over the Bank of Japan, under pressure from SCAP, was affected by the establishment (in 1949) of a Policy Board as the supreme organ for determining the Bank's policy. The Board was com-

[36] Bank of Japan, *The Bank of Japan*, pt. iii.

posed of representatives of ordinary banks, trade, industry, and agriculture, the Ministry of Finance, and the Cabinet Offices, as well as the Governor of the Bank himself. At first it was disliked by the Bank of Japan on the ground that it removed responsibility from the governor and directors. Later, however, the Bank came to regard the Board with favour since it served to qualify the authority of the Ministry of Finance over the Bank's credit policy.

The disposition of authority thus created provoked criticism which gathered strength as time went on. The need for a revision of the law governing the Bank of Japan was generally accepted, but a sharp cleavage arose between those who wished to confer a larger degree of independence on the Bank and those who considered that its policy should be subjected in detail to the authority of the Ministry of Finance. The conflict between the Bank and the Ministry of Finance was particularly evident in connexion with foreign-exchange control. The Bank regarded itself as the proper body to exercise this control and it objected to the fact that its authority was qualified by the close relations established between the Ministry and the Bank of Tokyo. There were other areas of dispute.

The controversy came to a head during the deliberations of the Committee of Research into the Financial System set up in 1956.[37] This Committee was appointed at a time when, through the increasing liquidity of the commercial banks, the Bank of Japan's authority over the extension of credit was in jeopardy. It agreed on measures required to strengthen that control, such as the compulsory reserve-deposit system afterwards adopted. But it was sharply divided on the question of the proper relations between the government and the Bank. One group, which included the representative of the Bank of Japan, thought that the main function of the Bank was to preserve financial stability, and it pleaded that success in that aim required that it should be accorded freedom in employing the necessary instruments of credit control. The proposals of this group if adopted would have loosened such authority as the Ministry of Finance possessed over the Bank's policy. The other group, including the repre-

---

[37] Bank of Japan, *Recommendations of Committee on Financial System Research Concerning the System of the Bank of Japan* (1960); and T. Shionoya, *Problems Surrounding the Revision of the Bank of Japan Law* (1962).

sentative of the Ministry of Finance, was concerned with the part that monetary policy played in the promotion of rapid economic development rather than with the preservation of financial stability. This group argued that the Bank's policy should be closely co-ordinated with the general economic aims of the government and with the fiscal, financial, and foreign-exchange policies as a whole. Effective co-ordination could be achieved only if the Bank were supervised by the Ministry of Finance which should have the power to give directions to the Bank about the use of the instruments of monetary control. It was asserted that if the Central Bank were independent, consistency in economic policy would be difficult to preserve.

This controversy, which clearly rests upon deep-seated differences of opinion about the functions of a Central Bank, and even about fundamental economic purposes, is still unresolved. Meanwhile the diffusion of monetary functions between the Ministry of Finance and the Bank of Japan continues to put obstacles in the way of reform. As we have seen, the Ministry of Finance's practice of issuing Treasury Bills at a rate of interest far below the market rate for short loans renders almost futile the efforts of the Bank to carry out 'open-market' operations. The whole episode is significant not only because of its technical interest, but also because it illustrates the extent to which intense rivalries between organs of State can jeopardize administrative efficiency. Yet it is equally remarkable that in Japan the existence of these unresolved conflicts between rival centres of power has generally been compatible with the successful conduct of affairs.

Postscript. When in the early 1960s the commercial banks were required to restrict their loans, which had been the chief source of finance for industrial development, industry turned to the securities market and sought to make use of the public's new disposition to invest in equities. But the securities companies to which the issues were largely sold overestimated the public's demand. The market became glutted and prices fell steeply. In 1964 restrictions on bank credit combined with depression in the stock market threatened to curtail drastically the supply of fresh capital. The government and the Central Bank thereupon provided large funds for buying up 'surplus' shares. It is ironical that a leading result of the Central Bank's efforts to restrain the loans of the commercial banks to industry is that it has itself been called upon to meet the needs of frustrated borrowers via the securities market.

V

Reform and Progress in Agriculture

JAPAN's economic progress in the modern era is commonly associated with the rise of industry and the appearance of a large foreign trade in manufactured and semi-manufactured products. Yet, as in other countries that have passed through an industrial revolution, the growth of the secondary industries was accompanied by far-reaching changes in agriculture. The nature of the industrial development cannot be understood without reference to these changes, since the present condition of manufacturing trades, their organization, the structure of wages, and the pattern of industrial relations, has been powerfully influenced by the circumstances of the rural economy.

We are here concerned only to depict the outstanding changes in agriculture since the Second World War, but we must permit ourselves a glance at the history of earlier times if we are fully to appreciate the most recent trends. The post-Restoration settlement, while it destroyed the feudal relationships and obligations of the Tokugawa régime, left intact the structure of agriculture and even the position of many of the peasants in relation to that of the landlord. As a result of the settlement, the ownership of the land became vested in those who had formerly paid tribute in kind (rice) to the feudal lords and were now required to pay a land tax in cash to the national government. Some of them were working farmers who now became peasant proprietors, but others were landlords who derived their income (or part of it) from rice rents received from their tenants. The inflation of the 1870s led to a redistribution of income in favour of these landlords, since their tax was fixed in terms of money at a time when the value of their rice rents rose steeply. The landlords applied this surplus income partly to investment in industry and trade and partly to the purchase of additional land and to the financing of their tenants. Throughout the modern era, and especially during periods of agricultural depression, the proportion of the arable land held on tenancies increased. By 1936 it amounted to 46 per cent of the total arable area. At that time 31 per cent of all farm households consisted of peasant proprietors, 42 per cent of farmers who leased some of their land from landlords and owned the rest, and 27 per cent of tenant farmers pure and simple.[1] It is estimated that before the war the tenant paid on an average about two-fifths of the value of his produce to the landlord in rent. Nearly four-fifths of the rent took the form of payments in kind or in the cash equivalent of a fixed proportion of the produce. The rent burden was heavy, for the tenant himself provided the farmhouse, equipment, seed, livestock, and fertilizers. He enjoyed little security of tenure. He commonly rented small and scattered patches of land, sometimes from more than one landlord. The landlord had the legal right of recovering possession without compensation, although in practice the harshness of the law was mitigated by custom or agreement.[2]

The typical Japanese landlord was a person of importance in the rural communities and up to the World Depression of the early 1930s, his economic strength was growing. But he was not a large landowner in the sense in which that term is understood in Western countries. Before the war there were nearly a million landlords who were classed as 'absentee' or 'non-cultivating resident' owners. Only a quarter of these non-working landlords had more than 3 *chobu* of land (i.e. about 7·4 acres), and many of them owned less than 1 *chobu*. Landlords with over 50 *chobu* (120 acres) counted as large. There were only 3,000 in this class, the majority of them in Northern Japan.[3] Most landlords had interests and occupations outside agriculture. In early Meiji times they were a source of capital for new industries. In more recent years professional, military, and commercial people found land a safe and profitable investment and a considerable proportion of the small landowners were men of this type. Many of the larger landowners had extensive interests in commerce, mining, and manufacturing industry.

The holdings of the peasants, like the estates of the landlords, were very small. In 1936 nearly half of them were less than 0·5 *chobu* in area and 94 per cent were under 3 *chobu*. A typical peasant with about 1 *chobu* held his arable land in about twenty

---

[1] S. Wakukawa, 'The Japanese Farm Tenancy System', in D. G. Haring, ed., *Japan's Prospect* (1946), p. 116.

[2] Ibid. pp. 141 ff.; Y. Kondo, *The Land Reform in Japan* (1952), pp. 2–9.

[3] Kondo, p. 17; N. Danno, *Japanese Agriculture since the Post-War Agricultural Reform* (Japan IPR, 1954), pp. 4–5; also Min. Agric. & For., *Abstr. Statist.* (various years).

small parcels. The chief crop was rice, which occupied over 56 per cent of all cultivated land. Much of this rice land carried a second crop—wheat, barley, or roots; and the upland farms bore crops of grain, vegetables, fruit, or mulberry trees. The rice yield per acre was one of the highest in the world, but this achievement required intensive manual labour, with very little help from machines or draught animals, so that the yield per person employed was very low. Japan's industrial and commercial development had not succeeded in relieving the rural over-population from which the country had long suffered.

The view that there was chronic underemployment in agriculture has been challenged, but the dispute turns largely on definition. It is true that the numbers engaged in agriculture could not be regarded in normal periods as excessive in the sense that, under the labour-intensive methods used, they were larger than those required at times of peak seasonal demand for labour (rice-planting and harvesting) to produce the output. Indeed, it may be argued that Japanese farming methods had adapted themselves to the labour force available. But if account is taken of the wide disparity between agricultural and urban incomes— in 1933–7 the ratio of income a head of the agricultural worker to that of the worker in manufacturing industry was only 34 per cent—then agriculture was clearly over-supplied with labour.[4]

The relation of agriculture to the growth of population must be examined further. At the time of the Restoration Japan's population was roughly about 30 millions. The number of agricultural households, it is estimated, was about $5\frac{1}{2}$ million, with $14\frac{3}{4}$ million agricultural workers, near four-fifths of the total working population. Between then and the outbreak of the Second World War, a period in which Japan's population more than doubled, the relative importance of agriculture in the economy steadily declined. By 1930 the proportion of those engaged in agriculture to total employed manpower had fallen to 48 per cent and by 1940 to 41 per cent.[5] Yet in spite of this relative decline, the absolute size of the agricultural population hardly changed at all. The area of arable land also increased comparatively little. From early Meiji until the eve of the Second World War the area under rice rose by only about 20

[4] Data from EPA. The comparison applies to factories with five or more workers.
[5] Kondo, p. 12.

per cent. Output, on the other hand, greatly expanded. The yield of rice per acre nearly doubled and that of other crops rose even more.[6] The increase in yields was brought about mainly by improvements in strains and by heavy application of fertilizers. During the Meiji era these consisted of natural organic substances, but subsequently the farmers made increasing use of chemical fertilizers, especially ammonium sulphate. Land productivity is estimated to have increased $2 \cdot 4$ times between the beginning of Meiji and 1939 through this increased investment in working capital. By these means agriculture succeeded to a large extent in keeping pace with the growth of population; during the 1930s only about a fifth of the rice consumed was imported. Up to this time accretions to fixed capital (apart from irrigation and drainage works) took the form mainly of instruments for processing the crops, such as oil-driven machines for threshing, and small electric pumps. The physical conditions of production in small fields, especially paddy fields, seemed to preclude the employment of power-driven machines for ploughing, sowing, and harvesting.

The increases in the productivity of the land were not unconnected with the modernization of Japan and the progress of her industry and commerce. Foreign trade gave her access to fertilizers, soya beans from Manchuria, phosphates from the South Seas, and ammonium sulphate from the West. After the First World War the expansion of her own chemical industry provided a local supply of ammonium sulphate. Agricultural research was fostered by the State and resulted in improvements in methods of cultivation and in strains of crops. Finally, easier communications by land and sea reduced the cost of marketing the produce and made possible the conversion of land to its most profitable uses. The progress in other branches of the economy brought new sources of income for farm households. The peasants had long engaged in many by-employments—fishing, handicrafts, and silk-raising. Their opportunities were enlarged by the growth of the domestic market and by the appearance of an export demand for agricultural products. The rise in the foreign demand for raw silk was especially important.

[6] Statist. Section, Dept Agric. & For., *Statist. of Rice*, quoted in R. Ishii, *Population Pressure and Economic Life in Japan* (1937), p. 165; Schumpeter, pp. 116–53, and Danno, p. 9.

By the 1930s two-fifths of the farming families raised silkworms. Family incomes could also be supplemented by employment in industrial establishments. The cotton mills and the silk-reeling mills were staffed by the daughters of the farmers, and male members of the families found temporary or seasonal work, most usually in small industrial firms and in the tertiary trades. In 1933–5 about 20 per cent of the total income of the average agricultural household was derived from non-agricultural sources,[7] although the proportion varied widely with the size of the holding. These non-agricultural sources of income enabled the Japanese farmers to share to some degree in the rise in the national income that accompanied Japan's modernization. Even so they could not completely offset the results of chronic underemployment characteristic of peasant communities in densely populated Eastern countries.

It is clear that throughout Japan's modern era agricultural and industrial developments were organically connected. The rural areas supplied a constant flow of workers not only for the factories but also for the multitude of small establishments in manufactures, commerce, and the constructional and service trades. It has been said that the typical farmer had five children, one of whom died before reaching maturity, two provided replacements for the farmer and his wife, and two migrated into urban employments. The presence of this reservoir of labour had a profound effect on the form of Japan's institutions. As long as the flow from the land continued there could be little hope of a flourishing trade union movement, and the low incomes earned in agriculture exerted a drag on industrial wages. The close personal ties existing between farming families and a large part of the industrial labour force produced a social situation that was unsympathetic to the appearance of official systems of social insurance. In periods of bad trade, urban workers flocked back to their rural families, and thereby relieved both State and industry of responsibility for their maintenance. The farmers thus carried the burden of industrial depressions. But they did not carry it in silence. During the 1920s tenant farmers' associations grew in number and strength and became increasingly involved in disputes with landlords over rents and security of tenure.

[7] Data about agricultural incomes from Min. Agric. & For., *Farm Household Economy Survey* (various years).

When Japan felt the impact of the World Depression, the causes of dissatisfaction were augmented, for not only were the farmers forced to shoulder part of the burden of maintaining those who would normally have found work in the secondary and tertiary trades, but the incomes from the land also declined. Finally, the collapse of raw-silk prices brought distress to millions. Rural discontent found expression in 'fascist' political movements, and these helped to overthrow parliamentary government and to produce the revival of militant nationalism which ultimately carried Japan into the Second World War.

During the 1930s Western observers of Japan, conscious of the increasing rigidities of their own society, often commented with approval on the resilience shown by the Japanese in adapting their economy to changes in market conditions. This adaptability was, indeed, a source of strength to the country in meeting the stresses of the World Depression; but it was, in large measure, associated with the desperate search for employment on the part of the surplus rural population and the weakness of the workers' bargaining power *vis-à-vis* their employers. It may be argued that the Japanese peasant was far better off than his counterpart in the rest of Asia and that until the early 1930s his standard of life had improved. This argument, however, was unlikely to impress the countryman who had become conscious that he had been asked to bear a disproportionate share of the fiscal burden in the past, just as recently he had been required to take the strain of the industrial depression. His anger was, therefore, directed against his rulers whose policies had produced these hardships, and especially against the industrial capitalists who seemed to him to have reaped the chief rewards of economic progress. He looked to the military, also rivals of the industrialists, to rescue him from his plight.

The Occupation authorities in 1945 were right in thinking that an impoverished peasantry would be a source of revolutionary sentiment likely to retard democratic advance and to lead to a revival of militarism. The virtual destruction of the landlords and the conversion of tenancies into peasant proprietorships, perhaps the most remarkable and enduring achievement of the Occupation, depended for their justification on that premiss. Yet a change in the system of land tenure, important though it might be both politically and economically, could not of itself solve the fundamental problems of the Japanese farming communities. Those problems were rooted in the continuing abundance of the working population in relation to other resources. In the end a solution had to come through an increase in opportunities for remunerative employment in industry and commerce, an increase that depended mainly on the growth of capital and on industrial enterprise.

Even before the war the Japanese government had taken tentative steps towards reforming the system of landholding, which the activities of the tenants' associations had shaken but not seriously disturbed. From 1922 there were arrangements for granting, from the Post Office Insurance Deposits Bureau, loans at low rates of interest to tenant farmers who wished to buy their land. The Agricultural Land Adjustment Act of 1938 was a more serious attempt to assist tenants by giving them a greater security of tenure, and land commissions were set up with powers to reduce rents considered exorbitant. The results of these measures were meagre and it was not until the Second World War that the structure of the rural economy was modified. Then a new era in the country's agricultural life began. An outstanding change of the war years was the redistribution of farm income between tenant and landlord. The Staple Food Administration Law of 1942 enforced the substitution of money rents for rents in kind and fixed the former at levels which, as inflation proceeded, bore little relation to the official price at which the authorities bought rice from the growers. The result was that the proportion of rent to gross farm income declined from 40 per cent before the war to about 10 per cent in 1945.[8]

Immediately the war was over the landlords sought to compensate themselves by trying to dispossess their tenants so that they might cultivate the land themselves. These attempts were soon frustrated by the land reforms introduced by the Occupation authorities. It is, however, worth observing that SCAP's policy can be regarded as having confirmed and carried further a tendency towards the elimination of the landlords which wartime policy had set in train.

Before the end of 1945 the Japanese government was ordered to introduce measures for the conversion of tenants into peasant proprietors, and ultimately the policy received expression in the

[8] Kondo, p. 20.

Owner-Farmer Establishment Law of 1946. This provided for the complete dispossession of absentee landlords and for the retention by other owners of tenanted land of only 1 *chobu* of cultivable land in Honshu, Shikoku, and Kyushu, and only 4 *chobu* in Hokkaido, while the holdings of owner-occupiers were limited to an average of 3 *chobu* in the three main islands and 12 in Hokkaido. Farmland in excess of these limits was to be purchased by the government and resold to 'eligible' farmers at prices based on the rental value of the land as registered at the tax offices.[9] Over 11,000 local land commissions composed of tenants, owners, and owner-cultivators, in the ratio of 5, 3, and 2, were set up to administer the Law under the supervision of prefectural and national authorities. Land purchased by tenants under this scheme was not to be resold for thirty years, except with special official authorization. The programme was to be carried out within two years. In 1947 pasture land was brought within the ambit of the reform. The rent of such land as continued to be held on tenancy was subjected to strict official control.

The vast and complicated transaction was almost completed by the end of 1949. By June 1952 the government had acquired nearly 2 million *chobu* of cultivated land and 450,000 *chobu* of pasturage and had resold most of this to the former tenants. By this process the proportion of the land farmed by tenants to the total cultivated area had been reduced from 46 to about 8 per cent.[10] Japan had become a land of peasant proprietors.[11] The transformation, though it depended initially on the determination of the Occupation authorities, could scarcely have been accomplished so speedily without the co-operation of the Japanese themselves, who, of course, were responsible for detailed administration. This suggests that the measure was gratefully received not only by the tenants but also by the nation as a whole.

The Law provided for what seemed at the time to be reasonable compensation for the landlords. The violent inflation which coincided with these transactions, however, meant that the land-

---

[9] Cohen, *Japan's Economy*, pp. 442–7; Kondo, pp. 21–25; Japan FAO Assoc., *Agriculture in Japan* (1953), pp. 34–37. The tenants engaged in cultivating the land had priority rights of purchase.

[10] Kondo, pp. 25–27. Later it fell to 5 per cent.

[11] For a detailed study of the social and economic aspects of the policy see R. P. Dore, *Land Reform in Japan* (1959).

G

lords were expropriated. As we have seen, few of them owned large estates. Most of them, while well off compared with their tenants, enjoyed only a modest competence of which they had now been deprived. It is true that this class was conservative in temper and during the 1930s had been closely linked with those responsible for Japan's military adventures. It may be argued also that most of the landlords had become economically functionless. In early Meiji they had taken the lead in fostering new agricultural methods as well as in financing local industries, but by the Showa era these activities had been largely assumed by officially appointed bodies or by co-operative associations among the working farmers. Finally, there is no doubt that the Land Reform was politically expedient, since it helped to damp down revolutionary sentiment among the peasants and to remove a source of unrest that might have shaken the stability of the Japanese government and so weakened the American strategic position in the Far East. Yet it is ironical that the dispossession of a rural middle class should have been undertaken at the behest of the government of a country that asserts so vigorously the rights of private property. Doubtless the emotive power of the term 'feudal', as commonly applied to traditional Japanese institutions, helped to remove any uneasiness among the American authorities about the results of their own actions in this field.

The transformation of the system of land tenure was by no means the only factor that affected Japanese agriculture in the post-war period, and in describing and interpreting the contrasts with the pre-war and early agricultural situation, we must have regard to other changes also. Indeed the causes of some developments that are commonly ascribed to the Reform are to be found elsewhere.

During the war agriculture lost manpower to the armed forces and to the munitions trades, and its output was affected by a shortage of chemical fertilizers and the diversion of arable land to non-agricultural uses. It was possible to replace chemical by natural fertilizers to a considerable extent, but only at the cost of additional effort on the part of the farmers. This intensified the shortage of workers, a shortage that could not be relieved by mechanization, as happened in England; for towards the end of the war even the simple implements normally used by Japanese farmers were hard to come by. The result was a considerable

decline, especially after 1942, in agricultural efficiency and output. In 1944 the index of agricultural production (1933–5 = 100)
stood at 77·6 compared with 110·6 in 1937. This steep decline
was accompanied by changes in the structure of production.
Policy was directed towards maintaining the output of the staple
foodstuffs, and much land was accordingly diverted from industrial crops and from uses considered inessential in wartime. While
the total cultivated area fell by about 3 per cent between 1937
and 1944, the area planted with the major food crops (rice,
wheat, barley, sweet and Irish potatoes) rose slightly, and the
output of those crops taken together was maintained up to 1944
at about the same level as before the war.[12] On the other hand,
there was a steep decline in the production of minor cereals,
pulses, vegetables, fruit, meat, poultry, and eggs. Further, the
area used for producing mulberry leaves, the chief non-food
crop, fell by some 47 per cent between 1937 and 1944.[13] In 1945
the collapse of the Japanese economy affected all branches of
agriculture and the index of production fell to under 60.

Agriculture recovered more rapidly from the effects of the war
than manufacturing industry. Its equipment had not suffered
the same physical damage as that of the urban industries, and
reconstruction was not impeded by questions of reparations, or
permitted levels of production, such as bedevilled early post-war
attempts to restart manufacturing industry. On the contrary,
both the Occupation authorities and the Japanese government
were equally anxious to increase supplies of agricultural goods
so as to avert the menace of famine. Official encouragement was
given to the restarting of the ammonium-sulphate factories
damaged by bombing, and imports of chemical fertilizers received priority. The manpower shortage in the countryside was
soon overcome, since the demobilized soldiers and the repatriates
found few opportunities for employment in industry. So, whereas
in manufacturing the recovery of production was hesitant until
after the outbreak of the Korean War, agriculture rallied quickly
after 1947. By 1952 the index of production stood at 111, and
although its subsequent movements were much influenced by

[12] The output of these staples (in brown-rice equivalents) was slightly greater on the
average between 1942 and 1944 than in the period 1935–7. Potatoes, especially
sweet potatoes, had increased, whereas cereals had fallen (B. F. Johnston, *Japanese
Food Management in World War II* (1953), pp. 93–128).

[13] Ibid. pp. 116–19, 253.

harvest fluctuations, in 1955 it reached 130.[14] The increase after the middle 1930s had been rather less than the growth in the total population during the same period, but it appears to have been about the same as that of the twenty years after 1914.

In estimating the significance of this increase in production, we must observe that there was a considerable growth, for the first time in the present century, in the size of the agricultural population. In pre-war days there were 5½ million farm households and the total (occupied) agricultural population was estimated at about 14 millions. By 1950 the number of households had increased to 6·2 millions and the agricultural workers to nearly 17 millions. Most of the increase took place immediately after the war when men were returning from overseas and opportunities for industrial employment were few, but the enlargement was maintained for several years. This reversal of the secular trend towards the decline in the importance of agricultural employment is one of the most striking features of the economic history of the period. It is true that between 1949 and 1955 the agricultural labour force as a proportion of the occupied population fell from 50 to 39 per cent, but the relative decline still left its absolute size greater than before the war.[15]

The additional numbers found employment in agriculture at a time when the area of arable land was declining; in 1952 it was about 7 per cent less than in 1941. Inevitably this meant that the size of the typical holding diminished. In 1946 there were 2,232,000 households with holdings of less than 0·5 *chobu*; in 1950, after the expansion in the agricultural population, there were 2,521,000 in that size group.[16] The increase in the numbers of these very small farms was attributed in some quarters to the Land Reform and to post-war legislation that prescribed an equal division of farm property among male heirs in place of the former system of primogeniture. In fact, however, the increasing fragmentation of properties was to be associated primarily with the increase of the agricultural population. In these circum-

---

[14] Min. Agric. & For., *Abstr. Statist.*; base period 1933–5.
[15] EPA, *Econ. Survey, 1955–6*, pp. 95–97; *Orient. Econ.*, July 1956, pp. 332–5; and Min. Agric. & For., *Abstr. Statist.* It is difficult to estimate accurately the number employed in agriculture because of the existence of numerous part-time workers and because of seasonal fluctuations in their numbers. Estimates from different sources vary considerably, but all series show the same trend.
[16] Min. Agric. & For., *Abstr. Statist.*

stances, it is not surprising to find that in 1954 labour (physical) productivity in agriculture was estimated to be only nine-tenths of pre-war.[17]

In certain other respects the changes introduced during the war and the immediate post-war period were not long maintained and some former tendencies were soon resumed. For instance, during the years of industrial and commercial chaos just after 1945, the contribution of agriculture to the total national income rose as high as 40 per cent, but after 1950, when the pace of industrial development greatly exceeded that of agriculture, the ratio of agricultural income declined and by 1954 it was back to its pre-war percentage of under 17. Again, the pre-war trend towards the diversification of agriculture reappeared and land reverted to crops which war-time policies had displaced. There was an exceptionally large increase in the output of fruit, vegetables, and milk and a notable development of types of farming formerly of little importance, such as stock-raising. On the other hand, the failure of the silk trade to regain its pre-war size meant that the production of cocoons and of mulberry trees remained very small. The output of rice, though fluctuating from year to year, showed a rising trend. In 1955 production was 9 million *koku* greater than in 1933, previously the record year, when it reached 70 million *koku*.[18] The annual average output of the period 1952–6 was about 10 per cent greater than in 1934–8.

Certain pre-war tendencies in farming methods were likewise resumed. The application of chemical fertilizers, which diminished during the war, was of necessity much increased after 1945, because former supplies of soya beans from Manchuria were not available. The farmers also began to use insecticides more lavishly and to introduce power machinery.

For a time the incomes and consumption levels of the working farmers compared much more favourably with those of the city dwellers than they did before the war. As late as 1953 the ratio of the agricultural worker's income to the average wage in manufacturing industry was 46 per cent compared with the pre-war ratio of 34 per cent.[19] One of the main causes of the improvement was the Land Reform which, if it made little impact on the technical organization of agriculture, exerted powerful distributional

---

[17] EPA, *Econ. Survey, 1955–6*, p. 97.   [18] *Koku*=4·96 bushels.
[19] Estimates made by Prof. T. Inoue of the Univ. of Utsunomiya.

effects. Tenants who acquired the ownership of land under the reform did so at a cost which the inflation rendered negligible. Even the land still held on tenancies (now only about 5 per cent of the total arable area) carried an annual rent of only 600 yen a *tan*,[20] a trivial burden when the gross income per *tan* was in the neighbourhood of 20,000 yen. The former tenants who were transformed into peasant proprietors now paid the land tax direct, but in the 1950s this was much lighter than before the war and their burden was very small indeed compared with their former obligations for rent. For working farmers as a whole the rent-tax ratio to the total farm income fell from 22 per cent in 1934–6 to 8 per cent in 1953.[21]

The relative increase in the price of food in the early post-war period was another favourable influence on agricultural incomes. The farmers, it is true, were unable to take full advantage of the scarcity of rice, their chief crop, because the price was subject to official control. Under the system in operation up to 1955, the government set a delivery quota for each farm and bought the stipulated quantities at controlled prices for distribution to the consumers. However, the growers were able to compensate themselves for the relatively low prices at which they had to dispose of this part of their supply by selling the rest at much higher prices in the black market. From 1955 the government ceased to require compulsory deliveries and entered into voluntary contracts with the farmers for rice supplies. The farmers were induced to enter into these agreements by the offer of advance payments at the time when the contracts were made.

The peasants' non-agricultural employments also brought them enhanced incomes. In the middle 1930s the ratio of non-agricultural to the total income of the farming community was, on an average, about 20 per cent. It fell to 10 per cent immediately after the war, but by the middle 1950s rose again to some 40 per cent.[22] This change was the result of a complex of causes not all of them favourable. For instance, it was attributable in part to the decline in silk-raising, which counts as an agricultural occupation. Further, the rise in the agricultural population forced members of farming families to take up additional by-employments in the household or occasional work in industry

[20] 10 *tan* = 1 *chobu* = 2·45 acres.   [21] EPA, *Econ. Survey, 1954–5*, pp. 166–7.
[22] Ibid. p. 165.

or trade, once opportunities became available. To some extent, therefore, the increased importance of non-agricultural income occurred merely as the result of the lack of sufficient full-time jobs on the farms. But there were positive gains. Better communications, notably the spread of bus services, widened the area within which the members of peasant households could find work. Again, the dispersion of factories during the war brought industrial work into the rural areas, and after the war this tendency persisted.

The effects of the agricultural changes on the well-being of the farmers were not evenly distributed. The former peasant proprietors obviously did not secure the same advantages from the Land Reform as those who formerly rented the whole or a large part of their arable land. Even among the latter benefits varied. Rents per acre previously depended upon fertility or situation, and the purchase price of the land, payable by instalments, was related under the scheme to the rents. But in the event the cost of acquiring the land was reduced as a result of the inflation, and the land tax imposed after the war was based on area rather than on productivity.[23] Thus peasants who formerly worked the most productive land benefited disproportionately from the abolition of rents. The effects of the reforms on the different types of landlord also varied. Those who were able to work the land formerly leased to others,[24] or those who were allowed to retain farms already managed by them, at least preserved a source of agricultural livelihood. But most of the non-working landlords completely lost their source of agricultural income and many small men in this class were impoverished.[25]

We have already emphasized that one of the objects of the social and economic reforms introduced by the Americans was to reduce the intervention of the State in economic life and to diffuse economic and political power. The Land Reform was not in all respects an effective instrument to this end. For to the extent that the landlord class had preserved its traditional functions, namely, providing credit to the peasants, introducing improvements in agricultural methods, and taking part of the strain of

[23] Nat. Research Inst. of Agric., *Summary Reps. of Researches, 1949*, pp. 54–56.
[24] This new class of working farmer accounted for a considerable proportion of the increase in agricultural households after the war.
[25] Danno, pp. 4–5.

bad harvests, its destruction compelled Japanese agriculturists to look to the State. This, however, was a continuance of a tendency that had long been present, and the effect of the change was qualified by the enlargement of the operations of co-operative societies formed among the peasantry. These societies had a long history and for many years before the war they had been engaged in the purchase of supplies, the sale of produce, and the provision of credit. During the war the agricultural co-operatives became instruments of government control, but after 1947 they reverted to their previous character and played an increasing part in the life of the countryside. In the early 1950s not only were most of the rice purchases of the government obtained through the co-operatives, but also 70 per cent of the non-controlled crops and 60 per cent of the chemical fertilizers were handled by them.[26]

At this point in the narrative it may be useful to summarize the main differences between the pre-war condition of Japanese agriculture and that of 1954–5. The outstanding changes were: (1) a 20 per cent increase in the size of the agricultural population and a 12 per cent increase in the number of agricultural households; (2) the conversion of tenants to peasant proprietors without their incurring any significant financial liability for this change in tenure; (3) the improvement in the economic position of the working farmers (especially the former tenants), partly through the Land Reform, partly through higher agricultural prices, and partly through new opportunities for non-agricultural employment which offset the loss of income brought about by the decline in silk-raising; (4) the diversification of agriculture through the development of livestock, fruit, and vegetable farming; (5) an increased application of working capital in the form of chemical fertilizers and of materials for the control of pests and diseases; (6) an increased use of fixed capital, mainly in the form of agricultural machinery, although by the middle fifties the mechanization of productive operations was still in its initial stage; (7) the destruction of the landlord class and the reduction of many of its members to the status of working farmers.

Despite these massive changes, however, the identities with the pre-war situation were almost equally impressive. The size of the holdings remained as small as before; indeed, the average had

[26] Japan FAO Assoc., *Agriculture in Japan*, p. 46.

slightly diminished. While production per acre had increased substantially, production per man-year had not advanced.[27] The incomes of farm households had risen, but although in the early 1950s they compared more favourably than before the war with those of the city dwellers, a wide discrepancy remained. Underemployment among the agricultural population was still heavy, and the functional relationship between agricultural over-population and industrial organization had been only mildly affected by the changes of the previous fifteen years. Surplus workers from the countryside still pressed into occupations in the small-scale secondary and tertiary industries, and the great annual flow of recruits helped to keep wages low in those industries and to inhibit the growth of powerful labour organizations among them.

After 1955 certain of the tendencies persisted. Agricultural production continued to rise, at first chiefly through increases in yields per acre. In 1960 the general index of agricultural production (base period 1950–2) stood at 137 compared with 103 in 1954 and 125 in 1955. In 1962 it went up to 141.[28] The output of rice, still by far the most important crop, was nearly 30 per cent higher in 1960–2 than in 1953–5; but the main increases after the middle 1950s occurred in the newer branches of agriculture which were concerned with livestock, eggs, milk, fruit, and certain types of vegetable. For example, compared with 1955 the production of milk in 1962 had increased two-and-a-half times and that of fruit had doubled. The change in the structure of agricultural production which reduced the importance of rice and other cereals had, as we shall see, very important effects on the organization of farming. In this period labour productivity in agriculture and household incomes also rose sharply, yet, since productivity in the non-agricultural sector grew much faster, incomes earned in agriculture rose more slowly than in industry and the widening disparity profoundly affected the position of agriculture in the national economy.

It has been emphasized that up to the middle 1950s many of the characteristic features of the past still remained, the small size of the holdings, the labour-intensive methods of cultivation, and the over-supply of manpower in rural areas. During the next few years some of the identities began to disappear. The

[27] EPA, *Econ. Survey, 1955–6*, p. 97.   [28] Min. Agric. & For., *Abstr. Statist.*

main influence for change was the remarkably rapid growth in the economy as a whole after 1955, for this by 1959 had transformed conditions in the labour market as well as the structure of demand for agricultural products. Agriculture found itself faced by problems that differed sharply from those of the past, and in the process of adaptation to its new economic environment it was forced to introduce striking innovations in technique. It is now, on the threshhold of revolutionary changes in its organization.

In the first place the rapid expansion of the secondary industries provided vastly greater opportunities than hitherto for the remunerative employment of members of rural families. In the past, as we have seen, despite the large migration to the towns, agriculture had retained a sufficient proportion of young persons to provide for the maintenance of the labour force. After 1955 the growth of the non-agricultural sector of the economy called for a much larger recruitment from the countryside, and agriculture found that it could no longer attract a sufficient number of school-leavers to maintain the size of its labour force. Before the war about 370,000 recruits, it was estimated, were necessary to maintain the size of agricultural households. In 1950 the number of school-leavers from country areas who found employment in agriculture reached 440,000, but the number fell to 264,000 in 1955 and 166,000 in 1959.[29] Even the eldest sons began to leave the land. In the past the eldest son could count on inheriting his father's land and knew that he would in future command the household income.[30] But the abolition of primogeniture by the Land Reform disturbed the family system and, in the face of the attractions of higher industrial earnings, weakened the eldest son's inducement to remain. Farming operations thus fell increasingly into the hands of the middle-aged and elderly, and the proportion of women in the agricultural labour force also increased. So not only did the number of persons engaged in farming decline but the quality of the labour force deteriorated. In absolute numbers the decline between 1955 and 1962 amounted to nearly 4 millions; as a proportion of the total occupied population it was from 39 per cent in 1955 to under 29 per cent in 1962.

[29] The ratio of labour replacements to withdrawals fell from 105 per cent in 1950 to 70 per cent in 1955 and 26 per cent in 1961.
[30] It used to be said: 'Even the cat's saucer belongs to the eldest son'.

Some of the young migrants left their homes for work in the cities. Others found it possible, because of the spread of industry to rural areas and to the improvements in communications, to take full-time non-agricultural work while continuing to live on the farm and to give occasional help to their parents.[31] This last practice led to a considerable increase in the number of part-time farming households. The statistical reports of the Ministry of Agriculture and Fisheries distinguish three classes of farm households: (1) those engaged full-time in farming; (2) those for which farming was the chief occupation but of which some members followed non-agricultural pursuits; and (3) those for which farming was a subsidiary occupation and which drew their main income from outside. In 1950 the proportions of households in these three categories were 41, 28, and 31 per cent respectively; at the end of 1962 the proportions were 26, 33, and 41 per cent.[32] For agricultural households as a whole the share of the total income derived from non-agricultural occupations rose from 28 per cent in 1950–1 to nearly 49 per cent in 1960–1. Most of the increase in the non-agricultural income came from wages rather than from industrial by-employments in the household; wages and salaries, which in 1951 had accounted for only 18 per cent of household income, accounted for 34 per cent of it in 1959–60.[33] For the first time in history (at any rate in a period of peace) agriculture was short of labour, and in view of the post-war fall in the birth-rate there was every prospect in the early 1960s that the rate of decline in its manpower would soon be accelerated.

The farmers responded to the manpower shortage by substituting capital for labour. The capital took the form mainly of agricultural machinery. During the 1950s, and especially towards the end of the decade, power-driven tractors and cultivators and other types of power machines were introduced in rapidly increasing numbers. The number of tractors (mainly small cultivators) rose from only 13,000 in 1950 to 89,000 in 1955,

---

[31] In a medium-sized factory producing motor components in Saitama Prefecture, one-third of the labour force in 1963 consisted of the sons and daughters of farmers, who continued to live on the farm and gave assistance to their parents in busy periods.

[32] *Japan Statist. Yb.*, *1962*, p. 71; and *Orient Econ.*, July 1964, p. 511.

[33] *Farm Household Economy Survey*; cf. also *Ann. Rep. on the State of Agric.*, *1961*, p. 40; *Orient. Econ.*, Mar. 1963, p. 141.

513,000 in 1960, and nearly 1½ million in 1963. The number of power-driven threshing machines trebled between 1950 and 1960 and there are now nearly 3 million in use.[34] Without mechanization it would have been impossible to increase grain production. The machines were not the only labour-saving innovations introduced at this time. The heaviest demand for manpower occurs in the late spring when the rice seedlings are transplanted. By the late 1950s the growth of the rice plants was being brought forward by the use of vinyl coverings for the seed beds, and experiments are now being made in the elimination of transplanting altogether by direct sowing. The use of insecticides sprayed from machines, and even from helicopters, and of chemical weed-eliminators has also been widely extended. Thus whereas in the past policy had been concentrated on raising production per acre, recently the main effort has been directed towards increasing labour productivity.

Meanwhile the structure of demand for foodstuffs in Japan was changing. A shift of demand from cereals towards meat, dairy-products, and fruit was evident in the early post-war years. After 1955 the tendency was much strengthened. In the late 1950s rice consumption per head of population was 16 per cent less than before the war while milk consumption had risen six times.[35] This tendency will almost certainly persist as incomes rise, for it has been calculated that the income elasticity of demand for milk is 1·23 compared with only 0·31 for rice.[36] The changes called for much additional fixed capital in the form of stock and buildings. Many highly capitalized and specialized enterprises have appeared (notably those for broiler and pig production) which bore little resemblance to the traditional peasant farm. New methods of fruit production came into being which dispensed with tedious manual labour, for example, that formerly used for wrapping fruit during its ripening.

These innovations in technique and organization carried further the tendency for Japanese farming to become more

---

[34] Data from Min. Agric. & For.; also *Orient. Econ.*, Dec. 1963, p. 618. Machines do not merely save labour; they may also reduce its supply price, for (it is said) their presence on the farm often persuades young men, now usually of a mechanical turn of mind, to remain in agriculture in the face of the attractions of urban employment.

[35] Japan FAO Assoc., *A Strategy for New Agriculture* (1962), pp. 5–6.

[36] Calculation of Prof. K. Tanaka of Waseda Univ.

highly commercialized. The Land Reform had resulted in an increase in the proportion of the rice crop that was marketed by the farmer himself, since previously the tenants had handed over as rent most of the rice which they themselves did not consume. Enterprises in the new branches of agriculture work almost entirely for the market. The proportion of the total agricultural output disposed of in this way rose from 62 per cent in 1952 to 75 per cent in 1960.[37] These changes, together with the growth in the proportion of household income derived from wages and other outside employments, raised the farmers' purchases from the non-agricultural sector of the economy. So the barriers between the agricultural community and the town dwellers were lowered and the outlook of the farmers and their responses to economic stimuli became assimilated to those of the rest of the population. By the early 1960s the farmers were expecting to share fully in the material benefits of economic development. The rise in their incomes encouraged this expectation, while the improvement in communications (for example, the spread of road transport and of radio broadcasting), as well as the increased outside activities of the farming families, made them familiar with new types of goods and new forms of expenditure.[38] In economic terminology, the 'demonstration effect' worked powerfully in rural areas. By this time the typical farm-house, at any rate in the Tokaido region, was very different from that of pre-war years. It was often equipped with up-to-date cooking appliances, refrigerator, radio and television sets, and other forms of consumers' capital. The motor bicycle and the bus had brought the towns within easy reach of remote rural communities. In changing the outlook and economic responses of the peasantry the trends towards democracy and egalitarianism have no doubt been influential, but it is probable that the new consumer goods have been more persuasive than new political ideas.

Farm-household members have now become mobile for the reason that they appraise the relative returns to farm work and industrial work more rationally than in the past. Their supply price to agriculture has been sharply raised. Formerly income a

---

[37] *Ann. Rep. on the State of Agric., 1961*, p. 19.
[38] The consumption of the average agricultural household was 74 per cent higher in 1961 than before the war (Min. Lab., *Wage Problems in Japan* (1962), p. 6).

head earned by farm households could remain at a much lower level than that earned by urban households without disturbing the allocation of labour, and the migration from farm to industry stopped far short of the point at which an identity of incomes was approached. In other words, equilibrium in the allocation of resources between the land and industry could exist despite the disparity in incomes. There were several reasons for this. When employment opportunities in industry were less extensive, the peasant valued highly the security represented by land ownership. Further, when he was comparing his income with that of the urban wage-earner, he did not distinguish between that part of his income that could be attributed to interest and rent from the part that could be attributed to his labour. In the third place, since large-scale industry, where relatively high wages were paid, recruited its labour from school-leavers rather than from adults, the opportunities for alternative employments available to the adult farmers were limited to small and medium establishments or to work as temporary labourers. In other words, the alternative labour market to which the adult farmers had access consisted of the low-paid sector of the industrial economy. Fourthly, the head of the farm household was inclined to regard the income of the whole household as his own when he was making comparisons with what he could earn elsewhere, and this attitude affected the disposition of the eldest son also.

In recent years these factors have become less powerful. The shortage of labour has raised very steeply the wages paid in small and medium establishments. Members of farming families are less ready than of old to accept their traditionally subordinate position to the head of the household, and, as we have seen, the abolition of primogeniture has altered the calculations of the eldest son. The commercialization of farming has led to a more rational appraisal of relative incomes, and the farmers have become conscious of the widening gap since 1954 between industrial wages and returns to agricultural labour. All this has stimulated mobility and there is every probability that the modification in the family system and in traditional attitudes will be carried much further.

So far, however, while the new forces have driven the younger members of the farm households to take up other employments, they have not yet become powerful enough to drive out the head of the household himself. The paradoxical result is that while the size of the agricultural labour force has been much reduced, the number of farm households has hardly changed. It is true that in 1962 there were about 300,000 fewer farm households than in 1950 (when their number attained a maximum), but there were still nearly 6 million of them, considerably more than before the war.[39] The structure of farming has been retained intact. As in the past, Japanese agriculture is still composed of a multitude of very small independent farms. In so far as this is not to be explained by the fact that the middle-aged or elderly head of the farm household is less exposed than the rest of his family to the inducements of other employments, the Land Reform must bear much of the blame. It is ironical that the post-war settlement, which was at first attended by economic as well as social and political advantages, by the late 1950s had become a serious obstacle to economic progress. In the beginning it had helped to raise productivity among the former tenants. Inducements to work hard were increased. Security of tenure encouraged them to make fixed capital investments and the abolition of the old system of landlordism stimulated commercial farming. But the legal restriction imposed on the sale or leasing of farms, and the strict control of such land as was still held in tenancy, by the late 1950s were hindering the reconstruction of farming tenures which efficiency then required. In particular, the economical use of new capital equipment was impeded. Agricultural machinery, especially the larger and more efficient tractors, cannot be used effectively on very small farms, especially when those farms are composed of scattered strips. As it is, Japanese agriculture, in terms of horse-power per acre one of the most highly mechanized in the world, is over-capitalized since each machine can be used only for brief periods.

A solution, it is realized, must be found by a consolidation of strips within each farm, and in the case of arable farms, by the creation of much larger units. These aims cannot be fully achieved without drastic changes in the law. Some farmers in their anxiety to increase their efficiency have found ways of surmounting the legal obstacles. There has been development of contract farming (that is, a system by which the smaller farmers assign the cultivation of their land to a single unit or group), and

[39] See Stat. App., Table 3, p. 264.

new co-operative ventures either for cultivation or for the use of particular items of equipment have appeared. Then in 1961 and 1962 the Diet amended the Land Law and the Agricultural Co-operatives Law so as to ease the restrictions on the sale of land and the prescribed maximum size of holdings.[40] Up to the present, however, no significant reduction in the number of independent farm households has taken place. There has been some increase in the number of farms in the larger size groups, but the trend towards the creation of full-time viable farms is still in its initial stages.

The government is fully alive to the problem. In its Income Doubling Plan for 1961–70 it forecast an increase in agricultural output of 2·9 per cent a year and a fall in the numbers engaged in agriculture of 2·8 per cent a year. For some time it has provided financial assistance towards mechanization, and in conjunction with the prefectural authorities, it has operated an extensive agricultural advisory service in which 10,000 persons are employed. But if capital and labour are to be as efficiently used as they are in industry, it is the system of land tenure that must be transformed and small-scale peasant farms replaced by large-scale commercial agriculture. Although the elimination of the disparities in income between different sectors of the economy is the accepted goal of policy, the authorities are naturally inclined to caution in pushing forward changes which represent a reversal of previous policies. No doubt the high prices which farmers can obtain by selling their land on what is now virtually a free market will overcome the reluctance even of the more conservative, especially as the shortage of farm labour will be accentuated as industry expands further.[41] But while this solution may be in accordance with the self-interest of farmers in areas within or adjacent to the great industrial centres of Japan, in other parts of the country (e.g. the north of the main island, Shikoku, and parts of Kyushu) where industrial development is still in an early stage, the path to efficiency through changes in land tenure may be more difficult to tread. There is danger of the appearance of a dichotomy between the areas of large-scale viable farming and

---

[40] Min. Agric. & For., *Japan's Agricultural Basic Law* (1962); cf. also R. P. Dore, 'Beyond the Land Reform' in *Pacific Affairs*, Autumn 1963, p. 272.

[41] Persons who already possess large holdings are still legally disqualified as purchasers, but because of the discretion recently given to local committees which administer the Land Laws, these disqualifications are probably ineffective.

those where the older methods persist. The contrasts in productivity and incomes may cease to be sectoral and become geographical as they are to some extent already.

The agricultural problem is being complicated by the current policy of trade liberalization. Since the war the government has purchased rice at a fixed price and has in effect subsidized its sale to consumers. What began during the war as a method of protecting consumers against increases in the cost of living, was transformed after the middle 1950s into a system by which the rice growers were guaranteed, at the taxpayers' expense, high prices for their products. The producers of other cereals, barley and wheat, have also benefited by a policy of price stabilization, and the typical Japanese farmer has continued to derive the greater part of his income from cereals. But with the shift in demand to other foodstuffs, the more alert farmers, as we have seen, have been diversifying their production. The rice policy will no doubt be continued in a modified form, but the abolition of import restrictions on other products might expose the more rapidly growing sectors of agriculture to fierce competition from abroad. Subsidies to that sector could hardly be adopted without breaches of international trade regulations. The newest and most thriving parts of agriculture might, therefore, become the most vulnerable. Dairy products and livestock present a particularly difficult problem. Japan has very little grazing land at present and the supply of domestically produced fodder is short. For this reason the growth of livestock farming has been accompanied by a large increase in imports of feeding stuffs. The further expansion of that industry, whether it is brought about by some form of protection or by enhanced efficiency, will require additional imports of these feeding stuffs in the future, unless, as has been proposed, the area of grazing can be extended by cultivating suitable grasses on the hills.

For social and political reasons it is unlikely that Japan will be willing to allow free market forces to determine the size of her agriculture or the allocation of its resources. With this simple solution denied to her (as to most industrial countries), the problems of agricultural policy, which must take account of the conflicting interests of different types of farmers and at the same time serve the general aim of agricultural efficiency, are extremely perplexing. In principle, it is true, they may not be very different

H

from those that trouble Western industrial countries, but they are more serious in Japan than elsewhere because of the still large size of the agricultural population and of its great political influence.

The provision of additional capital for buildings, equipment, drainage works, roads, and stock is clearly a condition of agricultural reconstruction and the existing financial arrangements reflect the needs of the past rather than those of the present. For many years, as part of the highly developed system of agricultural co-operation, local co-operative credit societies have existed, linked with prefectural and regional associations and ultimately with the Central Cooperative Bank for Agriculture and Fisheries. But the credit societies have to serve two purposes. First, they act as savings banks for the peasants and in this capacity they must compete, in the rates they offer on deposits, with the commercial banks. Secondly, they are supposed to provide loans at relatively low rates of interest to the farmers themselves. These purposes are difficult to reconcile and the societies have maintained their solvency only by investing a large part of their funds in the towns. Far from attracting new capital for agriculture, they have provided a channel for directing new savings into industry.[42] In the conditions of the past, this role was acceptable, but at a time when the creation of a viable agriculture depends on the transference from labour-intensive to capital-intensive methods, the system has serious drawbacks. Farmers unable to obtain loans from the co-operative societies and the organized market have been forced to borrow at very high rates in the unorganized market which consists of merchants, moneylenders, and mutual-loan associations.

It is unlikely that the supply of savings from the rural areas will grow very fast, despite the increase in the incomes of farm households, for with the equalization of rural incomes that resulted from the Land Reform and the approximation of rural to urban standards of expenditure, the marginal propensity to save on the part of the farmers has fallen. It seems therefore that the new capital must come from government sources. There is a tendency already for official financial institutions, notably the Agriculture, Forestry, and Fishery Finance Corporation, to enlarge their

[42] A point emphasized by Prof. Yuzuru Ito in an unpublished paper, 'Capital Movement and Farmers' Saving and Investment' (1962).

loans for land improvement, rural roads, and drainage, and the
Treasury has subsidized the purchase of farm machinery and
other forms of fixed capital.[43] If the agricultural revolution
(defined as the selective expansion of agriculture and the creation
of viable farms by the reduction in the number both of agricultural employees and of farm households) is to be successfully accomplished, the government will probably be forced to provide in
one way or another a high proportion of the funds needed.[44]
Here again the analogies with Western countries are close.
Another line of policy that might contribute powerfully to the
concentration of farms is the extension of social welfare. Peasants
cling to their land because of the security it seems to afford them
in a harsh, competitive world. Despite the continual growth in
the industrial demand for labour, this disposition on the part of
adult farmers is unlikely to be completely destroyed in the absence of adequate national provision against old age, sickness,
and poverty. Here is another illustration of the mutual inter-
dependence of policies in different sectors of the national life. In
the end, it seems likely that time, uniting the present generation
of farmers to their ancestors, will serve, in the absence of willing
successors, as an even more effective agent of the agricultural
revolution than the politicians and civil servants in Tokyo.

[43] A heavy investment in improved drainage is required in order to make possible
the use of larger and more economical cultivators.
[44] The minimum size for a 'viable' arable farm is thought to be 5 acres; at present
only 6 or 7 per cent of the farms are of that size or larger.

VI
Industrial Reconstruction and Development

THE growth of Japan's economy during the modern era was brought about mainly by industrialization, by the transference of an ever-increasing proportion of her resources from primary production to manufacturing industry. In the last decade, however, the 'Japanese economic miracle',[1] to use the now hackneyed term, has been achieved not merely by a remarkable expansion of manufactures, but also by a profound change in the structure of industrial production which has taken the form of a movement of resources to trades based on modern technology. These changes will be the subject of this and of the next three chapters. We shall begin by discussing the effects of the war on industry, the process of recovery after 1945, and the rising tempo of industrial growth after the middle 1950s. Against this background we shall then consider a representative sample of the leading trades with the object of throwing light on their organization, efficiency, and technical equipment.

First, let us glance at the statistical evidence of industrial growth. The index of the volume of industrial production shows that recovery from the depths to which the economy had descended at the end of the war was at first very slow. It was not until 1951 that the index rose above the level reached in the middle 1930s, but from then on the advance was at a pace that compares very favourably with what was achieved in the most progressive Western countries. In 1953 industrial production was over 40 per cent greater than in 1935; in 1957 it was well over twice as great, and in 1961 probably four times as great as before the war. Finally, despite a temporary slackening in the rate of increase during 1962, rapid growth was resumed in the following year. As already shown, the development did not proceed at a steady pace, for the long bursts of expansion were punc-

---

[1] Astonishment at Japan's progress is a recurrent sentiment in the West. In 1875 W. E. Griffis (*The Mikado's Empire*, i.291), referred to 'the recent marvellous changes in Japan'.

tuated by three short periods of hesitancy, in 1953–4, 1957–8, and 1962. But for our present purpose it is the rate of secular growth that is significant; over the last decade (1953–63) the annual average rate of increase in industrial production was much higher than anywhere else in the free world.[2]

The index referred to covers 'industrial activity', which includes utilities (gas, water, and electricity) and mining, as well as manufacturing. The output of the utilities between 1935 and 1962 rose at about the same rate as the average. As mining output had only doubled, it follows that manufacturing industry grew even faster than the index of industrial activity as a whole. In 1963, indeed, it was probably nearly five times that of 1935.

The rise in the volume of industrial production during the 1950s was accompanied by a great increase, though not a proportionate increase, in industrial employment. Between 1950 and 1963, the number of persons engaged in manufacturing industry rose from 6,250,000 to 11,290,000 and those in construction from 1,350,000 to 3,070,000. As a proportion of the occupied population the numbers employed in manufacturing and construction increased from 22 to 31 per cent. This is still rather lower than the corresponding proportion for Great Britain where the numbers engaged in primary production are very small, but it is, of course, much higher than before the war (1940) when the proportion in Japan was 24 per cent.[3]

The movements in the general index of production and in manpower give no indication of the great structural changes that have occurred in Japanese industry in recent times. Yet since these changes are functionally related to the growth in total output, they must be considered in some detail. Attention was drawn in Chapter I to the pre-war tendency towards an increase in the relative size of the capital-goods industries. The tendency was greatly strengthened during the war, and after the post-war collapse it was resumed. The changes can be measured. Between 1937 and 1955 the output of capital goods increased by over 50 per cent and that of consumer goods by under 40 per cent. During the next eight years while the output of consumer goods

---

[2] According to UN statistics, the index of industrial production (1953=100) in 1963 was 383 for Japan, 207 for West Germany, 241 for Italy, 202 for France, 136 for the US, and 135 for the UK.

[3] *Japan Statist. Yb.*; the proportion was 19 per cent in 1930 according to I. B. Taeuber, *The Population of Japan* (1958), p. 87.

grew two and a half times, that of capital goods nearly quadrupled. These proportions are indicative of changes in the importance of certain individual industries to which close attention must be directed. Immediately before the war the predominance of textiles, though less overwhelming than a decade earlier, was still unchallenged. In 1937 the textile trades as a whole were responsible for about 27 per cent of the gross value of factory production and for about 37 per cent of total factory employment.[4] During the war the size of the textile trades diminished and after 1945 their recovery was slow. In 1951 the volume of textile output was only half that of 1937, and it was not until 1959 that this group of trades reached an output equal to that before the war. In 1963 the output was probably about 60 per cent greater.[5]

This comparatively modest growth resulted in a steep fall in the relative importance of the textile trades. In 1961 they accounted for under 10 per cent of the gross production of the factory industries and for about 14 per cent of total factory employment. The experience of the various trades that composed the group was by no means uniform. The performance of the newer branches was much better than that of the older branches, a contrast that will be discussed in the next chapter.

The 'stagnation' of this formerly predominant sector of Japan's industry provides a key to the understanding of many of her economic problems during the 1950s. Other countries that manufacture and export textile goods, notably Great Britain, had a similar experience with this part of their industry, but the effect on Japan, especially during the early and middle 1950s, was exceptionally serious because of her previous specialization. That it has been possible for her nevertheless to make such a substantial advance in her total industrial output testifies to her remarkable versatility. Like other former specialists in textiles, she found her main compensation in metals and engineering. The output of these industries increased enormously during the years of war only to share in the general collapse after 1945. Until 1950 recovery was slow, but during the subsequent period of general

---

[4] Factories in this context are workplaces with 5 workers and over. The corresponding proportions for 1930 were 38 per cent and 55 per cent. The figures exclude the production and employment of publicly owned establishments (Dept of Comm. & Ind., *Factory Statist.*).

[5] See Statist. App., p. 268 below.

industrial revival the trades soon grew beyond their pre-war limits. The production of chemicals also increased very fast and in 1962 it was probably four times greater than before the war. These three groups of industries (metals, engineering, and chemicals) accounted in 1960 for about 59 per cent of the total value of factory production compared with 45 per cent in 1934–6. They employed 48 per cent of the factory labour force in 1960, compared with 36 per cent in 1934–6.[6]

Within these groups certain trades made outstanding progress. The iron and steel industry trebled its output between 1955 and 1962 and in the latter year it turned out five times as much as before the war. The electrical-apparatus industry, which extended its scope to include many new branches such as the manufacture of electronic equipment, increased its production by six times during those seven years. The shipbuilding industry trebled its output during the same period and the motor industry, which was still very small in the middle 1950s, emerged as one of Japan's major branches of manufacture. A marked expansion also occurred in the output of instruments of various kinds, such as clocks and watches and scientific instruments, while several new trades engaged in the manufacturing of cameras, binoculars, sewing machines, refrigerators, and washing machines developed very fast, especially after 1958. In the chemical industry the chief growth after 1955 occurred in the production of the various derivatives of the oil-refining process. In the ceramics group there was an enormous increase in the output of glass and cement, while the rise in the production of tableware was on a more modest scale. The food, drink, timber, and rubber industries also expanded substantially and branched out in new directions. In mining the growth was much less than in manufactures chiefly because its main constituent, coal-mining, was depressed. On the other hand, the production of electrical energy which more than doubled between 1937 and 1955, doubled again between 1955 and 1962.[7]

[6] Bank of Japan, *Econ. Statist.*, *1962*, pp. 221–2. The pre-war figures cover factories with 5 or more employees, including the working proprietors; the post-war figures up to and including 1960 cover those with 4 or more. For 1961 and later the figures cover factories with 30 or more employees; according to that definition the 'three groups' mentioned above had 58 per cent of factory employment in 1961.

[7] Sources of figures are *Japan Statist. Yb.*, *1962*, and Bank of Japan, *Econ. Statist. 1963*.

It is clear that in the post-war period Japan moved to an entirely new plane of industrial achievement. Before the war she was a specialist in textiles and in low-priced miscellaneous consumption goods. At that time, despite the advance in the output and quality of her metal and engineering products, she was still far inferior to the nations of the West in industries that depended on modern technology. After the war, and especially after 1955, she succeeded in developing the whole range of science-based industries with which contemporary manufacturing enterprise is associated. The quality as well as the quantity of her metal, engineering, and chemical products have placed her in the ranks of the most advanced nations of the world. In some products she has gained pre-eminence.

The factors chiefly responsible for this achievement have already been enumerated. They include *inter alia* the successful import of new techniques, the ample supply of good-quality labour available to manufacturing industry, and the high rate of industrial investment. Of these the second and third are examined in detail in other chapters and only particular aspects of them need be considered here. The first, however, deserves attention at this point in the discussion, since it is intimately connected with the massive innovation of the period.

In the early post-war years Japan's industry was suffering from her long period of technical isolation from the advanced countries, and the gap between her technical standards and those of the West had widened. This conclusion was certainly in accord with the opinion of informed foreign observers at the time. The consumer-goods industries, including the textile trades, were short of capacity, since much machinery had been scrapped during the war, and the data supplied to the World Bank in 1952 showed that a high proportion of Japan's equipment in the heavy industries was old and obsolete, while that installed during the war[8] was of an inferior quality. After 1952, however, the rate of re-equipment rose sharply. Japan used part of the proceeds of American 'special-procurement' expenditure to import new machinery, and much new plant was acquired by the electricity generating, iron and steel, shipbuilding, and textile industries. By 1955 the technical efficiency of these trades had much improved and the way was prepared for the expansion of the next

[8] Cf. *Orient. Econ.*, Mar. 1954, p. 125.

few years, which was especially great in shipbuilding and engineering. Already Japan had tried to close the technical gap by importing foreign 'know-how', and from then on her firms entered into numerous contracts with foreign firms for the use of the latest technical processes. By 1960 almost every substantial enterprise in the newer trades was a party to such agreements, which often provided not merely for the licensing of foreign patents but also for the presence of foreign experts in Japanese plants and the training of Japanese technicians abroad. Between 1950 and 1962 1,998 contracts for technical co-operation had been signed with foreign firms, nearly two-thirds of them American.[9] Most of the contracts related to projects in industries that have grown especially fast, notably iron and steel, petrochemicals, chemical engineering, electronics, and motor manufacturing. The result was that by the early 1960s the technical gap had been virtually closed in most branches of industry and Japanese firms were themselves beginning to devise important innovations.

Access to this new knowledge would have been useless if Japan had not been equipped to take advantage of it. Here she was assisted by the presence of well-qualified managers and competent technicians. Efficient management was a legacy of her former industrial organization which was reconstituted, as we shall see presently, soon after the end of the Occupation. For her adequate supply of technicians she owed a debt to her admirable technical schools and colleges. Similarly, her widespread system of education and training taken as a whole must be given credit for ensuring that her ample labour force was well prepared for industrial employment. Since 1960 the remarkable increase in the demand for skilled labour has emphasized more strongly than ever the importance of trained aptitudes in fostering industrial growth, and we discuss in Chapter XI the present educational practices and plans designed to maintain and improve the quality of her workers.

It would clearly have been impossible for Japan to assimilate the new techniques and to have put her labour to highly productive work if she had not been able to find very large new capital resources. We have already observed that the ratio of investment to the gross national product was exceptionally high

[9] EPA, *Econ. Survey, 1962–3*, p. 216.

after the middle 1950s, about 33 per cent between 1956 and 1960.[10] What is more, a very large share of the new investment was embodied in industrial equipment. On the other hand, there can be little doubt that the rapid growth in the capitalization of manufacturing industry occurred in some degree at the expense of investment in social overhead capital (the infrastructure). Comparatively little capital was provided for roads, housing, and welfare expenditure. Even the investment of industrial concerns was concentrated on plant and machinery; the director of a great new steel works excused the appalling condition of the roads and tracks that linked various shops by saying that the firm preferred to use all its capital for installing improved equipment. A point has probably now been reached where these deficiencies in the infrastructure must now be made good, unless industrial efficiency is to suffer, but so far the investment policy has earned high returns in the expansion of manufacturing output.

The introduction of improved techniques led to notable increases in productivity throughout industry. In the immediate post-war years output per employee was undoubtedly very low, and up to the end of 1952 it is probable that both in manufacturing and mining it was still less than before the war. At that time, however, a rapid recovery was taking place. It was officially estimated that in 1953 labour productivity in manufacturing was about 10 per cent greater than in the middle 1930s (1934–6) and in 1954 about 15 per cent greater.[11] From then on the improvement was very substantial indeed as the table on p. 111 indicates. It is evident from these figures that, while the rise in some of the newer industries, such as motor vehicles, was very large indeed, it was substantial even in long-established industries such as cotton spinning and ammonium-sulphate manufacture. For the whole period between 1950 and 1960 labour productivity in manufacturing is estimated to have risen by 5·5 per cent a year.

These figures cover firms of medium size as well as large firms,

---

[10] Cf. S. Okita, *Economic Growth of Post-War Japan* (1962), pp. 13–14. In 1959 the ratio was 35 per cent and in 1960 38 per cent. The average ratio of gross *fixed* capital formation to GNP was about 18 per cent in 1951–5 and 28 per cent in 1956–60.

[11] Estimates of Min. Internat. Trade & Ind. Labour productivity in mining was still much lower than pre-war at that time.

Man-Hours of Direct and Indirect Labour per Unit of Output

	1955	1960
Pig iron	4·40	2·49
Ingot steel (open hearth) . .	6·94	5·12
*Steel sheet	23·00	13·83
Cotton yarn (20s) . . .	31·60	24·70
Worsted yarn	86·51	54·44
Woollen yarn	55·11	51·57
Rayon staple	10·96	7·92
Motor passenger vehicles . .	390·92	143·70
Motor commercial vehicles .	800·62	200·02
Cement	2·49	1·26
Tyres and tubes . . .	181·27	141·90
Liquid chlorine . . .	22·65	9·58
*Newsprint	11·60	7·19
Ammonium sulphate . .	19·44	10·57
*Electric motors (standard) .	8·21	5·26
*Rayon filament . . .	62·76	53·04

* Direct labour, manufacturing.

Source: Yb. Lab. Statist., 1961. Between 1960 and 1963 average labour productivity in manufacturing rose by 23 per cent.

but they do not reflect the experience of small firms where measurement is extremely difficult. Yet since that sector is still important, it cannot be neglected in any account of the country's industrial progress. We have already referred to the pre-war dichotomy, common to other old-established societies which have undergone a rapid economic development, between the sector composed of highly capitalized large-scale plants with modern techniques, and that made up of the multitude of small workshops which operated without elaborate equipment. In the former were to be found the great establishments in the engineering and the heavy industries, the large, highly mechanized plants in the cotton-spinning, woollen, and rayon industries, and also a number of factories in certain traditional industries which had adopted modern techniques, for example, the *tabi* manufacturing industry. The small and medium workplaces were found both in old industries that served the Japanese consumer (such as the manufacture of certain foodstuffs, silk and rayon fabrics for Japanese dress, and pottery for domestic use), and in modern industries to which the small-scale organization could be economically applied (such as the manufacture of some kinds of electric lamps and of parts for bicycles and other engineering products). On the commercial and financial side these two sectors of the economy were linked through the great trading companies and banks of the *Zaibatsu*, for these formed the channel through which the small producers secured access to markets, finance, and technical knowledge. Yet, in spite of this link, the two sectors remained strongly contrasted with one another in the productive methods and type of labour which they employed. It was to be expected that as Japan's industrialization proceeded the economy would gradually lose its dual character. But as long as the over-populated countryside was able to provide an abundant supply of labour for industrial and commercial occupations, the process of assimilation was bound to be delayed. An American economist has estimated that in 1939 23 per cent of the manpower employed in manufacturing industry was to be found in workplaces with under 5 workers and 46 per cent in those with under 30 workers.[12]

The economic circumstances of Japan in the early post-war period did nothing to disturb this dichotomy. In many respects it became more pronounced. In spite of the dissolution of the *Zaibatsu* and other changes in economic organization which will be examined later, and notwithstanding the structural transformation already considered, the gulf between the two sectors remained wide. It is difficult to find comparable figures for the pre-war and the post-war periods, especially in the case of the very small workplaces. Such information as is available, however, suggests that while there has been an absolute increase in output and employment in all the size groups in manufacturing industry, the smaller and medium-sized establishments have remained of overwhelming importance in respect of numbers employed. Table 11 in the Statistical Appendix shows that in 1955 60 per cent of the workers in manufacturing industry were found in workplaces with under 100 workers, and even in 1960

[12] E. P. Reubens, 'Small-scale Industry in Japan', *Q. J. of Econ.*, Aug. 1947, p. 587. Mr Reubens produces evidence to show that pre-war estimates exaggerated the relative importance of the smallest workplaces (i.e. those with under 5 workers). Lockwood (p. 112) agrees that these earlier estimates (based on the Census of 1930) are unsatisfactory as *measures of actual employment*, but he holds that the Census figures are 'broadly representative of the labour force in terms of chief occupation' (see p. 12 above). However, all estimates of the numbers employed in very small workplaces are very uncertain; some put the figure much higher than Reubens.

the proportion was nearly 55 per cent.[13] The figures for very small workplaces in that table do not include the large number of retailers engaged in producing their own supplies, who are especially numerous in the food trades. Such figures are not, of course, an accurate guide to the contributions of the several size groups to the national product. Labour productivity is generally far higher in the large firms and plants than in the others. In 1959 establishments with 500 employees and over were responsible for 41 per cent of the total sales of manufacturing industry, although the employment they provided amounted to only 24 per cent of total manufacturing employment. In terms of value added the output per worker in the 1,000-and-over group was four times that in the 4–9 group and two and a half times that in the 30–99 group. Even though many medium-sized firms that acted as sub-contractors to great engineering companies improved their equipment and methods of manufacture very considerably during the later 1950s, in general the disparities between the large establishments and the rest have probably increased. For instance, between 1955 and 1959, when 'added value' per worker in manufactures rose by 35 per cent on an average, the increase was 25 per cent in the 4–9 group and 48 per cent in the 1,000-and-over group.[14] The effect of these contrasts in productivity on the pattern of wages will be considered in Chapter XI.

The survival of the small firms and of disparate conditions of employment during a period of rapid economic growth can ultimately be explained by the nature of Japan's factor-endowment. Both natural resources and capital have been scarce, while her labour supply has been plentiful. Capital has been applied lavishly to industries where technical conditions require heavy investment in equipment. But where the nature of the product permits manufacture by less highly capitalistic methods, production has been left to small and often, though not invariably, ill-equipped workplaces. Before the war the high concentration of new investment in certain fields was associated with re-

[13] These figures are from the *Census of Manufacturers* (Min. Internat. Trade & Ind.). They may not record all the employment in very small workplaces. Shinohara, *Survey of Japanese Literature on the Small Industry* (pp. 21–22), estimates that about 20 per cent of total manufacturing employment was afforded by workplaces with 1–3 workers in 1960.
[14] Data from Min. Lab.

armament. During the early post-war years, the demands under the American 'special-procurement' programme stimulated investment in the heavy industries, and the government directed a high proportion of the new capital into the large-scale industries, including electricity generating. Subsequently, the rise of new science-based industries required heavy investment in large plants. Yet, in spite of this investment, a large part of the growing labour supply still had to find work in lightly capitalized industries conducted in small and medium establishments.

By the early 1960s there were signs that the duality in the economy was approaching its term. Rapid economic growth had created a labour shortage in the sense that small and medium firms found that they were no longer able to attract labour at wages below those paid by the large firms. Labour-intensive industries, therefore, came under pressure, and articles of handicraft together with services rose steeply in price. Some small manufacturers engaged in the production of articles of luxury were able to regard this rise in costs with equanimity, since in the increasingly prosperous society demand for their goods was well maintained.[15] But others were faced with the alternatives of raising productivity to compensate for the increase in wages or of going out of business. In many industries their response to this challenge has taken the form of vigorous attempts to modernize their organization and equipment. Some of them have achieved this result by merging with their fellow-manufacturers, with the object of installing up-to-date capacity and raising their scale of operations. Others, while retaining their independent existence, have sought a solution of their problems by co-operation in the setting up of new industrial centres. These are not unlike the trading estates established in the Development Areas of Great Britain, although they differ from their British counterparts in being composed of firms in the same industry. In this they are faithful to an old tradition. Groups of specialist craftsmen are still to be found in particular villages or quarters of towns (such as the Nishijin silk weavers of Kyoto), and in the modern era it has been usual for small producers in a new industry to set up

---

[15] For instance, the doll industry of Saitama Prefecture, which is in the hands of numerous small parts-makers and assemblers, has remained very prosperous, despite the high prices charged for their products. These dolls are highly regarded as presents.

their factories in a particular locality (for example, the worsted weavers of Ichinomiya). Their example is now being followed by many groups of small firms. The government, under powers conferred by special legislation, has given financial help to these ventures in the form of grants, loans at low rates of interest from the official banks, and tax concessions.

The most significant development, however, is that large firms that have been accustomed to buy components from medium and small sub-contractors have been forced by increased competition to reorganize their supplies. This has generally resulted in a rise in the scale of operations, an increase in specialization, and an improvement in techniques on the part of the sub-contractors. The latter changes have been so striking as to induce some observers of the economic scene to claim that a new type of industrial organization has emerged. They refer to it as *Keiretsu*, by which they mean a closely-knit, vertical hierarchy of enterprises centred on a great concern which directs, organizes, and fosters a multitude of dependent sub-contractors. It seems likely that where this *Keiretsu* organization has appeared, it has had the effect of circumscribing co-operative activities among small and medium manufacturers. It is true that since the war there has been a proliferation of various types of association for the promotion of the interests of such manufacturers, and numerous laws have been made for their encouragement. But these firms have tended increasingly to resort to the city or local banks for loans rather than to make use of the facilities provided by their own co-operatives, while the strengthening of the vertical links between particular large and small enterprises has robbed the associations of some of their other functions. Many of them, in the words of a Japanese commentator, have lately become 'sleeping associations'.[16]

These changes are of outstanding importance. In the past, when skilled labour was plentiful and cheap, economic efficiency over a considerable sector of industry was attained by other means than those employed in countries where capital was plentiful and labour scarce. It could then be argued that Japan's advantages in competition with the industrialized West were to be found chiefly in labour-intensive industries, among which those composed of small and medium workplaces were prominent. But this

[16] Shinohara, *Survey*, p. 86.

conclusion is now far less well established than a decade ago, and it seems that further profound changes are imminent in the organization of some of the leading industries.

VII
The Textile Industries[1]

THE textile industries shared only to a modest extent in the post-war expansion of Japanese manufactures. It was not until 1959 that their output exceeded that of the pre-war period, and the possibility of their ever regaining their former predominance in the economy can be decisively rejected. In this respect, and for similar reasons, Japan has followed a course comparable with that of other leading industrial countries. Yet, despite the relative decline, textiles still employ more workers than any other industrial group distinguished in the Census of Manufactures and they occupy a more prominent place in Japan than they do in the United States, the United Kingdom, and other Western countries. Statistics for the group as a whole disguise the violent changes that have occurred in the constituents of which it is composed. During the first ten years after the war the recovery in rayon was much more rapid than that in cotton, wool, or silk. Between 1955 and 1960 most branches of the industry advanced, but the chief feature of the expansion was an immense growth in the production of synthetic fibres, yarns, and fabrics. After 1960 both cotton and rayon declined and progress in textile production was dependent almost entirely on synthetics. The failure of raw silk to approach its pre-war output demonstrates that even the most progressive economies have their depressed branches.

Thus the post-war period has seen the reconstitution of the textile industry on the basis of man-made fibres in the place of natural fibres. This is the first outstanding change. The second is the transformation in markets. From being a predominantly exporting industry, textile manufacture has become concerned primarily with serving the home consumer. About three-quarters of the output is now sold in the domestic market. The buoyancy of this demand is attributable partly to the growth in

[1] Data for textile production, trade, and capacity from Toyo Spinning Co., Inst. for Econ. Research, *Statist. Digest of Japanese Textile Ind.* (quarterly) and from All-Japan Cotton Spinners' Assoc.

I

population and partly to the increase in the consumption of fibres a head from 9·37 lb. in 1934–6 to 14·72 lb. in 1957 and 20·19 lb. in 1961. Yet even in the 1960s textiles provided a larger share of Japan's exports than they did of the exports of other industrial countries. But the proportion has steadily declined, from 53 per cent in 1934–6 to 37 per cent in 1955 and 23 per cent in 1963. The two outstanding changes referred to above are not independent of one another. As in other countries the substitution of man-made fibres for raw cotton was encouraged by the relative cheapness of the former. In Japan's case, moreover, the long-continued weakness of the export trade to which the decline in textile sales powerfully contributed, and the recurrent difficulties with the balance of payments, compelled her to seek the means for reducing dependence on fibre imports.

The individual textile industries must now be treated in some detail, and we shall begin with raw silk, once the major Japanese industry, now fallen into decay. The depression in the silk industry during the 1930s was the source of many of Japan's most serious economic problems, for its incidence was felt not so much in the main industrial centres but rather in the countryside. Two million farming families relied upon the sale of their cocoons for the greater part of their money income, and in the chief silk-raising districts the filatures provided much employment for the daughters of the farmers. As silk formed such a large item on the export list, a fall in silk prices meant inevitably a serious disturbance in the balance of payments. These problems returned in an exaggerated form to post-war Japan. During the war capacity was much reduced not merely in the reeling branch but, more seriously, in the cocoon-raising branch, for many mulberry trees were uprooted to make room for food crops. The capacity could doubtless have been restored, although in any event the process would have been slow. After the war, however, it soon became evident that the great export market had gone and that the loss had to be accepted as permanent. The American hosiery industry had changed over to nylon. All that was left was the relatively small demand from domestic and foreign weavers. The decline in the industry is shown in the statistical tables.[2] It will be seen that the production of raw silk recovered slowly in the first ten years of peace, that after the middle 1950s

[2] Statist. App., Tables 8, 9, 16.

it stagnated, and that in 1963 it amounted to only about two-fifths of the output of the middle 1930s. As home consumption by 1955 had been restored to the pre-war level and was afterwards maintained without much change, the whole loss was sustained in the export market. In 1934–6 the annual average export amounted to 522,000 bales, in 1961–3 it averaged 71,000 bales.[3] This means, in effect, that raw silk has ceased to be of much importance as an export industry. The ratio of exports to output has fallen from over two-thirds before the war to about one-quarter in recent years, and the share of silk in Japan's total export trade is becoming insignificant. Silk is exported in forms other than raw silk, notably as fabrics, but the production and export of fabrics have also fallen. In 1934–6 the annual average export was 85 million square yards. In 1961–3, despite some recovery after the early 1950s, it amounted to only 62 million square yards, about one-third of the total production.

The decline in world demand for raw silk was the chief, though not the only, cause of the collapse of Japan's sales. Before the war she supplied nearly three-quarters of the silk that entered international trade. During the post-war period China became a more dangerous competitor and Japan's proportion of the diminished total fell to under 60 per cent. The worsening of her position occurred mainly because the fall in demand was especially great in the types of goods and markets in which she formerly specialized. But a rise in costs was also responsible for the industry's difficulties. In the early years of peace high food prices brought keen competition for land formerly used for mulberries. At the same time the yield of cocoons per ton of mulberries remained for some years much lower than before the war and many workers formerly engaged in the tedious process of cocoon raising were attracted to more remunerative employments. For these reasons the reelers found that cocoon prices had risen disproportionately to the price of reeled silk. Improvements in productive methods were later effected which raised the output of cocoons per *tan* of mulberries well above the pre-war level.[4] But the competition for land for alternative uses became more intense, and as the agricultural labour supply moved from a con-

---

[3] Bale=132 lb. Data from the Central Raw Silk Assoc. of Japan, and *Japan Statist. Yb.*

[4] 1 *tan*=0·245 acres.

dition of surplus to scarcity, labour costs rose even more steeply.[5] The consequence was that cocoon prices continued to increase. Meanwhile, the reelers found that the strong demand for labour from the prosperous manufacturing industries meant that they could no longer obtain cheap female labour to staff the filatures. They responded by efforts to improve efficiency. Innovations such as the adoption of automatic reeling machines had a marked effect on both labour productivity and on quality, and costs were also reduced by introducing a two-shift system. By 1954 the output of filature silk per operative-month was twice that obtained before the war and by 1960 it had more than doubled again.[6] These measures, however, only partially offset the increasing cost of labour and cocoons, and many of the producers were persuaded by the uncertain prospects of the industry to enter other lines of trade. Employment in silk reeling, which declined from 350,000 in the middle 1930s to 76,000 in 1950, rose to 87,000 in 1953 and then fell steadily to 49,000 in 1960.

The technical changes in silk reeling produced structural changes in the industry that deserve notice. Before the war the optimum unit from an economic standpoint was probably a medium-sized filature with 150 to 300 basins, for this type of establishment was able to secure economies of scale and also to exercise sufficient supervision over cocoon suppliers to ensure uniformity in materials.[7] There were, in addition, a few very large firms with numerous mills, notably Katakura, and many small filature owners, besides a multitude of hand reelers. The changes of the early post-war period fell with uneven incidence on the several branches. The larger firms were able to meet the rise in costs more effectively than the rest of the filature owners by technical innovation and by substituting capital for labour; while the hand reelers, who employed few hired workers and were untroubled by the provisions of the Labour Standards Law, were at first little affected by the rise in wages. So the main bur-

---

[5] The number of sericultural households fell from 1,690,000 in 1938 to 810,000 in 1949, and to 645,000 in 1960. Recently efforts have been made to modernize sericulture by the establishment of large, co-operative mulberry farms, and by the adoption of various labour-saving techniques.

[6] Japan Silk Assoc., *The Raw Silk Industry of Japan* (annual) for information about production; also T. Ogura, ed., *Agricultural Development in Modern Japan* (1963), pp. 558–65.

[7] Cf. Schumpeter, pp. 515–16.

den of the contraction of the industry was borne by the medium-sized filatures.[8] Subsequently, with the progressive rise in the price of labour, the advantages of mechanization increased and even the hand reelers were drawn to other employments. In 1960 over four-fifths of all the raw silk was produced by 220 fully mechanized mills (that is, mills equipped with automatic reeling machines), most of them owned by large concerns. The rest was reeled by about 1,200 smaller filatures and a rapidly shrinking number of hand-reeling mills.[9]

The other chief branch of textiles, cotton, can also attribute its chief post-war troubles largely to a loss of export markets, and we must refer to its experiences in this field before describing the structural changes in the industry. Before the war cotton goods, chiefly piece-goods, were sold mainly, though by no means exclusively, in Asian countries. During the 1930s the tendency was for international trade as a whole in cotton goods to contract as the former importing countries expanded their own production, but Japan then succeeded in enlarging her exports, chiefly at the expense of Great Britain. After the war the general tendency towards a shrinkage in international trade in cotton persisted, and in this period Japan was among the chief sufferers.[10] By the middle 1950s the shortage of raw materials and equipment which had been the chief handicap in the early post-war years had been overcome, and it was abundantly clear that the limit was then being set by the lack of foreign demand. Japan no longer had access to her former market in China, and her sales to the Indian subcontinent appeared to have suffered a permanent decline through the successful competition of Indian textiles. Consequently in 1954 and 1955 cotton piece-goods exports (in quantity) were under half those of the middle 1930s, and yarn exports also had fallen very steeply. Later there was a revival, in yarns chiefly because of larger sales to South East Asia, and in piece-goods through the growth in demand from widely dispersed customers among which South East Asia and Australia were of special importance. Even so, although in

[8] Soc. for Econ. Coop in Asia, *The Smaller Industry in Japan* (1954), p. 15.
[9] In addition there are a small number of mills engaged in dupion reeling (double-cocoon reeling); this process is still only partly mechanized.
[10] Statistical data for textiles from Toyo Spinning Co., *Statist. Digest*; All-Japan Cotton Spinners' Assoc.; and K. Seki, *The Cotton Industry of Japan* (1956).

1961–3 yarn exports had nearly regained their pre-war quantity, piece-goods exports were still only half.

The exports of pure cottons (and indeed of other goods made of natural fibres) cannot nowadays be treated in isolation from those of yarns and fabrics produced from man-made fibres, for many of these products are substitutes for one another and in some degree they are produced by the same equipment. Some rayon staple is spun in cotton spinning mills, spun-rayon yarn is woven in cotton weaving sheds, and filament rayon on silk looms. The coming of pure synthetics added to these productive complications, and mixtures of natural and synthetic fibres have become a substantial part of the output of all branches of the textile industry. With these points in mind we may review the course of events in the rest of the textile export trade. Exports of rayon-filament goods were affected in the same way as cotton goods. Filament yarn exports began to approach the pre-war quantity only in the early 1960s. Exports of filament fabrics, after rising in the middle 1950s, later declined steeply, and in 1961–3 they amounted to under three-fifths of the corresponding export in 1934–6. On the other hand, the exports of spun-rayon yarn, a new trade just before the war, rose well above those of cotton yarn during the middle and later 1950s, and when they afterwards declined their place was taken by a quite massive export of rayon staple itself. The exports of spun-rayon fabrics grew very fast during the middle 1950s and in 1957–8 were only a third less than cotton piece-goods exports. Subsequently this trade also declined by about a third. Meanwhile a great new export in synthetics and mixtures developed. The foreign trade in this group of products has thus shown wide oscillations since the war. The only other textile industry with a substantial export trade before 1940 was the wool-using trade. For most of the post-war period foreign sales of both wool yarn and fabrics were very low and, despite a rapid recovery after 1954, in 1961–3 exports had still barely regained their pre-war volume. As in other countries, the wool-using industry employs many other fibres besides raw wool; these include synthetics, which have grown considerably in importance.

The blurring of the former distinctions between separate classes of products that has resulted from the introduction of man-made fibres has affected organization in the industrial group as a whole. The change may best be approached from the side of the cotton industry and deserves detailed discussion. Before the war the cotton industry was composed of several distinct branches. First, there were the great integrated firms which operated combined spinning-and-weaving mills and were responsible for a high proportion of the yarn output and for practically all the output of standardized grey cloth. Secondly, there were the specialist spinning firms, some linked with large firms of cotton merchants. Thirdly, there were the specialist weavers with medium-sized and small sheds. These produced wide cloth for home and export and also narrow cloth for Japanese dress. Finally, there was the small and diminishing hand-weaving branch.[11]

Among the integrated firms production was concentrated in a very few business units. In 1935 six firms controlled nearly half the spindles and produced about the same proportion of the yarn output. Eleven firms possessed nearly two-thirds of the spindles. The mills owned by this group were nearly all large and their size was tending to increase. The whole industry had been reorganized during the preceding decade and operated almost entirely with high draft ring spindles. There was the same concentration in the weaving branch. The 'Big Six' operated over half the total looms owned by the integrated branch of the industry and four-fifths of the looms were in the hands of eighteen companies. Their weaving sheds were equipped with automatic looms and the bulk of the output consisted of shirtings and sheetings for sale at home and abroad.

The specialist spinning firms, for the most part, possessed smaller mills than the integrated firms, although most of their capacity was also high draft. The yarn was sold mainly to the third group, the specialist weavers. In the middle 1930s these turned out, on ordinary looms, nearly all the narrow piece-goods and about three-fifths of the wide piece-goods in quantity; in value the proportion was probably about two-thirds. The specialists themselves fell into several groups, the fair-sized firms with 50 power looms or over, medium firms with 10–49 looms (mainly power looms), and small firms with under 10 looms (mostly hand looms). Their output consisted of a wide variety of cloth, including fancy goods, and during the middle 1930s the tendency was

[11] For description of the pre-war structure see Schumpeter, ch. xvi.

for this section of the industry to increase in relative importance both in the home and export markets. This was an indication of the fact that Japan was suffering from increased competition in the bulk trade from India and elsewhere and was moving into the manufacture of higher-priced fabrics. In the finishing branch of the industry, some of the integrated firms had their own establishments, but much of their cloth, together with all the cloth of the specialist weavers, was finished by firms that concentrated on one of the main processes—dyeing, bleaching, or printing. Many of these firms were quite small.

In the early years of the Second World War, the tendencies of the previous decade were reversed, for the official control imposed on production and sale resulted in discrimination in favour of the large firms. Even before the outbreak of the Pacific War the government, in its attempt to reduce Japan's dependence on imports, had insisted on a large admixture of rayon staple in the production of cloth for the home market. For the export market a system was devised which linked allocations of raw cotton with exports of manufactured goods. The administration of these controls was centred on the spinning companies, and the independent weavers of fabrics for export became in effect mere sub-contractors for those companies.[12] As the war proceeded, the controls were strengthened, and the cotton industry was drastically contracted and completely reorganized. Compulsory amalgamations were effected among the spinning companies with the result that production was concentrated on fourteen integrated groups, most of which had interests in other branches of textiles as well as in cotton spinning and weaving. Among the independent weavers and the finishers also production was concentrated in selected mills. The complex structure of the industry, formerly well adapted to the diverse markets that it served, was destroyed.

Even the firms that survived changed over in part to the manufacture of non-textile goods. The shortage of metal led to the scrapping of much equipment, and many spindles and looms were dismantled and shipped to the continent or the South Seas where the government hoped that they would be used for serving local markets. At the end of the war the number of operable spindles had been reduced from over 12 million to little more

[12] Seki, p. 193.

than 2 million. The looms owned by the spinning firms had fallen from 108,000 to 24,000 and those of the independent weavers from 255,000 to 112,000.[13]

The reconstruction of the industry after 1945, though encouraged by SCAP, was impeded by the shortage of raw materials. In 1946 imports of raw cotton were financed by the Commodity Credit Corporation and later other loans from American sources, official and private, were provided. Imports of Indian cotton began in 1947 and of Egyptian in 1948. For several years the industry remained subject to rigid official control. The financial arrangements with the Americans were administered by the government and the Bank of Japan, and until February 1949 the exports of piece-goods against which the loans were made were conducted entirely through a government agency. The government also controlled the reorganization of production. At first spinning was confined to the ten large spinning firms that had survived the war. Then in 1947 twenty-five new firms (*shinbo*) were allowed to produce yarn, and after 1950, when the restrictions were much relaxed, numerous small-scale spinners (known as the *shin-shinbo*) began production.[14] The controls were finally abolished in 1951.

Meanwhile there had been a growth in production and equipment and this continued at an accelerated pace after the outbreak of the Korean War. By 1952 the number of spindles reached $7\frac{1}{2}$ million, of which 64 per cent were owned by the 'Big Ten', 21 per cent by the *shinbo*, and 15 per cent by the *shin-shinbo*. The growth of the industry was checked by the textile recession of 1952, but it was soon resumed and by the end of 1956 there were about 9 million operable spindles. This represented the limit of the expansion and later, partly as a result of the policy of sealing redundant spindles, and partly because of a rise in productivity, the number of operable spindles declined to under 8 million (1961–2).[15] The same happened to rayon-staple spindles which increased rapidly to nearly 3 millions in 1957 and

---

[13] Seki, p. 312.   [14] Ibid. pp. 37–47.

[15] The Textile Industry Equipment Adjustment Law of 1956 provided for the sealing of a proportion of every spinner's capacity in the cotton, rayon, woollen, and worsted industries. Under that law large numbers of these spindles have been stopped; for example, in 1962 1 m. cotton spindles were regarded as permanently stopped and $1\frac{3}{4}$ m. were idle under arrangements for temporary sealing; in all 30 per cent of the capacity was out of service.

were then cut back to under $2\frac{1}{2}$ millions. In the weaving branch of the cotton industry, which in this period became increasingly occupied with man-made-fibre yarns, the number of looms owned by the spinning-weaving firms rose from 24,000 at the end of the war to 81,000 in 1955 only to decline to 62,000 in 1962. On the other hand, the looms owned by the independent cotton weavers nearly trebled between 1946 and 1957. In the latter year they numbered 300,000 and since then they have slightly increased.

Although the old structure of the industry was in some measure restored after 1952, certain important contrasts remain. Despite the diminished output of yarn, there were more spinning firms in the late 1950s than before the war. This is explained by the entry of the small firms of specialist spinners in the early post-war period.[16] Yet although these newcomers for a time threatened the predominance of the large spinners, they lost ground during the textile depression of 1952. By the middle 1950s the 'Big Ten' had over three-fifths of the total spindles and nearly two-thirds of the looms owned by the integrated concerns. Within the spinning-weaving section the high concentration of output on a few firms has not been disturbed by the changes of the last twenty-five years, although a considerable fringe of small spinners still remains.[17]

On the other hand, the specialist weavers appear to have increased their proportion of the pure cotton cloth output. In the years 1961–3 they accounted on average for about three-quarters of it (in quantity) compared with under three-fifths in the middle 1930s. This was a corollary of the change in the character of the output and particularly of exports. Exports of standardized goods—the products of the great integrated mills—have declined to a much greater extent than those of cotton fabrics as a whole. For example, the trade statistics show that post-war exports of grey cloth compared much less favourably with pre-war exports of those goods than did the exports of bleached, dyed, yarn-dyed, and printed fabrics, and in general there has

---

[16] The newcomers into the spinning industry came mainly from other branches of textiles. They included independent weavers, knitted-goods manufacturers, rayon-staple spinners, silk spinners, rope makers, and textile-machinery manufacturers (Seki, p. 131).

[17] In 1935 the 'Big Six' owned 48 per cent of the spindles and 53 per cent of the looms belonging to spinning-weaving concerns.

been a steady upward trend in quality. The rise in the relative importance of specialist weavers is in continuance of the pre-war tendency, and as the specialists are mostly medium-sized or small firms, the effect has been to diminish the degree of concentration on the weaving section of this industry. It would be misleading to examine these structural changes wholly by reference to the output of pure cotton goods. Both the integrated and the specialist weaving sections of the cotton industry now use yarns and fibres other than cotton far more extensively than before the war. Besides pure cotton goods their output consists of spun-rayon cloth, filament-rayon cloth, and cotton mixtures, including synthetics. These varieties form a much higher proportion of the specialists' output than of the integrated firms' output. This is another reason for the relative improvement in the position of the former.

Yet, although the great integrated concerns in what is commonly regarded as the cotton industry itself appear to be less important than formerly, it would be an error to suppose that they have had to content themselves with a more modest place in the textile industry as a whole. In fact they have to a large extent compensated themselves for the decline in cotton by moving to other interests. This brings us to a consideration of the structure of the man-made-fibre industry. As in other countries the manufacture of filament rayon and staple fibre is an activity of very large firms and large plants. In Britain until recently it has been in the hands of firms financially distinct from those in the natural-fibres industries. In Japan, on the other hand, cotton firms have had an important share in the actual manufacture of filament rayon and staple fibre, including high-tenacity filament for motor tyres, and they have lately moved into the manufacture of pure synthetics. This is what might have been expected, for new developments in large-scale industry in Japan have usually proceeded from existing firms. For many years past it was common for large cotton firms to have interests in the wool and silk-spinning trades and, when rayon was introduced, they played a leading part in the development of the manufacture. By 1955 cotton-spinning firms owned over two-fifths of the rayon capacity. The rest was in the hands of firms either specialized to the man-made-fibre production or closely associated with chemical firms. Similarly, although synthetic production was developed initially by firms formerly concerned with rayon and chemical manufactures, cotton spinners also have moved into this field in recent years.

The complexities of the present organization may be illustrated by a few examples.[18] The Toyo Spinning Company in 1962 was one of the three leading firms in the spinning-weaving section of the cotton industry. Apart from its output of cotton yarn and fabrics, it was one of the largest producers of woollen and worsted yarn, woollen fabrics, rayon filament, staple fibre, and spun-rayon yarn, and it has lately taken up the manufacture of synthetic goods. Kanegafuchi, a peer of Toyo Spinning in cotton, had an even wider range of interests, some of them outside the textile field. It owned plants producing cotton yarns and fabrics, woollen and worsted yarn, woollen cloth and felt, raw silk, spun silk and fabrics, rayon staple, spun-rayon yarn, rayon fabrics, and synthetic resins. Recently it has started to produce nylon. The third largest cotton spinner is Dai Nippon Spinning. This firm long possessed interests in all branches of the natural-fibres textile industry. Its concern with rayon staple dates back to 1935 and it was the first cotton spinner to produce pure synthetics. It took this step in 1950 when it began the manufacture of vinylon. These are all old-established cotton firms. The pioneer in rayon filament was Teijin, established in 1918 as part of the old Suzuki concern. It began to produce rayon staple on the eve of the Second World War and after 1945 high-tenacity rayon and acetate rayon. Later it began the manufacture of synthetics with a polyester fibre, which soon became its chief product and it recently established a plant for nylon manufacture. Toyo Rayon, set up by Mitsui in 1926 for the production of filament, followed much the same course as Teijin. It took up the manufacture of rayon staple just before the Second World War and of high-tenacity filament just afterwards. The chief step in its postwar career occurred in 1951 when it started the production of nylon of which for many years it remained the chief producer. Recently it has turned to the manufacture of polyester fibres and to the production of basic materials for the synthetics. As with some other rayon companies it has tended to abandon its original field in order to concentrate on these new activities.

---

[18] *Orient. Econ.*, Aug. 1963, pp. 459–69; Japan Chemical Fibres Assoc., *Rayon and Synthetic Fibres of Japan* (1963).

Most of the companies engaged in synthetic production have technical agreements with firms overseas, Toyo Rayon with Du Pont, Teijin with ICI, and Asahi Chemical (which makes cupra-ammonium and viscose rayon, acrylon nitric fibres, nylon, explosives, food products, and various chemicals) with the Dow Corporation of the United States. The textile firms have not been content with a horizontal extension of their range of production. Some of them have moved back into the manufacture of materials required for synthetic fibres and forward into finishing and making-up, often by means of sub-contracting arrangements. Similarly, firms that built themselves up as producers of materials or semi-products have advanced into the manufacture of more highly finished goods.

During the pre-war decade Japan's cotton industry had become technically very efficient, at any rate in the main processes of spinning and weaving. Practically all the spinning mills used high drafting and the equipment of the weaving sheds owned by the integrated firms consisted almost entirely of automatic looms. The destruction of most of this equipment during the war presented the firms with a difficult problem of reconstruction. But in the process of solving this problem, the leading producers were able to equip themselves with up-to-date machinery, and after 1952 heavy investment in new plants, both in the cotton and in the man-made-fibres industries, was undertaken. The government, in an effort to render Japan less dependent upon imports of raw materials, gave special encouragement to the rayon and synthetic-fibre industries by providing finance at low rates of interest and by reducing the tax burden.[19] In the cotton industry many detailed technical improvements were effected, notably the conversion of carding engines, drawing frames, and roving frames to large package types, the change-over of roving frames to the simplex system, and the introduction of super-high drafting and of pneumatic cleaners.[20] The most recent technical progress has taken the form of continuous automated spinning. As a result productivity per spindle and per operative has much increased. A comparison with pre-war standards is obviously difficult because of changes in the type of product. It appears, however, that although in the late 1940s production per man-hour was very low in cotton spinning, by 1950 it had probably

[19] *Orient. Econ.*, Feb. 1956, p. 74.   [20] Ibid. May 1955, p. 240.

surpassed the pre-war level. After 1952 the advance was rapid and production per man-hour in the middle 1950s was probably between one-quarter and one-third greater than before the war.[21] Since then rationalization and innovations in spinning methods have brought further advances, and between 1955 and 1960 labour productivity increased by over one-fifth. The progress is continuing. The Japan Cotton Spinners' Association estimated that the output per spindle (16 hours running) rose by 26 per cent between 1958 and June 1963. Output of cotton cloth per loom in the combined mills rose by about 7 per cent in the same period.[22] In the specialist-weaving mill section it is more difficult to estimate movements in productivity or efficiency, but it is probable that in recent years they have also shared to some extent in the recent advance.

Although technical efficiency in most branches of textiles had probably surpassed pre-war levels by the early 1950s, in other respects the industry was slow in regaining its pre-war competitive strength. Before the war the expert buying of cotton and skill in blending kept raw-material costs low, and cheap labour was available for the processes preparatory to spinning. After the war the exchange and import controls deprived the spinners of their former opportunities for the selective buying of cotton. These difficulties were accentuated by changes within the merchanting section of the industry. That section, which was formerly dominated by a small number of great firms engaged both in importing raw cotton and exporting piece-goods, sustained grave damage from the war. Its overseas organization was destroyed, its financial resources were depleted, and for many years after the war its recovery was impeded by the continuing controls over foreign exchange and imports. The place of the big firm was taken for a time by numerous small merchants who lacked both the experience and the financial resources of their predecessors. Even after the reconstitution of the large merchant houses, the opportunities for mass marketing in which they had formerly displayed their efficiency were reduced by the loss of trade in standard types of goods. The specialized merchant houses, therefore, sought compensation by diversifying their trade, and new patterns of industrial relationships were estab-

---

[21] *Orient. Econ.*, June 1956, p. 275 and EPA, *Econ. Survey, 1954–5*, p. 57.
[22] All Japan Cotton Spinners' Assoc., *Monthly Rep.*, Nov. 1963, pp. 86–100.

lished among firms in different sections of the industry. There was concentration among the merchant houses themselves and also a tendency towards vertical integration set going by the great cotton spinners. These firms assumed control over the formerly independent weavers and finishers either by engaging them to work on commission or by entering into exclusive contracts with them for supplying yarn and purchasing the finished products. Some of these arrangements were made direct with the weavers, and others through the medium of small merchants who themselves have been reduced to the position of spinners' agents.[23] The great firms have also penetrated in much the same way into the making-up trade which has developed very quickly. Thus the formerly closely-knit relations between the different sections of the industry have been largely restored although the distribution of power has changed.[24]

[23] N. Inaba, 'Integration of Enterprises in Japan', *Ann. of Sch. of Business Admin., Kobe Univ.* (1960), pp. 48–51.
[24] Y. Arakawa, 'Small Wholesalers in Cotton Textiles Marketing in Japan'; in T. Yamanaka, ed., *Small Business in Japan* (1960), pp. 257 ff.

VIII

The Engineering Industries

THE enlargement of the engineering industries during the early and middle 1930s was stimulated by investment in rearmament and in the foundation of centres of heavy industry in Manchuria. But it did not depend wholly on public expenditure or national policy concerned with strategic aims, and progress was by no means limited to the branches that directly or indirectly obtained their orders from the State. Several other engineering trades made striking advances, notably the manufacture of bicycles, light electrical apparatus, and textile machinery. On general economic grounds one would have expected Japan's relative advantages to lie in the production of the lighter products, especially labour-intensive goods. Yet even in some of the heavy branches, such as shipbuilding, Japan was a cheap producer.

Throughout the industry during this time there was a remarkable growth in technical efficiency. By the middle 1930s Japan was competent to turn out the complete equipment for power stations, and she had ceased to depend on foreign countries for imports of the commoner types of machine tools. She still lagged behind Western countries in the production of some products, for example, motor cars; but her industry was rapidly extending its scope. Her relatively cheap skilled labour and her well-trained technicians enabled her to go a long way towards overcoming both her technological inferiorities to Western nations and also her disadvantages in regard to supplies of certain raw materials.

With the outbreak of the Sino-Japanese War in 1937 the expansion of this group of industries, though not of every constituent in it, was accelerated. After 1941 the new or enlarged plants of the old-established firms were joined by the plants of other industries converted to wartime production. In 1944 the output of engineering goods reached its peak. In volume it was then more than three times the output of 1937, or four and a half times that of the middle 1930s. The growth was accomplished not merely by the expansion or adaptation of the large-scale sector of industry, but also by the enlistment of small producers, including those located in country areas, as sub-contractors. As in other countries, however, the industry became distorted from the pattern of peacetime needs. The trades that served the export markets and the home civilian demand, such as the manufacture of bicycles or of textile machinery, declined as their plants changed over to munitions production. On the other hand, there was an immense expansion in the output of machine-tools and aircraft. In some respects Japan was jeopardizing her future. She had depended upon foreign countries for information about technical advances. For instance, in the electrical industry, as in several others, her producers had links with American and European firms that gave her access to new devices and scientific discoveries. The war snapped these links and the gap between Japanese and Western standards of technical accomplishment widened.

In spite of the damage sustained by many of the large engineering plants, Japan emerged from the war with a greatly increased capacity in this group of trades and with a more widely diffused knowledge of engineering skills. Yet the task of redeploying her resources for meeting the demands of the post-war world was far more onerous than that faced by her main competitors. Having lost her former export trade, she was deprived of access to supplies of imported raw materials essential to the heavy industries. With her financial system in ruins and reserves exhausted by inflation, it was difficult for her manufacturers to obtain capital for reconstruction. The uncertainties that arose directly from her defeat were especially perplexing for the engineering firms. SCAP's policy in regard to the 'level' to be permitted to various types of production was aimed particularly at trades that were deemed to contribute to Japan's capacity for making war, such as shipbuilding. These were subjected to onerous restrictions. Similarly, the proposal to distribute plant as reparations was formulated with an eye on the heavy engineering industries, and firms could not make a start on any programme of reconstruction until the fate of their plants was known. Finally, the policy of dissolving the *Zaibatsu* added to these uncertainties, because the engineering industry had been dominated by those concerns.

The attempts of the Japanese government to deal with the

K

financial problem of reconstruction have already been described. We have also seen how Allied Occupation policy towards industry changed when the cold war started. As 'economic democratization' and the reparations problem fell into the background, the reconstruction of engineering made some headway. After the outbreak of the Korean War, and with the final abandonment of the early post-war plans for removing plant as reparations, Japan's production of engineering goods began a rapid advance. As she was the only country with spare engineering capacity at this time, orders poured into her factories and shipyards. In 1951 the output of machinery rose far above the 1937 level. The heavy demands arising from the Korean War were sustained in the next few years by substantial investment in the textile and the heavy industries, including the public utilities. In 1953 the index of machinery production reached 267 (1934–6 = 100). The decline in American 'special procurement' and the deflationary policy of the government in 1954 led to a slight fall in output; but towards the end of 1955 the industry entered upon a period of extraordinarily rapid expansion. Output doubled between 1955 and 1957, and after a check during the recession of 1958 it doubled again by 1961. Growth continued during the next two years though at a somewhat diminished rate. In 1963 the production of engineering goods was about five times that of 1955 and ten times the pre-war level. Engineering had become Japan's greatest industry. Its progress in the late 1950s is attributable to the convergence of several factors: the high rate of fixed investment in manufacturing industry, the rapid spread of new industrial techniques, the rise in personal incomes which greatly enlarged the demand for durable consumer goods, and the penetration of foreign markets by a wide diversity of engineering products ranging from ships to electronic apparatus and cameras.

The rate of growth was unique in the history of engineering and it could not have been attained if the industry had failed to extend its range. It is true that some of the older branches, such as shipbuilding, machine tools, textile machinery, and electrical machinery, expanded very fast, but the most remarkable feature of the period was the appearance of trades that had hardly existed or were of minor importance before the war or even in the early 1950s. These included the production of motor cars, electronic apparatus, instruments such as cameras and binoculars, and several types of durable household goods.

In foreign markets the changes had been equally notable. In the 1930s Japan sold the greater part of her machinery export to North East Asia, especially to Manchuria. This was a corollary of her heavy investment in that area. There was only a small export, chiefly of light engineering goods and electrical apparatus, to parts of the world that lay outside her political control. In the post-war period the North East Asian markets virtually disappeared, but the export trade of the 1950s and early 1960s was greater than formerly and far more widely extended. It included the sale of heavy plant and industrial machinery to South and South East Asia and also a large trade in both heavy and light engineering products to North America, Europe, and Australia. The very rapid growth of this group of exports—sevenfold between 1953–4 and 1962–3—was the chief cause of the expansion in Japan's export trade as a whole. Before the war machinery made only a small contribution to the trade; in 1962–3 it accounted for over a quarter of its total value.

The changes in organization were less revolutionary. Before the war the technical units in the engineering industry consisted of, first, a few very great plants each with a wide range of products and, second, a large number of medium-sized and small plants. The former were to be found chiefly in the heavy industries, although they also shared in the output of the lighter products. The small and medium plants were of several kinds. Some of them belonged to sub-contractors who worked for the large plants. Others were engaged in producing either parts for assembly in medium-sized assembly factories or light finished goods, such as cheap electric lamps, made to the orders of merchants. The small plants suffered less than the large plants from the air raids, and after the war they were able to equip themselves with machine tools from dismantled munitions factories.[1] As at this time the rehabilitation of the large factories was proceeding tardily, the importance of the small producers in the industry was considerably enhanced. After 1950, however, most new investment was directed into a relatively small number of large plants, and during the period of deflation in 1954 the small firms were hard hit. This was especially true of sub-contractors to large firms.

[1] Industr. Bank, *Survey Fin. & Ind.*, Jan.–Feb. 1954, p. 10.

During the boom that began in the later part of 1955, when capacity in the large plants became fully occupied, a greatly increased quantity of orders was placed with the small producers. They stood up well to the recession of 1958 which dealt a serious blow to the small firms in the textile and consumer-goods industries,[2] and they shared also in the benefits of the exceptionally rapid industrial growth during the next three years. The small and medium plants, therefore, occupied as important a place in engineering production during the post-war period as in the late 1930s. In the middle 1950s, for instance, four-fifths of the output of sewing-machine parts and three-fifths of the output of bicycle parts were being made by small and medium firms, and in these industries the high degree of specialization on the part of each producer resulted in very efficient manufacture.[3] Even in the shipbuilding industry medium-sized contractors made a notable contribution to the enlarged output, and in some of the most rapidly growing trades of the later 1950s, such as motor-car manufacture, the large firms surrounded themselves with subcontractors for the production of components.

Conditions are now changing. In the past when the wages paid by sub-contractors were low and flexible, the large manufacturers were able to buy components from them at low prices in normal times and to compel them to shoulder the burden of temporary recessions. The growing shortage of labour has narrowed the gap in wages between large and small establishments and has reduced wage flexibility. The profits of the small producers, therefore, have been much compressed and their prospects dimmed. At the same time the liberalization of trade and the growing intensity of competition are forcing the large firms themselves to seek for new cost-reducing measures. It is likely that they will find their remedy in rationalization which will involve the reorganization of components-manufacture into larger units. It is also likely that the leading engineering firms themselves will find it expedient to specialize to a much greater extent than has hitherto been customary; this is a question to be considered later.

SHIPBUILDING

We may now proceed to an examination of a few of the chief branches of the industry, namely the shipbuilding, electrical-

---

[2] EPA, *Econ. Survey, 1958–9*, p. 141.   [3] Ibid. *1954–5*, p. 70.

engineering, motor-vehicle, bicycle, sewing-machine, and camera trades. We begin with shipbuilding. During the 1930s the Japanese mercantile marine grew fast and at the beginning of the Pacific War it amounted to more than 6 million gross tons. The Japanese shipbuilding industry which constructed most of this fleet had been stimulated by government financial assistance rendered under a Scrap-and-Build Plan, as well as by large orders for naval vessels. The annual launchings of merchant ships during the five years before the outbreak of the Second World War averaged about 330,000 gross tons. During the war the capacity of the industry was vastly expanded and, apart from a large tonnage of naval vessels and wooden ships for coastal navigation, about 3,200,000 gross tons of steel merchant ships were built.[4] The last stages of the war, however, were disastrous. Nearly all the ocean-going ships were sunk by Allied action and at the end of the war shipping and shipbuilding were subjected to rigid control by the Occupation authorities. SCAP was intent upon permanently destroying Japan's ability to make war, and to this end it was proposed that the merchant fleet should be limited to $1\frac{1}{2}$ million gross tons of steel ships and that no vessel should exceed 5,000 gross tons or should have a maximum speed of over 15 knots.[5] Much shipbuilding equipment was to be seized as reparations and the remaining yards were required to occupy themselves chiefly with the construction and repair of ships for coastal navigation.

Even this limited programme of work was frustrated in the early post-war years by the lack of financial resources among shipbuilding firms. At that time the government was the only source of funds for reconstructing the heavy industries and it established a Ship Corporation whose functions were the execution of a recovery programme and the supply of funds for this purpose to the extent of 70 per cent of the cost of building. Up to 1948 construction remained limited to small coastal vessels. The change in Allied policy towards Japan in that year, however, had immediate consequences for shipping and shipbuilding. By 1950 SCAP's control over these industries was finally relinquished, and Japan was then for the first time able to proceed with the

[4] Cohen, *Japan's Economy*, p. 196.
[5] H. Yamamoto, 'The Recovery Method of the Japanese Shipping Industry in the Post-War Period', *Kobe Econ. & Business R.* (1954), p. 90.

large-scale reconstruction of her ocean-going fleet.[6] Soon afterwards the boom in world shipping, set going by the Korean War at a moment when Western shipyards were fully extended, brought demands from foreign ship owners and Japan became an important exporter of ships. For financing this new programme money was provided by the government, chiefly through the United States Aid Counterpart Fund. After 1952, when this source of finance dried up, the Japan Development Bank became the chief provider of funds at low rates of interest. Then in 1953 the government took powers which allowed it to subsidize interest payments, above a minimum of 5 per cent, on loans made by the commercial banks to the shipbuilders. This government assistance kept the industry active throughout the early 1950s, even after the Korean boom was over, and a substantial export was maintained. At this time Japan's costs were high compared with those of Western countries, but her delivery dates were shorter than theirs and her builders were assisted in meeting foreign competition by the application of the 'link' system to this branch of the export trade.[7]

Meanwhile, the industry had invested heavily in new equipment and had greatly improved its constructional methods. Between 1950 and 1955 some 22,000 million yen were invested in new capacity.[8] The number of berths capable of constructing large ships was much increased, and the 'block' building system and modern welding technique, in substitution for riveting, were widely adopted.[9] Japan became as well, or even better, equipped than most European countries for building large tankers. At the same time technical improvements were effected by the industries that supplied materials to the shipyards. In the early post-war years steel consumption by Japanese shipbuilders per unit of tonnage had been 10 per cent higher than that of the British shipbuilders, because of the unreliability and lack of uniformity in the steel plates.[10] By the middle 1950s this disadvan-

---

[6] Yamamoto, pp. 91–94.

[7] Industr. Bank, *Survey Fin. & Ind.*, Mar.–Apr. 1955, pp. 9–15. For a description of the 'link' system, see p. 230 below.

[8] *Orient. Econ.*, Jan. 1957, p. 22.

[9] Yards capable of building ships over 20,000 gross tons increased from 14 in 1954 to 20 in 1956; among these 13 were capable of building ships of 30,000 tons and over compared with 6 in 1954 (ibid. Dec. 1956, p. 595).

[10] Soc. for Econ. Coop. in Asia, *The Major Industry and Its Technique in Japan* (1954), p. 26.

tage had been removed and the product had gained a reputation for excellence. There were advances too in marine engineering assisted by technical arrangements between large Japanese firms and foreign manufacturers of diesel engines and turbines. Japan was thus well placed to benefit from the rise in the world demand for ships that began in 1955 and her shipbuilding industry could view with complacency the abandonment of the 'link' system. Two years later her competitive position was considered so strong that the government was able to remove the subsidy which had been given for compensating builders for the high market interest rates on loans, while the Development Bank imposed more onerous terms. In 1956 Japan became the world's largest shipbuilder, a position that she has since maintained. Between that year and 1961 she contributed 23 per cent to the total mercantile tonnage launched. She became a pioneer in the building of large ore carriers and giant tankers (65,000 dead-weight tons or more), and in 1962 she launched the first super-tanker of 131,000 tons. Mass-production methods were successfully introduced for the manufacture of small and medium turbines.[11]

The high rate of construction enabled Japan to restore her mercantile marine to its pre-war size by 1959 and subsequently to enlarge it considerably. Many of the new ships, however, were sold to foreign owners. Indeed, between the end of the Second World War and 1962 rather more than half the tonnage was exported, and after 1956 foreign sales of ships made up over three-fifths of the tonnage launched and accounted for about one-tenth of the country's total exports. For nearly a decade Japan has been the world's chief exporter of ships and her superiority has progressively increased. Furthermore, her yards have built up a large business in the repair and remodelling of ships for foreign as well as domestic owners.

The success of Japan in this industry can be more readily understood if it is realized that from the beginning shipbuilding has occupied a key position in Japanese engineering. In the West the rise of the modern shipbuilding industry, which occurred at a time when many other branches of engineering were well established, was roughly coincident with the appearance of the new steel industry, and close financial links were forged between

[11] *Japan Trade Guide, 1963*, pp. 83–87.

steel firms and the shipbuilders. In Japan modern shipbuilding, fostered by government subsidies and protection, was among the earliest branches of engineering to attain importance, and its initial development preceded the establishment of a steel industry which for the greater part of its life was largely under government ownership and control. So although some shipyards were in the hands of the same groups that also owned the few private steel works, in the main the financial links between steel and shipbuilding were slender. On the other hand, the shipbuilders were pioneers in the application of modern engineering techniques to the wide range of products used in ships. This was because, at the beginning, there were few specialist firms capable of producing the components required. The shipbuilders were, therefore, obliged to concern themselves with the manufacture of the supplies they needed. As time went on they turned to the production of other goods that made similar demands on productive technique, and they became leaders in mechanical engineering and in the manufacture of heavy electrical equipment. The great electrical manufacturing firm, Shibaura (now the Tokyo-Shibaura Electrical Company), developed out of a leading shipbuilder, Ishikawajima, in the first decade of this century, and the Mitsubishi Electrical Manufacturing Company grew out of the Kobe Dockyard (a Mitsubishi enterprise). In recent times one of the chief motor-car manufacturers, Isuzu, was set up as a subsidiary of Ishikawajima.[12] This wide spread of interests is, of course, characteristic of most of the leading firms of Japan.

The pioneers have to a large extent retained their predominance in shipbuilding. A high proportion of the ships launched after the Second World War were produced by a few great concerns and their associated sub-contractors, notably the Mitsubishi Shipbuilding and Engineering Company and other successor firms of the old Mitsubishi, Hitachi, Kawasaki, and Ishikawajima. In fact, nine-tenths of the post-war tonnage, including all the large ships, was built in 24 yards owned by 19 companies with 2,800,000 out of the 3 million tons of capacity. In addition, there were in recent years 14 yards owned by 7 firms engaged in building vessels from 500 to 4,000 gross tons, and about 260 small yards which produced coastal fishing boats and other small craft.

[12] Industr. Bank, *Survey Fin. & Ind.*, Mar.–Apr. 1962, pp. 1–7.

Both the small yards and the sub-contractors shared in the benefits of the boom, especially as the 'block' system required that much work should be given out to specialists. The workers too enjoyed a more than average rise in wages. Their numbers, however, changed little between 1952 and 1962, except for a moderate increase in the 'temporary' employees. This stability, at a time of soaring output, was achieved by an improvement in the quality of labour (as a result of systematic training schemes), technical innovation, and the skilful planning of operations. Expert British visitors to the Japanese yards have marvelled not so much at the absence of demarcation troubles as at the ability of the management virtually to dispense with work-inspectors. Greater productivity meant that between October 1958 and July 1961 the labour cost in building a 47,000 ton tanker fell by 19 per cent and total cost by 16 per cent.[13]

Thus within a few years Japan's position as shipbuilder was completely transformed. In the early 1950s she was a high-cost producer and the activity of her industry depended on various types of subsidies and upon her possession of idle capacity at a time when the builders of other nations were full occupied. In those years it seemed reasonable to suppose that her prosperity as a shipbuilder could not outlast the boom, for the high cost and the inferior quality of her steel made her long-run competitive position unfavourable. Yet by heavy investment in new plant and by revolutionizing her organization and technique she attained by 1956 a level of technical efficiency that matched, and in some respects exceeded, that of her rivals abroad. Despite many natural disadvantages, she became the largest producer and exporter of ships. This pre-eminence has since been confirmed and will not easily be wrested from her. Yet, even though progress is likely to continue, it can hardly be expected that the very high rate of growth that was experienced during recent years can be long maintained. Since the ambitious Japanese entrepreneur is not content with less, in this industry he has characteristically sought to preserve the tempo of his advance by further diversification. Shipbuilders have turned increasingly towards the rapidly expanding trade in industrial machinery, and in the case of the eight largest firms, between 1956 and 1960

[13] Example based on information supplied by Mr S. Miyamoto.

the proportion of their output of industrial machinery to their total output (in value) rose from 32 per cent to 54 per cent.[14]

ELECTRICAL MACHINERY AND APPARATUS

The manufacture of electrical machinery and apparatus, which first became a considerable branch of industry in the years just before the First World War, grew rapidly in the next two decades. By the eve of the Second World War Japan was not only capable of supplying most of the products required for industrial and domestic use, but she also had a large export trade in a few types of apparatus, such as electric lamps. The growth of the industry and the extension in the range and quality of its goods were accompanied by a rise in the output of electric power to which it made an essential contribution.

Many of the chief firms were originally offshoots of *Zaibatsu*-owned undertakings in shipbuilding or mining.[15] At the outset these concerns were engaged mainly in turning out electrical goods for other constituents in the same *Zaibatsu*, but after a time they began to produce for the market. The members of the electrical industry from its first years established close relationships with foreign companies from which they obtained technical knowledge and sometimes capital. The Tokyo Electric Light Company, an affiliate of Mitsui, had close links before the First World War with the General Electric Company of the United States, and during the early 1920s several other leading companies entered into relations with foreign manufacturers, e.g. Mitsubishi with the Westinghouse Electric Company and Furukawa with Siemens-Schuckert. In the inter-war period a high proportion of the production of machinery and apparatus (about three-fifths of the total) was in the hands of six great concerns, most of which produced not merely a wide variety of equipment for power stations and factories but also light electrical apparatus.[16] Nevertheless, small and medium-sized firms found a place in the industry both as sub-contractors to the big firms and also as specialist manufacturers. For instance, at

[14] Industr. Bank, *Survey Fin. & Ind.*, Mar.–Apr. 1962, p. 5.

[15] Examples of the succession from shipbuilding were given in the previous section. An example of the succession from mining is the Hitachi Electrical Company which was originally formed to repair electrical machinery used by the Hitachi Mining Company.

[16] Industr. Bank, *Survey Fin. & Ind.*, July–Aug. 1954, p. 3.

that time, the electric-lamp industry comprised three types of producer: first, the Tokyo Electric Light Company which manufactured high-grade lamps, together with most of their components, in a few large and well-equipped factories; second, about a dozen medium-sized firms which produced standard types of lamps from parts and materials bought from specialist suppliers; and finally, numerous small factories and workshops engaged in making cheap lamps, miniature bulbs, and automobile bulbs. The output of the first two groups was sold mainly in the home market, but most of the output of the small producers was exported.[17]

During the early part of the war the capacity of the industry was much enlarged, and the 'Big Six' (reduced to five in 1939 by the amalgamation of the Tokyo Electric Light Company and the Shibaura Engineering Works) built several new factories and absorbed a number of small firms. In the later years of the war the capacity of most of these factories was concentrated on the production of munitions and the output of many types of electrical apparatus declined. In the period of economic chaos that followed the war the industry encountered serious difficulties. The dissolution of the *Zaibatsu* struck a particularly heavy blow at this industry which was so intimately bound up with their interests, and the shortage of investment funds meant that there was little demand for the kind of equipment required for the generation and transmission of power. A high proportion of the diminished output consisted of apparatus for domestic use and much of it was turned out by the small producers. Revival in the heavy branches did not begin until 1951 when it was at last possible to proceed with plans for developing the electricity-power supply. From then onwards recovery was rapid.[18]

By this time the industry had largely re-established the forms of organization and the system of inter-firm relationships which the war had destroyed. One of the obstacles to the recovery of the industry in the immediate post-war years was the backwardness of Japan's technique. She had depended upon foreign associates for access to new devices and discoveries, and when she was deprived of this assistance during the war her standards of technical proficiency were lowered. During the early and middle 1950s, however, the former links with foreign companies

[17] Schumpeter, pp. 544–8.
[18] Industr. Bank, *Survey Fin. & Ind.*, July–Aug. 1954, pp. 3–10.

were rejoined and new ones forged. The flow of technical information to Japan was thus resumed, under contracts with such firms as Escher Wyss, Westinghouse, International General Electric Company, Siemens-Schuckert, Brown Boveri, and Philips. At the same time the fabric of financial and commercial relationships that was so seriously damaged by the dissolution of the *Zaibatsu* was to a large extent repaired. By the middle 1950s Tokyo-Shibaura Electric had established close links with the Mitsui Bank, and Mitsubishi Electric with the Mitsubishi Bank. As a Japanese commentator has said of this industry, 'the pre-war relationships with the *Zaibatsu* have been continued under a changed form in the post-war period'.[19] Not all the business, however, went to the old firms. Several newcomers appeared as the industry struck out fresh branches, such as electronics and electrical components for motor-cars, and one of them, Matsushita, became by the end of the decade the largest manufacturer of light electrical apparatus. Even Matsushita was linked financially with the *Zaibatsu* and derived much of its financial support from the Sumitomo Bank.[20]

By the late 1950s and early 1960s the electrical apparatus industry, as in pre-war days, was dominated by a few great firms each with diverse interests, some of which extended far beyond the electrical industry. There was, of course, some difference of emphasis among the leaders. For example Hitachi, Tokyo-Shibaura, and Mitsubishi Electrical Manufacturing were dominant in heavy electrical machinery and together with three other firms they produced about three-fifths of the output of that type of product. Matsushita and Sanyo were leaders in the light electrical apparatus and electronics production. With the expansion of firms such as these the early post-war tendency towards an increase in the relative importance of the small and medium producers was reversed. Yet these still continued to enjoy a considerable share of the manufacture of light electrical apparatus, e.g. lamps, batteries, and small electrical machines. Their survival depended not only on their lower wage costs, an advantage that tended to disappear, but also on the economies they derived from specialization, economies which the large firms often sacrificed for diversification.

[19] Industr. Bank, *Survey Fin. & Ind.*, July–Aug. 1954, pp. 3–10.
[20] Personal inquiry. In 1962 Matsushita employed 35,000 persons in its 56 factories.

The electrical industry made an outstanding contribution to Japan's industrial growth after 1955. By then its reconstruction in respect of reorganization and technical competence had been completed, and it was fully prepared to respond to two powerful stimuli that were applied during the next few years. The first came from the country's heavy investment in industrial equipment and the second from the steep rise in the demand for household electrical apparatus. The result was not only a great increase in the quantity of output, but also an improvement in its quality and an immense extension of its range. A number of virtually new industries came into being, notably the various branches of electronics. During the early 1960s, when the steep growth in certain types of durable consumer goods showed signs of slowing down, new opportunities were found in the manufacture of computers and of apparatus for automation.

The statistical evidence of growth in this group is very impressive. In terms of value added, the output in 1962 was about nine times that of 1955. This rate of increase was nearly twice as fast as the growth in output of other industrial machinery and three times as fast as manufacturing output as a whole. For some products the increase was stupendous; for radio sets it was eight times, for television sets forty times, and for electrical refrigerators a hundred times. From a modest position in this group of products Japan had moved in the space of seven years into the company of the leading producers. Her importance may be illustrated by the fact that as a manufacturer of electric cables she is second only to the United States.

In the past the electrical-machinery industry, at any rate the branches concerned with generators, transformers, and motors, had always found its chief market at home, and up to the middle 1950s exports of lighter products, such as lamps, in which there were considerable foreign sales before the war, remained small. The expansion of the industry in subsequent years, however, was accompanied by a rapid growth of exports which in 1961–2 were seven times those of 1955 (in value) and comprised 10 per cent of the output. The electrical industry thus became an important contributor to Japan's export trade; its share of the total rose from only 2½ per cent in 1955 to 8 per cent in 1961, which was about the same as that of cotton fabrics. The trade included a substantial amount of heavy machinery and communications

equipment sent mainly to South East Asia, but by far the greater
part of it consisted of light electrical apparatus, lamps, trans-
istors, and various household appliances, which found markets
all over the world. By this time Japan had become renowned as a
cheap producer of light electrical goods of high quality. She had
reduced costs not merely by improvements in technique but also
by the extensive substitution of female for male labour. For heavy
equipment, however, especially that for thermal generation, her
competitive strength is more doubtful and is soon to be tested by
the exposure of her market to foreign imports.

MOTOR VEHICLES

Up to the middle 1930s the Japanese motor-car industry was
of small account and the country relied upon imports for most of
its needs. Even the small domestic production consisted mainly
of cars and lorries assembled from imported parts by local
branches of Ford and General Motors. Apart from these, Japan-
made cars were few in number (under 10,000 a year) and poor
in quality. In 1936 manufacturing equipment was bought from
the United States and American engineers were engaged by
Japanese firms to develop the industry. After the outbreak of the
Sino-Japanese War the government made determined efforts to
free Japan from dependence on imports, and both in Japan and
in Manchuria the leading *Shinko-Zaibatsu*, Aikawa of Nissan and
of the Manchurian Industrial Development Company, organized the expansion of the industry. By the time of the Pacific War
Japan had become almost self-sufficient in the supply of lorries,
although little progress had been made in the production of
passenger cars. In 1940 the output of cars and lorries together
reached about 50,000. After the war the industry had to be
created anew. There was an abundance of engineering capacity
that could be diverted to this manufacture, but Japan was deficient in up-to-date equipment and technical knowledge. As in
the electrical-engineering industry, remedies were sought in
technical-assistance contracts with foreign firms, such as Austin,
Hillman, Renault, and Willys Overland, and as a result foreign
makes of cars were produced under licence. In addition, several
firms began to turn out light cars, trucks, and passenger vehicles
of their own design.

The first considerable stimulus to the industry was provided by the Korean War when the United States Forces placed large orders for trucks, and for many years there was a substantial 'special procurement' demand. The recovery of the economy as a whole increased the requirement for trucks which, because of the import controls, had to be satisfied from home production. At this time Japanese manufacturers were still handicapped by the high cost and poor quality of certain types of steel as well as by the small scale of their operations. So their products compared unfavourably both in quality and price with those of Western firms. For example, in 1956 Japanese-made trucks were 30 per cent dearer than their foreign equivalent and for passenger cars the comparisons were even less favourable. But the industry, including the components manufacturers, was at that time being extensively re-equipped with up-to-date plant, and by the end of the decade it was ready to meet the rapid growth in demand both for private cars and commercial vehicles that then occurred. Output rose from 110,000 in 1956 to 263,000 in 1959 and 990,000 in 1962, besides 1,800,000 three-wheelers, motor cycles, and motor scooters. It is expected that output will continue to grow fast during the rest of the decade and will reach 1,855,000 four-wheeled motor vehicles by 1970.[21] The proportion of private cars in the total output, which was small during the middle 1950s, rose sharply after 1959, and this tendency is likely to be strengthened as personal incomes rise.

The export trade in automotive products, which still accounts for a comparatively small proportion of the output (in 1962 about 5 per cent of finished four-wheeled vehicles and 9 per cent of the output of motor cycles), is expected to become one of the leading items of the export list by the end of the decade. Before these results can be achieved, however, certain problems will have to be solved. The industry grew up under the shelter not only of a high tariff (40 per cent *ad valorem* on cars and 30 per cent on trucks), but also of import and exchange restrictions. Except in the case of three-wheelers and motor cycles, Japan's costs and prices are high by international standards, and the abolition of the import restrictions may expose the industry to dangerous competition. Further, the country's roads are still unsuited to the motor age, and these must be improved if the potential demand for cars is to be realized. The second problem

[21] Income Doubling Plan estimate. But in 1964 the output was already 1,700,000.

is now being vigorously tackled by the government, which is investing heavily both in urban road improvements and in the construction of trunk roads. A solution of the first problem must be found in the rationalization of the industry. Despite the recent advances in technique and organization, the scale of operations of the typical Japanese motor firm is still small by Western standards. The largest producers, Toyota and Nissan, manufacture several basic models in each class. This, however, is not the most serious obstacle to realizing the economies of scale. Like motor manufacturers in other countries, the Japanese firms rely on outside suppliers for most of the components they require. But whereas in Great Britain and the United States most of these components manufacturers are themselves operating on a very large scale, in Japan the motor firms follow the common practice in the engineering industry of drawing their supplies from numerous tied sub-contractors, many of whom are very small. The practice was rational enough in the days when the labour costs of small firms were low, but it has lost some of its former merits because of the recent rise in wages in that sector of the economy. Even where large components-manufacturing establishments have been built up, such as Denso which is controlled by Toyota, economies of scale are not fully realized because of the very wide range of components produced. Already, however, the pressure of competition is compelling more intensive specialization among the larger suppliers and is gradually modifying the sub-contracting system as hitherto practised. Until the reorganization is completed the liberalizing of trade may temporarily check the growth of some sections of the motor industry.

BICYCLES

During the 1930s Japan was the world's chief producer of bicycles. Half of her output was exported and, in the machinery and vehicle group, cycles were the most important item in the export list. The industry declined during the war, for the plants and the labour force were diverted to war production. After 1945 recovery was not long delayed, and by the early 1950s the pre-war output had been surpassed. The rapid recovery in production can be attributed in part to the fact that war factories, now without markets, had ample supplies of machine tools which either could be diverted to cycle production *in situ* or could be sold to former manufacturers of cycles or cycle components. The new equipment permitted the production of cycles of an average quality superior to those made before the war.[22] The industry shared in the rapid expansion in Japanese engineering that occurred after 1956, and in 1963 the output of complete cycles reached 3,160,000, more than three times the output of 1950.

During the 1930s the cycle industry was composed of a small number of substantial and medium-sized firms engaged in the manufacture either of the completed cycle or of parts, and also of numerous small specialist workplaces, each of which undertook the production of a component or the performance of a process of manufacture or assembly to the orders of wholesale merchants. The very cheap bicycles produced for export (mainly in the form of parts) came from these small producers. By the middle 1950s the organization had been considerably modified, though by no means transformed. The number of workplaces was fewer than before the war and the importance of the very small manufacturers had declined. This occurred partly because of the loss of foreign markets for very cheap bicycles and partly because of the competitive advantages enjoyed by the larger factories equipped with efficient machine tools. Nevertheless, although factories with 100 workers and over employed about half the total labour force engaged in workplaces with 10 or more employees, a large section of the trade remained in the hands of specialist manufacturers of parts or assemblers, some of whom operated on a very small scale.[23] It is estimated that in 1954 there were 400 factories with 10 or more workers, besides probably 1,000 domestic workshops. The town of Sakai, near Osaka, was dotted with cycle workshops and small factories. The low administrative expenses and cheap labour recruited by these producers compensated in some measure for their inferiority to the large factories in equipment and technique. More recently, however, they have come under pressure because of the rise in their wage costs and of the change in the nature of the demand. Up to the middle 1950s the Japanese bicycle was a heavily built machine, used for transporting goods as well as persons. The former function has now been assumed by motor vehicles, and it has been

---

[22] Soc. for Econ. Coop. in Asia, *Smaller Industry in Japan*, pp. 39–40.
[23] Ibid. pp. 40–41.

necessary for the industry to turn to the manufacture of lightly built machines. The change has compelled the manufacturers to adopt innovations in design, materials, and manufacturing technique, and the organization of the industry has been modified in order that the benefit of these new methods can be secured. Nevertheless, the specialist sub-contractor still retains much of his importance.

The recovery in foreign trade failed to keep pace with the rise in output. During the early 1950s exports were less than one-third of the pre-war quantity and in 1953 they accounted for only one-tenth of the total production. After that year there was some improvement, punctuated by violent short-term fluctuations. The greater part of the exports in recent years has consisted of parts rather than completed bicycles. Yet even if these exports are included, it is evident that the cycle industry has lost much of its former importance as an exporter. Before the war Japan's competitive strength in this trade was displayed chiefly in the manufacture and sale of the cheap, low-grade bicycle to West Africa and other countries where incomes were very small. The demand for that type of product has fallen away since the war, and in the market for higher-grade bicycles her relative advantages are less conspicuous.

SEWING MACHINES

While the cycle industry is an old-established industry that has successfully adapted itself to post-war market conditions, the manufacture of sewing machines is new. Before 1935 output had been insignificant, and the home market both for industrial and for household sewing machines was supplied by imports from the United States. In the years just before the war Japan's production began to expand. It reached a peak in 1940 when 150,000 machines were produced. Like other industries that served a civilian market, sewing-machine manufacture declined precipitately during the war and only machines for industrial use continued to be made. Immediately after the war, however, a remarkable expansion began. By 1947 production was already near to the pre-war peak and in 1951 over a million machines were produced.[24] In 1956 output reached 1,720,000 units, as well as a small production of machines for industrial use. From

[24] Industr. Bank, *Survey Fin. & Ind.*, Sept.–Oct. 1955, pp. 1–2.

then on there was a steady and continuous advance and in 1963 the output was over three and a half million, excluding industrial machines. At first most of the output went to the home market, but after 1948 a substantial export trade began. It reached 840,000 units in 1951 and 1,180,000 in 1954, or 86 per cent of the total output. The value of this trade was then exceeded, in the machinery group, only by that of ship exports. Thus the new industry depended predominantly upon demand from abroad. At a time when Japan's export trade as a whole was stagnating, foreign sales of these goods increased from year to year. A high proportion of the exports was sent to the United States. Subsequently exports rose more slowly than production, but in 1962–3 they still represented well over half the output and they contributed nearly as much to the total export trade as pottery or rayon fabrics.

This remarkable development must be explained. It can be well understood that the home demand for sewing machines should have been very high for some years after the war, for the Japanese had to replenish their stocks of clothing and the increasing use of Western-style dress called for a large supply of sewing machines. This, however, does not account for the growth of exports. At the end of the war, as we have already seen, Japan had a surplus of engineering capacity. For many years none of this could be used for munitions and restrictions had been imposed on various other types of production. Japan therefore had ample capacity and skilled labour to devote to the manufacture of products of this kind. In the chief manufacturing countries of the West, on the other hand, engineering capacity was fully stretched and the post-war demand for durable consumer goods such as sewing machines could not be satisfied. A ten-months' strike at the American plants of the Singer Sewing Machine Company in 1949 gave Japan her opportunity to enter that market.[25]

In the conversion of her productive capacity to new uses after the war, Japan showed a characteristic adaptability, and sewing-machine manufacture fully demonstrated this quality. It was not merely the pre-war sewing-machine makers who reconverted their factories to this production. The industry enlisted many new recruits. Some of them consisted of large firms engaged in various

[25] Ibid. pp. 2–3.

branches of engineering (e.g. the Mitsubishi Electrical Company). Some were firms hitherto engaged on quite different types of production, such as the Fukusuke Tabi Company.[26] Others were small firms of engineering sub-contractors who turned to the production of parts for sewing machines. These small firms were very numerous just after the war, and although there was a reduction in their number in later years, even in the early 1960s there were some 300 specialist makers of parts. This organization had been fostered by the government, which instituted standards for sewing-machine parts and introduced a system of inspection which saw that they were maintained.[27] At the same time certain firms became the focus of a co-operative system of production in which numerous producers participated.

As in other branches of the Japanese economy, this combination of large-scale organization at the centre with a wide diffusion of the actual processes of production led to the emergence of a highly efficient industry. The several types of producers of which it is now composed may be classified as follows: first, a few large integrated concerns which produce a high proportion of the parts they require; secondly, medium-sized firms which process the arm-beds and assemble the products; and thirdly, the assembly firms which buy parts from small specialists. With one exception, these assemblers also are very small firms. From the early 1950s the medium and small firms were responsible for most of the output of household machines, while the large firms tended to concentrate on industrial machines.[28] Co-operative organization played its part in the conduct of the export trade as well as in the organization of production. When low-priced Japanese exports gave rise to a threat that anti-dumping duties would be imposed in the United States, the industry formed an association for handling exports jointly so as to prevent offers of goods at exceptionally low prices.

This organization was consistent with considerable innovating activity as well as with the large-scale production of standardized machines. After 1956 most of the increase in production occurred in the improved 'zigzag' machine class, and iron castings gave place to parts fabricated from light alloys.[29] The pre-

---

[26] *Tabi* are Japanese-style socks.   [27] EPA, *Econ. Survey, 1954–5*, p. 70.
[28] Industr. Bank, *Survey Fin. & Ind.*, Sept.–Oct. 1955, pp. 3 ff.
[29] *Orient. Econ.*, Feb. 1963, pp. 106–13.

sent structure of the industry, however, may prove vulnerable to the changes in the wage structure. Small firms have flourished hitherto because they were able to recruit workers at relatively low wages. This advantage they have to a large extent lost, and the recession of 1961, when many of the small firms went out of business, may come to be regarded as a turning-point in the trade's history. As in other industries, adverse conditions have forced the smaller firms into a position of extreme dependence on the large manufacturers whom they supply. It seems, moreover, as if commercial trends are also becoming less favourable for them, for overseas orders are being placed to an increasing extent with large makers by the American distributive concerns with which these are closely linked.

CAMERAS

Japan's relative advantages in international trade were found for many decades chiefly in goods the efficient manufacture of which depended on manual skill and competent organization. Among the older industries, those engaged in producing bicycles, toys, fancy goods, pottery as well as textiles, satisfied these criteria. Since the war she has added a group of trades which not only make demands on her traditional qualities but also call for scientific and technical knowledge and an ability to work to fine limits. These trades include the manufacture of cameras, binoculars, and other optical goods, watches, clocks, and scientific instruments. All these have become prominent in the export trade during the last decade. The manufacture of cameras will be taken as an example.

Before the war, in spite of the propensity of the Japanese to take photographs, the camera industry was small and its products of indifferent quality. During the war technique improved under the influence of the military demand. In particular, there was a marked advance in the quality of lenses. After the war the skilled labour and technical resources were quickly adapted to the creation of what was in fact a new industry. At first the inducement towards this production came from the demands of the Allied Occupation troops, but soon a substantial export trade to the United States was created.[30] Output (in units) rose from about 50,000 in 1947 to well over 1 million in 1955 and to

[30] *Sumitomo Bank R.*, Jan. 1956, pp. 20–21.

3,120,000 in 1962. In recent years nearly half the output has been exported. In addition to the manufacture of ordinary cameras, Japan has also built up since the middle 1950s a large production and export of motion-picture cameras and projectors. Between 1955 and 1963 the value of exports of optical goods as a whole increased six times and in the latter year came to 46,000 million yen, about the same as motor vehicle exports and nearly half the value of the exports of ships. A high proportion of these goods was sent to North America.

The structure of the industry changed considerably during the period of its expansion. All the leading producers had pre-war connexions with the optical, camera, or photographic industries, but they were small until the war brought about an enormous increase in the demand for optical equipment for military purposes. After 1945 they diverted their capacity to production for the civilian market.[31] In the early 1950s about 90 concerns were producing cameras. By the end of the decade the number had fallen to under 50, and four-fifths of the production was concentrated in 9 large concerns. Methods of production were diverse. There were 5 firms which undertook the whole process, although even these relied to some extent on sub-contractors for part of their components supply. The remaining firms confined their activities either to manufacturing parts or to assembly.

The reasons for Japan's success in this industry are of interest because of the light they throw on her industrial potential as a whole. For very cheap cameras, as for other goods which depend on mass-production techniques, Japan cannot match the United States. But the manufacture of the high-grade camera, while it requires a degree of standardization and the use of precision machinery, also calls for much patient labour for testing and inspection. This is not yet an industry to which automation can easily be applied. Japan is endowed with precisely the kind of resources that fit her for this production, especially the production of lenses, and, as in other trades in the same category, she has pressed home her advantages.

[31] *Orient. Econ.*, Mar. 1957, pp. 135–42.

IX

Steel, Chemicals, Fuel and Power

IRON AND STEEL

THE modern Japanese iron and steel industry, in its origins and development, was a product of State initiative. The first iron and steel works of a Western type, the Yawata Works, was founded by the government in the early years of the present century and was operated as an official undertaking. Most of the other firms that entered the industry later on also depended in varying degrees upon government financial assistance or protection. When Japan launched her rearmament programme during the 1930s it was considered desirable to extend government control over industries of strategic importance, and the iron and steel industry was an obvious subject for the application of this policy. Accordingly, in 1934 the Nippon Seitetsu[1] was formed to take over and operate the Yawata concern along with six other important enterprises. The State held most of the capital in this new company and the various *Zaibatsu* the rest. At the time of its formation the Nippon Seitetsu was responsible for nearly all the country's output of pig-iron, more than half the ingot-steel output, and over two-fifths of the finished-steel output of Japan and Korea. After the outbreak of the Sino-Japanese War in 1937 a great expansion of capacity was undertaken both by the official concerns and by outside companies. Nor was growth limited to Japan Proper. In Manchuria also there was a steep increase in capacity, especially pig-iron capacity, under the leadership of another government concern, the Showa Steel Company. The aim of the policy was not merely the expansion of output, but also the creation of a well-articulated industry in which the producers in Japan Proper were supplied with pig-iron and ore from Manchuria (together with some ore from Karafuto) and coking coal from North China, while firms in Japan Proper produced the finished steel required for Manchurian as well as for domestic development. At this time Japan

---

[1] Japan Iron and Steel (Co.).

was also obtaining ore from Japanese-owned mines in Malaya, scrap from the United States, and pig-iron from India.

The policy of expansion and integration was pressed much further after the outbreak of the Pacific War. The result was the creation of a great industry, by far the largest iron and steel industry outside Europe, the United States, and Russia. In the early 1930s Japan's output had been quite small; in 1932 it was about 1 million tons of pig-iron and under $2\frac{1}{2}$ million tons of ingot and cast steel, while the Manchurian and Korean output did not exceed half a million tons of pig-iron a year. By 1943 Japan's output of pig-iron amounted to nearly $4\frac{1}{2}$ million tons and her output of ingot steel to over $7\frac{1}{2}$ million tons.[2] The Korean and Manchurian output by then had risen to about $1\frac{1}{2}$ million tons of pig-iron and half a million tons of steel.[3] The successful execution of this expansionist programme depended upon the maintenance of the lines of communication between Japan on the one hand and North and South East Asia on the other. When towards the end of the war these lines were cut by the Allies, the Japanese industry was deprived of much of its raw materials and semi-products. By the end of the war most of the plants in the industry were still intact, but production had fallen very low through a shortage of material supplies.

For several years after the war recovery was slow. Imports of raw materials were narrowly limited by the shortage of foreign exchange and by the policy of the Occupation authorities, who contemplated permanent restrictions over the future size of this as of other strategic industries. At the same time domestic supplies of fuel were small because of the deterioration of mining equipment and the dispersal of coal-miners. In 1946 the output of pig-iron amounted to only about 200,000 tons and of steel to 560,000 tons. During the next year the Occupation authorities allowed coking coal and ore to be imported from the United States and elsewhere, and the government provided subsidies from the Reconstruction Finance Bank. These measures made a revival possible. By 1949 output had risen to $1\frac{1}{2}$ million tons of pig-iron and over 3 million tons of steel, broadly equivalent to

---

[2] EPA, *Japan. Econ. Statist.: Industrial Production* (various years); and Japan Iron & Steel Fed., *Statist. of Iron and Steel Ind.* (various years) for statistical data in this section.

[3] Jones, *Manchuria*, p. 153.

the output of 1933 and 1934. The institution of the Dodge Deflation Plan threatened to check the recovery, but after the outbreak of the Korean War in June 1950 the advance was resumed
at a much increased rate. Japan's iron and steel industry, along
with her other heavy industries, was among the chief beneficiaries of the boom that the war engendered, and large orders
were placed by the Allied governments as well as by private
customers. Even when the general boom collapsed, the home
demand for iron and steel persisted and output continued to rise.
By 1953 it was higher than the wartime peak and after a slight
fall in 1954 it rose again. In 1956 pig-iron output reached 6·3
million tons and ingot and cast-steel output 11·1 million tons.
This represented an increase over 1937 of 90 per cent in the case
of steel and 160 per cent in the case of pig-iron. Among the
finished-steel products, the advance was especially great in
sheets, plates, and tubes. At the same time the quality was improved and the range of products extended to take in special
steels and highly fabricated goods.

During the next two years growth was checked by the recession of 1957–8, but then there followed one of the most remarkable periods of development ever experienced by an iron and
steel industry in any country. Between 1958 and 1963 the output
of pig-iron increased by 170 per cent and that of steel almost as
much. In 1964, when her steel output rose to nearly 40 million
tons (26 per cent more than in 1963), Japan became the world's
third largest producer. She was surpassed only by the United
States and Russia. This extraordinary growth was associated
with the exceptionally heavy industrial investment of the period
and especially with the expansion of engineering. Yet Japan's
ambitions as an iron and steel producer are by no means
satisfied, for according to the plan for Doubling the National
Income it is expected that by 1970 the industry will turn out
48 million tons of steel, 45 millions for the home market and
3 millions for export. When this result is achieved, Japan's steel
consumption a head will be equivalent to that of the United
States in 1958.

Japan's rise to a position as a major steel producer is perhaps
the most surprising development in her economy during the last
decade, for not long ago it was a commonplace to assert that her
lack of the essential raw materials and the high cost of fuel would

inevitably put narrow limits on her accomplishments in this industry. How her success has been achieved, therefore, deserves close attention, and we must examine the post-war changes in technique and organization that have enabled her to surmount her natural disadvantages. These changes have indeed been profound. As we have seen, before and during the war output in Japan Proper was very highly concentrated in the government-owned Nippon Seitetsu and in a small number of other concerns owned for the most part by the *Zaibatsu*. The Occupation policy of destroying concentrations of economic power led to the break-up of the former and to the destruction of the economic empires of which the outside iron and steel companies were members. The properties of the Nippon Seitetsu were distributed between the Yawata Company, which had been the nucleus of the combine, and a new concern called the Fuji Iron and Steel Company. The shares owned by the government were sold on the market, and many of them passed into the hands of banks and financial institutions formerly part of the *Zaibatsu*. As a result of this and of other measures of reorganization, there emerged in the post-war world three major integrated producers, Yawata, Fuji, and the Nippon Kokan Company, a concern which before the war had specialized in tube production. In 1953 these three concerns between them produced over four-fifths of the country's pig-iron, 55 per cent of the ingot steel, and about the same proportion of the finished steel.[4] The remaining output of pig-iron and steel was then in the hands of ten large concerns (of which the Kawasaki Steel Corporation, Sumitomo Metal Industries, and the Kobe Steel Works were the chief) and of a considerable number of smaller producers operating open-hearth furnaces and rolling mills. There were also many small re-rollers. The number of producers in the last two categories increased substantially during the early post-war years when capital for modernization was not yet available in adequate amounts.

The second group of steel firms included some long-established

---

[4] Yawata was the largest producer with $1 \cdot 4$ m. tons of pig-iron, $1 \cdot 9$ m. tons of ingot steel, and $1 \cdot 6$ m. tons of finished steel. Fuji, which had a high proportion of newly-built equipment, produced $1 \cdot 65$ m. tons of pig-iron, $1 \cdot 45$ m. tons of ingot steel, and $1 \cdot 2$ m. tons of finished steel. Nippon Kokan's output was $0 \cdot 8$ m. tons of pig-iron, $0 \cdot 9$ m. tons of ingot steel, and $0 \cdot 6$ m. tons of finished steel. These figures are for 1953 (S. Kawata, *Japan's Iron and Steel Industry* (1954), *passim*).

steel producers, but their position had been shaken by wartime changes. Most of them had formerly obtained their pig-iron from abroad, especially from Manchuria, and the collapse of the Japanese empire and the shortage of foreign exchange meant that after the war they had to look for supplies within Japan herself, either among the integrated concerns or the smaller pig-iron producers. Their difficulties were increased because foreign scrap, used extensively in their furnaces before the war, could not easily be obtained. Further, many of their finishing plants had been located for the convenient handling of Manchurian semi-products and for this reason also the change in Japan's economic position left them seriously handicapped. The responsibilities of the war and of the Peace Settlement for the weakness of this section of the industry must not, however, be exaggerated. Technical advances which had increased the advantages of vertically integrated plants would anyhow have rendered obsolete the former relationships between the Manchurian and Japanese branches of the industry. Yet this fact merely emphasized the inadequacies of the specialist steel producers in the post-war world.

At this time there were other difficulties common to the industry as a whole. All the producers were faced by serious obstacles in acquiring raw materials. Before the war, Japan had depended upon imports for 87 per cent of her ore and for a high proportion of her coking coal. At that time nearly 40 per cent of her ore came from China, Manchuria, and Korea; Malaya supplied most of the remainder. For imports of coking coal Japan depended wholly upon China and Saghalien. After 1945 these sources of supply were denied to her. Although she succeeded in increasing her domestic production of ore, she still found herself in extreme dependence on distant foreign countries both for ore and fuel. With the rapid increase in her output of steel towards the end of the decade the proportion of imported ore to total requirements rose to nearly three-quarters and in the case of coking coal to about half.[5] The coal imports were drawn chiefly from North America and in recent years from Australia, and the ore mainly from Malaya, the Philippines, and India. Japan was also obliged to import about half of her scrap requirements, mainly from North America. Compared with its position before the war,

[5] *Fuji Bank B.*, Mar. 1961, p. 19. In 1961–4 the proportions were much higher.

therefore, the iron and steel industry had to meet the costs of a longer haul for its materials and it had become far more vulnerable to fluctuations in freight rates. Further, the rise in mining costs at home added to the steel makers' problems.

In the early 1950s the cost of coking coal per ton of pig-iron in Japan was double that in England or West Germany.[6] Indeed international comparisons of steel costs in general were then very unfavourable to Japan. It was estimated that in 1951–2 she needed twice as many man-hours as Great Britain and seven times as many as the United States to produce a ton of pig-iron; for steel the factors were 2 and 5 respectively. The effect of these disparities on costs was not balanced by her lower wages. Labour costs per ton of pig-iron were 20 per cent higher in Japan than in Great Britain and the United States; for steel produced from molten pig-iron the disparity between British and Japanese costs was about the same, although it was less for steel made from cold pig-iron.[7] In quality some of her products (e.g. steel sheets) were less reliable than those of Western manufacturers.

The Japanese industry responded to the challenge by a thorough reorganization. In 1951 an ambitious modernization plan was introduced by the government.[8] This plan provided for the creation of new sintering plants (for the treatment of low-grade Japanese ore), the renovation and extension of blast-furnace capacity, the construction of new integrated plants, including a very large works of the Kawasaki Steel Corporation at Shiba, and, in particular, the installation of new equipment for rolled products, including continuous strip mills and plate-rolling mills. Efforts were also made to reduce dependence on ore imports by using increased quantities of iron sand, which is abundant in Japan. Until recently this material was smelted only in electric furnaces, but methods were worked out for using it in blast-furnaces and in recent years about $1\frac{3}{4}$ million tons were consumed annually.

The first modernization plan was followed by a second and far more ambitious plan which was carried out between 1956 and 1960. This was aimed primarily at the construction of several additional vertically integrated plants located and equipped so

---

[6] Kawata, *Japan's Iron and Steel Industry*, p. 89.
[7] EPA, *Econ. Survey, 1953–4*, p. 61.   [8] Kawata, pp. 62–83.

as to handle imported materials with the utmost economy.[9] By the end of the period Japan had assimilated the most advanced techniques of iron and steel production. She had built large fleets of ore and coal carriers which greatly reduced the cost of transport from overseas, and she had equipped herself with very efficient means for discharging the cargoes at the sites of the iron and steel plants.

In consequence, Japan's competitive position in this industry was transformed. Technical advance had led not merely to an improvement in the quality of the products but also to a reduction in processing costs. At the same time the re-siting of the industry and the improved arrangements for handling imports lowered the cost of the materials required for pig-iron production to about the same level as that in Europe. Fuel costs fell steadily and steeply throughout the decade.[10] In an industry regarded as progressive in all countries, Japan's advance in technical efficiency was exceptionally great, and the former wide disparities in labour productivity between herself and the West were narrowed. It could no longer be said that her advantages in lower wages were more than offset by low productivity. On the contrary, by the end of the decade Japan by international standards had become a cheap producer of steel.[11] This applied particularly to the ordinary grades, but she had also advanced as a producer of special steel. About one-fifth of her output was electrically smelted.

The reorganization that accompanied the technical progress of the industry left the three leaders of the early post-war period still in the van. In the course of the next decade, however, they were joined by six other vertically integrated firms. The whole group was responsible in 1961 for 95 per cent of the pig-iron output, 74 per cent of the crude steel, and 75 per cent of the hot rolled steel; most of the firms were also engaged in the manufacture not only of a wide range of fabricated steel products but also of chemicals and cement.[12] The latest recruits to the original small band of vertically integrated concerns had diverse origins. Some had formerly operated blast-furnaces and steel furnaces

[9] Industr. Bank, *Survey Fin. & Ind.*, Mar.–Apr. 1960, pp. 3–5; *Sumitomo Bank R.*, Mar. 1963, p. 10; and J. Bienfait, *La Sidérurgie japonaise* (1965), pp. 35–52.
[10] Between 1955 and 1961 the consumption of coking coal per ton of pig-iron fell by 17 per cent (Jiji Press, *Japan Trade Guide, 1963*, p. 66).
[11] *Fuji Bank B.*, Mar. 1961, p. 19.   [12] Ibid. pp. 20–29.

and now acquired rolling mills, while other old-established producers of finished steel and engineering products went into the primary sections of the industry either by the creation of new capacity or by absorbing existing firms. The rationalizations did not end there. Most of the open-hearth steel producers and rollers who remained outside these groups were brought into association with them by financial or personal links, and their activities became integrated with those of the great concerns which in effect controlled them. For example, most of the independent rollers were left with cold rolling, being supplied with hot rolled coils by the great strip mills. This reorganization was, of course, a condition for the efficient operation of the newly established plants.[13]

It might have been expected that the concentration of production in a few groups would have led to the same rigidity in prices and costs that has long characterized the British steel industry. Yet here, as in other branches of her economy, Japan succeeded in preserving flexibility depite the growth in the scale of operations. This was demonstrated during the recession of 1962. Japan's industry then found itself with serious over-capacity, for home demand declined just when the very heavy investment of the second steel plan and some of the investment scheduled in a third plan had come to fruition. In some countries the practice in such circumstances is to strengthen cartel arrangements with the object of holding prices. The Japanese producers certainly set up what is called a 'recession cartel' for rolled products, but competitive forces in their economy are still too strong for them to be able to maintain prices in such conditions, and there were steep price reductions in all classes of steel.[14] These reductions encouraged the revival of the consuming industries and by the spring of 1963 production was again rising fast. Nor did the Japanese steel makers during the recession lament that the rise in unit costs precluded them from selling abroad profitably. On the contrary they cut prices on their foreign sales as well as on their domestic sales, with the result that their exports rose in quantity by 70 per cent over those of 1961.[15] Japan can still call on quali-

[13] Inaba, pp. 51–57.
[14] Medium shapes (6×65 mm.) fell from 61,000 yen a ton at the peak to 27,500 yen in September 1962 and heavy plates from 54,000 yen to 31,250 yen. Steel bars fell 40 per cent in price between the peak of 1961 and June 1962 (*Fuji Bank B.*, July 1963, p. 18).   [15] Ibid. pp. 17–22.

ties of enterprise and audacity to meet the challenge of recession as she did in confronting economic disaster after the war. If ever she spurns the challenge and runs for shelter, her age of economic grace will come to an end.

The creation of the modern iron and steel industry has required a large investment, the equivalent of about £130 million for the first plan, £600 million for the second, and £240 million for the third, now in process of completion.[16] Most of these funds have been found outside the industry and a large proportion of them have come from government agencies, especially the Japan Development Bank which has furnished loans at relatively low rates of interest. Between 1955 and 1960 the World Bank lent £55 million for the construction of steel plants. It may be 'said that although the post-war iron and steel industry falls formally within the private sector, its development has been guided by the government with the help of financial arguments which in a time of capital scarcity have been very persuasive.

The world shortage of steel up to the middle 1950s enabled Japan to build up an export trade far greater than in pre-war days. At that time the exports, which amounted to about 400,000 tons of finished steel, went mainly to Manchuria, China Proper, and Kwantung. They represented about 10 per cent of the finished steel output. During the early 1950s the exports were much in excess of this figure. They rose sharply after 1950 and in 1952 they reached 1,650,000 tons. After a decline in 1953 they again increased and in 1955 amounted to about 2 million tons, well over one-fifth of the total output. These goods found markets all over the world, especially in India, South East Asia, the United States, and even the United Kingdom. The boom of the late 1950s diverted the attention of the steel makers from foreign markets, and exports tended to decline until 1960 and 1961 when they rose well above 2 million tons, about one-tenth of the output. After that their growth was remarkable and in 1963–4 they averaged 6 million tons a year. A high proportion of the sales (a third in 1963 and two-fifths in 1964) went to the United States. Most of the exports consisted of finished steel and secondary products, in contrast to the imports which were mainly of pig-iron.

The changes in Japan's position in the steel trade during the post-war period can scarcely be understood without reference to

[16] *Sumitomo Bank R.*, Mar. 1963, pp. 10 ff.

the changes in world market conditions. Her foreign sales were heavy during the early and middle 1950s, not because she was a cheap producer but because she could deliver steel at a time of great scarcity and because her exports were in effect dumped.[17] In recent years Japan's costs have fallen to levels that make her fully competitive with the steel of any other country. Although it is probable that her chief relative advantages will continue to lie in exporting highly finished manufactured products rather than crude steel, this is not inconsistent with the expectation that by 1968–70 steel exports will rise to some 10 million tons a year.

CHEMICALS

The chemical industry was one of the most rapidly growing branches of manufacture both in size and range during the 1930s. Whereas at the beginning of that decade Japan depended upon imports for a substantial proportion of her chemical fertilizers and of the chemicals needed by her textile industries, on the eve of the Second World War she had become almost self-sufficient. For many years the government had interested itself in the development of the industry, largely for strategic reasons, and some branches owed their initial growth to official assistance or protection. Nevertheless, by 1937 Japan had become competitive with foreign countries in many classes of chemicals, and she had worked up a fair-sized export trade in a few of them, e.g. the sale of dyestuffs to China. At that time the chief products of the industry consisted of nitrogenous fertilizers (especially ammonium sulphate), which were essential to the maintenance of the agricultural output, sulphuric acid used in the manufacture of various chemicals and for processes in the textile and metal industries, caustic soda and soda ash for the rayon, glass, and soap trades, dyestuffs, and pharmaceuticals.

By the end of the Second World War the output of these goods had been much reduced because of bomb damage, the shortage of power and raw materials, and the conversion of many plants to the manufacture of explosives. The recovery of the industry

---

[17] The Japanese steel makers were expected by their government to earn foreign currency to pay for their imports of raw materials, and at times they sold their steel abroad at much lower prices than those charged at home. For instance, in 1956 the f.o.b. export price of heavy plates was £60–£70 a ton compared with a home price of £90–£100 a ton; for angles the respective prices were £50 and £90.

was very uneven. The restoration of plants in the ammonium-sulphate and other chemical-fertilizer trades was given priority by the Occupation authorities in the interests of food production, and funds were provided for this purpose by the government's financial agencies. So this section of the industry was one of the earliest to recover, and by 1949 the pre-war output had been surpassed. Expansion continued for several years, and in 1955 the output of ammonium sulphate was more than twice the annual average output of 1936–7. The upward trend continued until 1959 when 2·6 million tons were produced. Since then there has been a slight fall attributable chiefly to the expansion in the output of other nitrogenous fertilizers, particularly urea, which in the early 1960s provided more than a quarter of the country's nitrogen production. The development of urea manu-facture, in which Japan leads the world, gave her the third place as a producer of nitrogenous fertilizers.

During the early 1950s by international standards she was by no means a cheap producer of these goods, but she raised her efficiency by innovations in processes, and although it is extreme-ly difficult to make international cost comparisons in this indus-try, the probability is that her costs are now in line with those of Western countries. She has certainly been very successful in foreign trade and in recent years she has exported about a third of her output of ammonium sulphate and nearly two-fifths of her output of urea. It is true that the producers of these goods follow a discriminatory pricing policy. This practice, however, is not confined to Japanese manufacturers, and since the government fixes the domestic price of fertilizers in the interests of the farmers, the discrepancy has been less than that shown in the fertilizer prices of some other countries.[18] Most of the sales have been made to neighbouring areas, especially Korea, Formosa, and the Philippines, a trade in which Japan enjoys freight advantages in competition with Western producers. Of late years she has sold fertilizers to more distant countries, for example, South East Asia, Australia, and South America. A rise in the use of chemical fertilizers by farmers in the underdeveloped regions of Asia, Africa, and South America, would certainly open the way to much larger sales in the future.

The branches of the chemical industry that provide products

[18] *Orient. Econ.*, May 1963, p. 268.

M

required for textile manufacture, such as caustic soda and dye-stuffs, were also seriously damaged by the war and found their recovery for a time handicapped by changes in the sources of supply of raw materials or in markets. The branches that depend on salt suffered from the cutting off of cheap supplies from China, and the loss of the China market for dyestuffs also had a damaging influence. Many of these difficulties, however, were overcome by the middle 1950s; and in subsequent years the rapid growth of a wide range of manufacturing industries that use chemicals for various processes brought expansion to all the older branches of the industry, including pharmaceuticals. But these developments were modest compared with the massive growth, especially after 1958, of new organic chemicals, particularly synthetic resins and polymers, which provided materials for the rapidly expanding plastics and synthetic textile industries. The growth of this new branch of chemicals coincided with the introduction of a great oil-refining industry from which the organic chemical plants now derive the bulk of their raw materials. In recent years the close association between these two branches has altered the character and organization of the chemical industry as a whole. By 1961 organic chemicals, a minor branch of production up to 1955, accounted for over half the total value of chemical production in Japan.

Until the introduction of the organic chemical branch, the Japanese industry, unlike the chemical industries of Western countries, was in the hands of numerous producers and the scale of operations was far lower than that found abroad. When Japan took up the manufacture of synthetic resins and polymers (in which the economies of scale are very considerable) a consolidation of interests and the establishment of close financial and technical links with the oil refineries became expedient. So there came into being during the late 1950s several *Kombinats*, as they were called, each composed of several large firms in different branches of the chemical and oil industries.[19] The chief *Kombinats* were centred on the old *Zaibatsu*. For example, Mitsui had long operated a chemical industry based on coal from the Miike mine in Kyushu. In 1955 it became linked with an oil-refining firm at Iwakumi (in the far west of Honshu) and created a *Kombinat* called the Mitsui Petro-Chemical Company. In 1956 six Mitsu-

[19] *Fuji Bank B.*, Sept. 1962, pp. 26–32; Inaba, pp. 57–60.

bishi concerns joined with Shell in founding the Mitsubishi Petro-Chemical Company, the operations of which were centred on a refinery at Yokkaichi. Sumitomo and Furukawa established similar *Kombinats*, and two steel producers, Yawata and Fuji, set up organic chemical plants which used the by-products of their furnaces.

All these concerns entered into very close relations with foreign chemical and oil companies which made available to them up-to-date technical knowledge and in some cases capital. The import of new technology by means of such arrangements played an essential part in overcoming the technical inferiority which was one of the most damaging legacies of the war and in promoting the subsequent expansion. Thus by the early 1960s the Japanese chemical industry, which ten years earlier had been mainly concerned with the production of fertilizers, had become highly diversified and its output in terms of value added was greater than that of textiles.

FUEL AND POWER

The post-war experience of Japan's fuel and power industries was similar in many respects to that of the corresponding industries in other industrial countries. Like the rest of the world, Japan was affected by sweeping changes in the primary sources of power and these gave rise to serious social and economic problems. The troubles of the coal industry were especially perplexing; they recall to the British observer the difficulties of his own coal-mining industry in the inter-war years.

It has never been possible to regard Japan's coal resources as one of her major assets, for the seams are thin and the quality of the product generally poor. Nevertheless, during the 1930s, under the influence of an expanding industrial demand, the output grew steadily and in 1937 it reached 45 million metric tons. A little was exported, but on balance Japan was an importer of coal, chiefly from China. Although these imports represented under a tenth of the home supply, they were qualitatively important, for they consisted mainly of coking coal for the blast-furnaces, a variety in which Japan was deficient. During the early years of the war the expansion of the output continued, but this was at the expense of the future. It was achieved by the neglect of development work and the concentration of mining operations on the most easily won coal. When the war came to an end, the industry passed through a period of chaos. Much of the mining labour was dispersed, and for a time little could be done to repair the ravages of the war. Output in 1946 and 1947 was little more than half the pre-war output, and production per worker fell to 72 tons a year compared with 216 tons in 1935.

Recovery started in 1948 and by 1951 output approached the pre-war (1937) peak and in 1953 exceeded it. Subsequently there was a decline and in 1955 output was only 43 million metric tons.[20] Even that output was reached only by the employment of a far greater labour force than before the war. The government provided financial assistance towards the re-equipment of the mines, and attempts were made to counter the worsened physical conditions by the introduction of power cutting and loading machinery and by the adoption of improved systems of mining. Yet while these innovations by 1955 had restored the *hourly* production per worker to that attained before the war, they were not sufficient to offset the effect on labour productivity of a reduction in the working hours by about 30 per cent. In 1955 the annual output per worker amounted to only 155 metric tons (compared with 216 metric tons in 1935). There was little improvement until 1960 and pre-war productivity was not exceeded until 1961.[21] As real wages in coal-mining had increased, the costs of the mining companies went up substantially, and Japanese prices during the 1950s compared very unfavourably with those of foreign countries. For much of the decade American coking coal could be delivered at Japanese ports at a price far lower than that charged for Japanese coal.

The total output rose very slowly. It attained a maximum of about 54 million metric tons in 1961 and 1962, and reliance on imports increased until in those years they represented about 20 per cent of home production. Meanwhile the vastly increased demand for power that accompanied Japan's industrial expansion was being supplied mainly by oil, most of which was imported in a crude state and refined in Japan. These imports (crude oil and petroleum products together) rose from 2·4 million kl. in 1950 to 12·1 million kl. in 1955, 25·6 million kl. in

[20] The annual average output of the period 1952–6 was 44 m. metric tons compared with 43 m. metric tons for 1935–8.
[21] Information from Min. Internat. Trade & Ind.; also *Japan Statist. Yb.*

1959, and 56·3 million kl. in 1962. In 1950 oil provided only 6 per cent of the country's power, in 1959 30 per cent.[22]

From the middle 1950s the government had encouraged the reorganization of the coal industry in the hope of improving its competitive position with other fuels, and in 1959 an official plan for the rationalization of coal-mining was formulated. But it is probable that it was the pressure of adversity as much as the persuasion of the plan that led the coal-owners to close many marginal mines and to concentrate production on the more efficient. The pace of rationalization was accelerated as it became clear during 1960 that the coal industry could no longer expect adequate protection against cheaper fuels, a point that was subsequently brought home by the abolition of import controls over crude oil and in the compulsory reduction in the price of coal by government edict.[23]

Rationalization and mechanized mining were responsible for a substantial rise in productivity in the early 1960s, but as in the previous decade this rise was insufficient to offset completely the increase in wages and other expenses.[24] Consequently the competitive position of coal *vis-à-vis* oil continued to deteriorate. The improvement in productivity, however, at a time when the total output was growing very slowly, created a serious problem of redundancy among the miners. The enlarged post-war labour force, which reached a maximum of 369,000 in 1950, fell to 274,000 in 1955, and to 179,000 in September 1962.[25] This steep decline led to serious unemployment and social discontent in the mining areas and forced the government to intervene. In 1962 it provided additional subventions to assist the coal-owners to reorganize their industry and for retraining unemployed coal-miners so as to fit them for work in other industries. A statutory minimum monthly wage for underground workers was fixed by the Ministry of Labour, a measure without precedent in Japan.[26]

The grim prospects of the industry were emphasized in the report of the officially appointed Coal Investigation Group, which in 1962 declared that coal could no longer be regarded as

[22] Industr. Bank, *Survey Fin. & Ind.*, July–Aug. 1960, p. 14; and *Fuji Bank B.*, June 1961, pp. 18–26.

[23] *Orient. Econ.*, Feb. 1963, p. 94.   [24] EPA, *Econ. Survey, 1961–2*, p. 303.

[25] *Japan Statist. Yb.*

[26] The wage was fixed on the recommendation of the Central Minimum Wages Commission (Japan Inst. of Lab., *Japan Lab. B.*, Feb. 1963, pp. 4–5).

competitive with oil and that, if free choice were permitted to consumers, by 1967–8 the domestic demand was likely to fall to 30 million tons or less. It is improbable that the industry will be left entirely to the mercy of free market forces. Even so it is certain that coal will continue to recede in importance as a source of energy and that oil will advance. The official prediction is that by 1970 oil will supply nearly 50 per cent of energy requirements, compared with just under 30 per cent in 1959, while the share of coal will fall from 38 to 29 per cent. Even if there is discrimination in favour of coal by the public utilities (as the Coal Investigation Group advised) with the effect of raising the output to about 57 million metric tons by 1967–8, the labour force is likely to shrink to 120,000, since further concentration on high-productivity mines is proposed.[27]

It is sometimes thought that Japan can view the worsening conditions in her coal industry with equanimity because of her resources of water power. These resources are certainly very great and they have long been extensively exploited for generating electric power. Even before the war Japan's output of electricity was not far short of that of the United Kingdom. There was a further increase during the early years of the war. Then followed a period of stagnation which lasted until 1949. In that year development was resumed, financed by loans from the United States Aid Counterpart Fund. In 1952 the government drew up an elaborate plan for the construction of new generating stations. It provided large funds for this purpose, and the industry also obtained foreign loans from the World Bank and from financial houses. Elaborate works were set in hand and much equipment was imported from the United States. In 1955 (fiscal year) production reached 65,000 million kwh., well over twice the pre-war output. By the fiscal year 1961–2 it had doubled again.

Japan has never relied on water power alone for the generation of electricity, for she has always needed thermal plants to maintain output during the winter months when the rainfall is inadequate. Since the war, despite the building of many new hydro-electric stations, most of the increase in electricity has been provided by thermal plants. Whereas in 1937 over 70 per cent of the current was generated by water power, in 1963 the pro-

[27] *Orient. Econ.*, Feb. 1963, p. 94; Industr. Bank, *Survey Fin. & Ind.*, Jan.–Mar. 1963, p. 6.

portion was under 45 per cent. The change is attributable to several causes. The exhaustion of the most easily harnessed sources of water power meant that the capital cost of new hydro-electric stations had become very heavy, especially as the rate of interest on loans was high. In so far as these interest charges were reduced by government assistance or by loans at less than market rates, the effect was to subsidize the industry at the expense of the taxpayer. On the other hand, the cost of post-war thermal generation was moderated, despite the high cost of domestic coal, by the availability of relatively cheap imported oil which the power stations used in increasing quantities. It is natural that the electricity industry, faced as it is by the prospect of continually rising capital costs, should repudiate the suggestion that in order to sustain the coal industry it should place long-term contracts with the mines. This issue is of considerable economic importance because it is estimated that by 1970 the ratio of water power to thermal power will be 4:6 compared with 6:4 in 1959.

The post-war period saw a change in the organization of the industry. During the 1930s the generation of electricity was becoming increasingly concentrated in a few very large concerns, several of which had raised capital in the United States or Great Britain. After the outbreak of the Sino-Japanese War, the government took control of the generation and transmission of electricity and set up a semi-official corporation, the Japan Electric Power Generating and Transmission Company, to execute its policy. Such a concentration of economic authority was repugnant to the Occupation authorities. In 1951 the semi-official concern was dissolved, and its generating and transmission properties were distributed among nine regional supply companies which had hitherto been engaged only in distribution. In September 1952, however, the government, intent upon stimulating a more rapid growth in the industry and conscious that private capital was unlikely to be available, created a new instrument for its purpose, namely the Electric Power Development Company. This officially-owned firm, which sells its current to other concerns for distribution, has been responsible for some large new stations. Among its first tasks was the construction of a great generating plant on the Tenryu River. Thus it might seem that the former concentration of authority has been in some measure restored. But this is a half-truth, and what has been far more evident in recent years is the defects of a system that leaves much of the development and the operation of the electricity supply with a number of virtually unco-ordinated regional concerns and fails to provide for a national power network. It may well be that efficiency will dictate the re-establishment of national control.

The changes described have affected most significantly Japan's dependence on external sources of power. In pre-war days and in the early 1950s this dependence was marginal, for the bulk of the energy consumed was supplied by coal and water power and there were small contributions from lignite and wood. The declining relative importance of water power for generating electricity, and the tendency for oil and imported coal to replace domestically produced coal, by 1959 had brought about a situation in which over one-third of the total energy was derived from imports. By 1970 it is expected that the proportion will have risen to three-fifths.[28] Mineral fuel in recent years has become one of the chief items on the import list, in 1963 nearly 18 per cent of the total value of imports. It may be that in the distant future atomic energy will free Japan from this reliance on foreign sources of power supply, but as elsewhere it is improbable that atomic power stations will be able to compete with conventional power stations for many years to come.

Sources of Energy as Proportion of Total Supply
(*in percentages*)

	1959	1970 Estimate
Water power	27·6	19·5
Coal	37·8	28·7
Oil	29·5	49·6
Wood	4·0	1·3
Natural gas, lignite, &c. . .	1·1	0·9
	100·0	100·0

Note: The table does not include the estimated output of atomic energy for 1970, but this is likely to be very small. Sources of energy other than coal are given in coal equivalents.

Source: Fuji Bank B., June 1961, p. 21.

---

[28] *Fuji Bank B.*, June 1961, p. 18.

X

Industrial Organization and the *Zaibatsu*

THE industrialization of a materially backward country is usually accompanied by a high concentration of economic power either in the State or in a few private entrepreneurial groups. The reasons for this association are not far to seek. In such a country the supply of entrepreneurial ability is narrowly confined, while capital needed for development can be rapidly accumulated only if incomes are very unequally distributed or if the State can enforce savings on the necessary scale. So there is nothing surprising in the emergence of a few dominant business houses during the period of Japan's industrialization. It is true that their form, their internal organization, and their relations with each other and with the government bore the impress of the country's social and political traditions, and that the actual direction of their development was determined by opportunities afforded by national policy. Yet, in essentials, the *Zaibatsu*, though remarkable business constructions, were neither so peculiar nor so sinister as is sometimes made out.

The organization and growth of these business groups have been described elsewhere,[1] and here only a few of their most important features will be considered. Some had their roots deep in the past. Mitsui, Sumitomo, and Yasuda had been prominent in Japan's economic life long before the opening of the country. Others emerged at the time of the Restoration from among *samurai* who had formerly administered the commercial and industrial undertakings of the feudal lords and later acquired control of them; Mitsubishi is in this category. Again, some appeared from among new firms who successfully exploited the opportunities of the Meiji era. For example, Furukawa and Asano began their modern career when they came into possession of mines and industrial establishments previously owned by the government.

[1] Lockwood, especially pp. 214–32; Allen, 'The Concentration of Economic Control in Japan', *Economic J.*, June 1937; Mitsubishi Econ. Research Inst., *Mitsui, Mitsubishi, Sumitomo* (1955), pp. 3–12 and *passim*.

All the *Zaibatsu* benefited substantially from their official connexions. The administrative talents, technical expertise, and capital resources needed for the execution of the government's expansionist policy were not widely diffused in Japan, and the State could not dispense with the services of the few who possessed them in financing its own activities or in building up the economy. So the *Zaibatsu* gained high rewards in their role as the essential agents of the government. They received profitable public contracts. Valuable government properties were from time to time made over to them in return for financial help. They rose on the tide of economic expansion to which they themselves markedly contributed, and by the time of the First World War the ascendancy of certain houses was well established. Their economic power as it increased enabled them to exert an influence on political trends, and during the 1920s some of them forged close links with the chief political parties. Their preeminence excited resentment among other groups in Japan, especially the army and the rural communities, and in the upheavals of the early 1930s their political influence was constricted. In the face of popular criticism the older and larger *Zaibatsu* tried to make themselves less conspicuous and withdrew from some lines of activity. They were now obliged to share the economic domain with certain newcomers favoured by the military. Of these *Shinko-Zaibatsu*, as they were called, the most important was Nissan. This concern originated in 1928 when G. Aikawa took over the Kuhara Mining Company and it subsequently played a leading part in the development of the heavy industries in Manchuria as well as in Japan Proper. Another *Shinko-Zaibatsu*, Nakajima, came to the front during the later 1930s when it was associated with the rise of armaments manufacture.

On the eve of the Second World War the four leading *Zaibatsu* (Mitsui, Mitsubishi, Sumitomo, and Yasuda, in that order of importance) were to be distinguished from the others[2] not only by their size and by the wide scope of their interests, but also by the fact of their predominance both in finance and in industry and trade. Their banks and their trust and insurance companies, which included the chief institutions in these several fields, provided a channel through which the savings of the general public were directed into the industrial and commercial undertakings

[2] Such as Asano, Furukawa, Aikawa (Nissan), Okura, and Nomura.

in the same group. Through these financial institutions the liquid resources of a great mass of concerns could be mobilized whenever the need arose, for example when heavy investment was required in some new branch of economic activity. Since there was only a small market for industrial securities among the general public, a manufacturing company that had no finance house behind it was liable to fall into a position of dependence upon a bank in another group.

In the industrial sector the *Zaibatsu* were especially prominent in the heavy industries (coal and metalliferous mining, metals, engineering, shipbuilding, and chemicals), although they also participated in the ceramics, textile, and paper industries. They had enormous real-estate interests, and the largest trading and shipping undertakings were under their control. It was not only the large-scale sector of the Japanese economy in which the *Zaibatsu* played a conspicuous part. Through their trading companies they handled the products of multitudes of small firms which they often financed, equipped, and largely directed.

The scope of the various *Zaibatsu* differed in detail. In the case of Mitsui and Mitsubishi the range of interests was extraordinarily wide—mining, numerous manufacturing industries, banking, trust and insurance, trade, warehousing, real estate, and shipping. Mitsui, the greatest of them, had been especially active in developing its trading interests and the famous Mitsui Bussan Kaisha (MBK) played an outstanding part in the conduct of domestic and foreign trade. Mitsubishi also had a large trading company, Mitsubishi Shoji Kaisha, and it was especially important in the engineering and shipbuilding industries. Sumitomo's main strength lay in mining, non-ferrous metals, and electrical engineering. Yasuda was primarily a financial house, although it had large interests in textiles, electricity supply, real estate, and warehousing. The lesser *Zaibatsu* tended to confine their strength to a narrower range of interests. Asano was concerned chiefly with the heavy industries, especially iron and steel and cement, Furukawa with mining, electrical engineering, chemicals, and rubber, Okura with engineering, metals, chemicals, and trading (including heavy investments in Manchuria), Nakajima with aircraft and munitions, Nomura with banking and trust business, and Nissan with engineering and chemicals, both in Japan and Manchuria. There were several other firms which were dominant in certain localities or in particular industries, notably Katakura in the raw silk industry.

One reason why the *Zaibatsu* excited the curiosity and suspicion of the outside world was to be found in the peculiarities of their internal organization. These vast and efficient businesses, equipped with all the contrivances of twentieth-century technology, rested on institutional foundations laid down in the 'feudal' past. Mitsui and Mitsubishi resembled the Fuggers of Augsburg rather than the anonymous giants of the era of the Western managerial revolution. Ownership was vested in a family or group of families, and the activities of every family member were regulated according to Japanese social practice by a family council which, in the case of Mitsui, framed its decisions in conformity with the ancient code of the house. Financial control over the network of businesses was exercised through a top holding company, usually called the *honsha*. This controlled the major operating subsidiaries under which there was an intricate network of sub-subsidiaries and affiliated companies. Major policies and the chief appointments to the *honsha* were determined in the family councils on the advice of the leading executives.[3]

Personal relations within the business hierarchy were governed by the Japanese tradition which prescribed absolute loyalty to superiors; but the extent to which the family members themselves exercised administrative authority varied from *Zaibatsu* to *Zaibatsu*. In Mitsubishi, for instance, the influence of the Iwasaki family remained very strong. In Mitsui, on the other hand, control over policy even before the Restoration had passed mainly to *banto*, or managers. But even the greatest of these *banto* could expect to retain their positions only so long as they were successful in promoting the welfare of the house.

The rivalries between the older *Zaibatsu* and the *Gumbatsu* (military)—rivalries which in the early 1930s had been accompanied by violent denunciations of *Zaibatsu* policy and even the assassination of leading *banto*—gradually gave place to cooperation between them in strengthening Japan's military power. By 1937 the *Zaibatsu* (the 'old' and the 'new' alike) had been called upon to promote the expansion of the munitions industries and to act as agents for the government in organizing the economy for war. After the outbreak of the Pacific War this

[3] Cf. T. A. Bisson, *Zaibatsu Dissolution in Japan* (1954), p. 24.

co-operation became unqualified. The *Zaibatsu* alone had the resources needed for the task and as the war proceeded economic power became increasingly concentrated in their hands. While the civilian industries in which the smaller firms played an important part contracted, the heavy industries, already largely in *Zaibatsu* hands, expanded. The concentration of the banking system during the war left the *Zaibatsu* banks in an even more dominating position than they already occupied. At the same time, *Zaibatsu* personnel were closely engaged in the administration of official controls. The result was that by the end of the war these great houses had much increased their share of the economic activity of the country. Figures can throw only a dim light on the position they had then obtained. It is to be noted, however, that whereas in 1937 the 'Big Four' owned 15 per cent and ten leading *Zaibatsu* 25 per cent of the total paid-up capital in the heavy industries, in 1946 the proportions were 32 and 49 per cent. In finance and insurance, the corresponding figures were, for 1937 23 and 24 and for 1946 50 and 53 per cent. The ratio of the loans of the four great *Zaibatsu* banks to those of all ordinary banks rose from 44 per cent in 1937 to 66 per cent in 1945. It is estimated that at the end of the war Mitsui employed 1,800,000 persons in Japan Proper and probably over a million more overseas. Mitsubishi is thought to have employed about a million.[4]

It is not disputed that the *Zaibatsu* contributed 'strength, efficiency, and sureness of purpose' to Japan in her period of rapid economic development.[5] They were the chief sources of investment capital and the spearhead of the nation's enterprise. This, however, was not an aspect of their activity with which the Occupation authorities in 1945 felt much sympathy. To them the *Zaibatsu* represented a major obstacle to the construction of a liberal society and a competitive economic system. These great houses had armed Japan for her conflict with the West and they had impeded (so the Americans believed) the rise of democratic institutions at home. Their destruction was an essential part of the general policy of social and political reform. If, in the process, economic efficiency were for a time diminished and recovery delayed, that was a price which Japan must be prepared to pay

[4] Mitsubishi Econ. Research Inst., *Mitsui, Mitsubishi, Sumitomo*, pp. 5–10.
[5] Bisson, p. 32.

in the interests of the future welfare of her people and of international peace. Some Japanese believe that the Americans were also moved by a desire to weaken the country's competitive strength in foreign trade, but it is doubtful if that motive ever exerted more than a minor influence over what was done. Indeed there is evidence that once American business circles had realized the full implications of SCAP's policy, they became deeply suspicious of it and did not refrain from bitter criticism. According to one commentator, they feared that 'an active anti-monopoly program abroad [might] presage increased anti-trust activity in the United States'.[6]

It must not be imagined that Japanese opinion was universally opposed to the American policy. Even in the ruling cliques the *Zaibatsu* had their enemies, and their shadow frustrated the growth of independent enterprises. Socialists and Liberals in general supported the view that the existence of the *Zaibatsu* was incompatible with the emergence of democratic institutions. But these circles, while supporting dissolution, believed that the State itself should take over and manage the *Zaibatsu* properties. This proposal found widespread support among those Japanese who realized that the disappearance of the *Zaibatsu* would leave a 'power vacuum' that the government alone could fill. However, the Occupation authorities were not disposed to consult Japanese preferences. They were intent upon dissolution.

Their policy passed through several stages. In the first days of the Occupation the authorities proceeded on the assumption that their purposes could be accomplished by a few sweeping measures. Then, as the complications of the task of remodelling the country's economic institutions were more widely understood, an elaborate series of measures was devised and vigorously applied. In the course of 1948, however, when the cold war began and the American administration became concerned with economic recovery rather than reform, its hostility towards the *Zaibatsu* and towards monopoly in general diminished. Nevertheless, the policy was not abandoned but was pursued in a modified form until the end of the Occupation. By then Japan's economic structure had suffered a profound change and some of its most prominent features had been permanently removed.

The policy was carried out by a series of related measures

[6] E. M. Hadley, 'Trust Busting in Japan', *Harvard Business R.*, July 1948, p. 427.

which were directed, first, towards destroying the power and
wealth of the *Zaibatsu* families, secondly, towards the dissolution
into numerous independent enterprises of the great mass of concerns within each group and, thirdly, towards the preservation
of the competitive, atomistic, structure so created. The *Zaibatsu*
directly affected by this policy consisted of the 'Big Four' and six
others. The properties of the family members were frozen immediately after the Occupation began, and the family securities
together with those owned by the top holding companies were
transferred to a Holding Company Liquidation Commission set
up by the Japanese government in obedience to SCAP's orders.
The Commission's main function was to dispose of these securities among the public in the hope of achieving a wide distribution
of industrial ownership. The *Zaibatsu* family members were
required to cease for ten years from participation in the businesses
formerly under their control, and there was a 'purge' of most of
the former leading *banto*. Next, a group of major subsidiaries
which themselves had controlled a large number of manufacturing, trading, and other undertakings was dissolved. Among the
outstanding companies in this group were MBK and Mitsubishi
Shoji, and the fragmentation of these great trading concerns provided the chief ground for the Japanese suspicion that the policy
was aimed primarily at weakening their country's competitive
power in foreign markets.[7] The attack was also directed against
the major subsidiaries in mining and manufacturing, although
here it did not display the ruthless determination that characterized the policy when applied to the trading companies.

   The dissolution, as it affected industry, was not limited to
Zaibatsu companies. It was extended to a number of semi-official
concerns, or so-called 'national policy' companies, whose existence in the eyes of the more zealous reformers constituted a
serious offence against economic liberalism. Most of these concerns had been founded during the 1930s when the Japanese
government was increasing its control over the economy for
strategic purposes. The companies included the Nippon Seitetsu
(Japan Iron & Steel Company) and the Japan Electricity
Generating & Transmission Company.

   In banking and finance the existing structure was only slightly
disturbed, although the chief banks, in common with other

---

[7] MBK was dissolved into 170 separate concerns and Mitsubishi Shoji into 150.

Zaibatsu companies, were required to change their names so as to emphasize their independence of former associates. The mildness of the authorities towards the banks can be explained partly by the intricate technical problems to which dissolution gave rise and partly because the policy had exhausted itself by the time SCAP was ready to deal with this sector.

The authorities were determined that the personal and financial links between concerns formerly in the same group should be effectively severed. So restrictions were imposed on the holding of shares in other companies and on interlocking directorates. Further, the contractual arrangements that had existed between the several member companies within each group were brought to an end; these arrangements had taken the form of undertakings or agreements by which the major business decisions and appointments in a particular company depended upon approval given by another. These measures were strengthened by the enactment in April 1947 of an anti-monopoly law which prohibited or narrowly limited the rights of firms to resort to restrictive practices or to devices designed to restrain competition and to create monopolies.[8]

The results of the measures were far-reaching. The wealth and power of the *Zaibatsu* families were in fact destroyed, for although compensation in the form of government bonds was paid for the properties which they surrendered, the value of this payment was almost wiped out by a capital levy and by the subsequent inflation. The dissolution of the top holding companies of the leading *Zaibatsu* and of many of their major subsidiaries together with the breaking of the personal, contractual, and financial links among them succeeded in producing a fragmentation of these great concerns. The leading executives were prevented for several years from any direct participation in the management of the successor companies which now came under the control of relatively junior officials.

In the course of these operations a vast quantity of securities passed into the hands of government agencies. The Holding Company Liquidation Commission acquired shares worth about

---

[8] The data on which this account of the *Zaibatsu* dissolution is based are: Holding Company Liquidation Commission, *Laws, Rules and Regulations concerning the Reconstruction and Democratization of the Japanese Economy* (1949) and *Final Report on Zaibatsu Dissolution* (1951); Bisson; and Mitsubishi Econ. Research Inst., *Mitsui, Mitsubishi, Sumitomo*.

9,000 million yen at original paid-up values, and securities of about the same amount came into possession of the Finance Ministry (as the result of the capital levy) and of other public authorities. But these sums were dwarfed by the quantities of new issues which were required for financing industrial reorganization during the inflationary period and were mainly taken up by government agencies. In the end about '70,000 million yen of company shares was handled in disposal operations directed by the government'.[9] Of this vast amount the securities handled by the Holding Company Liquidation Commission represented only a small proportion and the disposal operations of that body must obviously be viewed in the light of the conditions created by the inflation. As we have seen, the original intention was to bring about a wide dispersal of securities as an essential condition for ushering in a liberal competitive society, and the Holding Company Liquidation Commission was the instrument chosen for this task. At the outset those familiar with Japanese economic and social conditions feared that the plan for disposal would encounter insurmountable obstacles in a country where private investors had been unaccustomed to enter the market for industrial securities. In the event the task proved to be at once less onerous and less significant. Disposals proceeded very slowly at first, but by 1950 some two-thirds of the shares held by the HCLC had been sold. Many passed to the employees of the companies and a fairly wide distribution was achieved. But an even greater number of securities had been sold by the Finance Ministry and other official agencies. In addition there was the great mass of new issues. It seems probable that most of these shares were acquired by banks, insurance companies, and other institutional investors, among which the former *Zaibatsu* financial houses were especially prominent. In the final result it appears that although the policy had led to a somewhat wider dispersal of security holdings, industrial ownership at the end of the Occupation still remained highly concentrated.

The dissolution policy retarded Japan's economic recovery, for it disorganized the main centres of economic initiative upon which she had hitherto relied and it introduced uncertainties into the business of decision making. SCAP's implied acceptance

[9] Bisson, p. 115.

N

of this opinion is shown by the diminishing vigour with which the policy was applied after the economic recovery of Japan became an aim of American policy. It is tempting to relate the speed of recovery in different sectors of the economy to the extent to which they had been affected by the dissolution measures, to argue that the stagnation of the export trade long after industrial production had revived was largely attributable to the destruction of the great trading companies. But this argument has little substance. The long frustration of Japan's trade revival can be attributed primarily, though not exclusively, to other causes.

We must now consider how far the formal results of the dissolution policy correspond with changes of substance in the country's economic organization. There can be little doubt that by the end of the Occupation the once closely-knit Japanese economy had been wrenched apart. But the policy had not been equally effective in all its aspects and its incidence on the several *Zaibatsu* had varied. The effect on the position of the families had certainly been catastrophic and probably permanent. Some of their real property and personal possessions could be, and later were, returned to them. Many of these assets, however, as well as the compensation received for the securities, had been used in the payment of taxes, and the family ownership of and control over the great business aggregates were at an end. Thus it appeared that in each group the original focus of activity had been finally destroyed. Yet we must recall that long before the dissolution, effective management had been largely in the hands of officials, and the question remains whether the destruction of the families meant also the end of centralized control. This question must be approached by stages. First, the dissolution of the central holding companies and the main subsidiaries still left the industrial and mining companies of the former *Zaibatsu* as the leading undertakings in their several fields, even though some of them had been split up into a number of independent firms. Secondly, the former *Zaibatsu* banks and insurance companies, though weakened, remained among the chief financial institutions of the country. Thus, except in trade where the policy of fragmentation had been most ruthlessly pursued, although the empires had been dissolved, the successor states were still dominant entities.

The problem of how far these successors were really independent, to what extent the old ties between them had actually been cut, is not easy to solve. With the 'purging' of the high executives management had passed into the hands of younger men. Yet it is acknowledged that the former chief *banto*, even in the hey-day of the dissolution policy, were consulted privately on matters of high policy by those in charge of the several businesses. The Japanese tradition of the elder statesman offered powerful opposition to the designs of the SCAP reformers. Further, the authorities were powerless to dissuade the managers of the successor companies from meeting together to discuss their common problems when they found advantage in doing so. Nor were the former financial links always severed so completely as had been intended. We have already noted that a high proportion of the new issues made by industrial companies during the inflationary period were acquired by banks and finance houses formerly in the same group. In the same way the financial business of these industrial companies continued to be handled as a rule by the bank with which they had previously been associated.

It was evidently found almost as difficult to destroy the cohesion of the *Zaibatsu* concerns as to compel oligopolists to compete. But general statements are liable to mislead. The several *Zaibatsu* were not equally resistant to the policy nor equally affected. Of the major *Zaibatsu*, Mitsui, the greatest of them, suffered most. Its empire had centred on its trading company and this was completely shattered. The Mitsui Bank, which alone of the *Zaibatsu* banks suffered a measure of dissolution, emerged in a weaker state than its rivals. It was not able to afford as effective assistance to other Mitsui companies as that given by the Mitsubishi and Sumitomo banks to their former associates. So Mitsui's industrial companies had to go elsewhere for accommodation during the reconstruction period. Finally, either because of its size or because of a stronger impulse of personal ambition among the managers of its undertakings, the emotional ties with the house were rather weaker than was the case with the other *Zaibatsu*. Certainly, the executives to whom the control of the successor companies passed, seem to have enjoyed their independence and to have displayed reluctance in accepting restrictions upon their full liberty of action.

On the other hand, in Mitsubishi the bank rather than the trading company had been at the centre of the concern, and the bank came out of the dissolution period in a comparatively strong position. Moreover, the Iwasaki family in recent times had exerted a greater influence over the policy than the Mitsuis, and among the *banto* strong personal loyalties towards the family had persisted. For all these reasons, in Mitsubishi the old ties, though loosened, were not broken. The same was true of Sumitomo, whose centre of interest lay in heavy industry and whose constituent companies retained their identity and much of their strength. In this *Zaibatsu*, control had always been highly centralized and personal relations among the executives remained close. Sumitomo had not participated largely in foreign trade, and, having its headquarters in Osaka away from the excitements of the capital, had not become deeply involved in political affairs. So it escaped some of the virulence that Mitsui had aroused in Occupation circles. As for Yasuda, this *Zaibatsu*, which had always concentrated on banking and allied interests, was divorced from its industrial and other properties, but, under the style of the Fuji Bank, it was left as one of the chief forces in Japanese finance.

The dissolution policy appears to have gained its chief enduring successes among the lesser groups and the *Shinko-Zaibatsu*. We have seen that the lesser *Zaibatsu* differed from the 'Big Four' in that their interests were not equally spread between finance and industry. In the period of reconstruction the individual companies, therefore, were unable to seek financial help from an associated bank, and there was no focusing point for the successor companies as a body. The *Shinko-Zaibatsu*, for their part, had specialized in armaments production or in colonial and Manchurian enterprise. Japan's defeat and the loss of her empire undermined their strength. Their dissolution left in being some very important industrial concerns, such as the Hitachi Engineering Company, formerly part of Nissan, but these were without affiliations with any group.

If at the end of the Occupation, the *Zaibatsu* still retained more than a shadowy existence, they were certainly not then equipped to serve as centres of initiative in the reconstruction of Japan's economy. Yet this did not mean that initiative was now widely diffused, as the Americans had hoped. On the contrary, the immediate effect of the dissolution was to produce an even more highly centralized economic system than before, at any rate so far as the large-scale sector of the economy was concerned. Responsibilities formerly discharged by the *Zaibatsu* were now concentrated in the State. Government officials stepped into the places once occupied by the great *banto*. This transference of power was confirmed by the shortage of private capital for reconstruction. As shown in Chapter IV, for many years resources for that purpose could be provided only by the government or its agencies, at first through the Reconstruction Finance Bank, and later through the Bank of Japan, which supplied the commercial banks with funds needed for financing industry. Thus the whole economy was reduced to extreme dependence upon the central authorities, an odd consequence of measures directed towards liberalizing the country's economic organization and based on a firm rejection of nationalization and State control.

This situation persisted until the end of 1954, but from the end of the Occupation the *Zaibatsu* began to mobilize their forces in an attempt to regain some of their lost ground. The reasons are clear. The underlying conditions that had led to the emergence of the *Zaibatsu* were still present, even in an exaggerated form. At a time when the country was deeply concerned with modernizing its industrial equipment and with closing the wide technical gap between itself and the West, capital was scarce and technical and administrative expertise was still concentrated in relatively few undertakings. Those whom the dissolution placed in charge of the chief enterprises had every inducement to seek, by conjunction with former associates, a solution for the problems, expecially the financial problems, which in isolation they found overwhelming. Their loyalties had not been destroyed and, for the most part, they were led by habit and disposition to co-operate in rebuilding the edifices demolished by foreign edict.[10] Events favoured them. The boom in the heavy industries that accompanied the Korean War and persisted in the years that followed was greatly to the benefit of the mining and manufacturing concerns formerly owned by the *Zaibatsu*. Then the deflation of 1954 wiped out or debilitated many new

---

[10] When I visited the head office of a former *Zaibatsu* bank at this time, I noticed that it was housed in the same building as the offices of numerous other companies which, before dissolution, had belonged to the same group. My comment on this propinquity provoked the reply: 'We are now, of course, entirely separate, but it is convenient to be able to visit our former associates so easily.'

concerns that had risen on the tide of post-war inflation. As had happened in similar circumstances in the past, the *Zaibatsu* were then left with greater relative strength.

The general attitude of the successor firms towards the houses of which they were once members was demonstrated by the hasty resumption of their old names as soon as the Occupation came to an end.[11] By the middle 1950s regrouping was well under way. Personal links among former member firms were strengthened by the appointment of common directors and there was a pronounced tendency for the proportion of each company's capital held by others in the same group to increase. At the same time consultations among the leading executives became more systematically organized and the reconstruction of the trading companies was begun. Just as the immediate effects of the dissolution differed in detail from *Zaibatsu* to *Zaibatsu*, so the pace and extent of the rehabilitation varied. Sumitomo, always the most compact group, was the earliest to recover. Very soon after the abolition of the head company, an informal group composed of the chief executives of the former main subsidiaries came into being. The *Hakusuikai*, as it was called, held regular meetings from the outset, and as the political climate became more genial it developed into a body for the discussion and formulation of policy. Meetings of subordinate officials were also organized and the old Sumitomo companies readily co-operated in financing research activities.[12]

Mitsubishi was not far behind. Although the interests and properties of this *Zaibatsu* were greater and more diverse than those of Sumitomo, the new pattern of association as it evolved differed only in detail. Mitsubishi also came to rely for the co-ordination of policy on regular meetings of the leading executives drawn from all firms in the group, and accordingly the *Kinyokai* (Friday Club) came into being. Other inter-group meetings were arranged for officials of lower status or for those concerned with particular common problems. Links were forged through intercorporate stockholdings and interlocking directorates. Like the other *Zaibatsu*, Mitsubishi introduced the practice of rotating personnel among its various businesses and is

---

[11] Except by the Fuji Bank, the successor of the Yasuda Bank.
[12] This part of the narrative is heavily indebted to a series of articles entitled 'Zaibatsu Leadership Race', *Orient. Econ.*, Feb.–June 1961.

said to have followed it more systematically. Mitsubishi concerns
working in the same field, though often keen rivals, have nevertheless been persuaded to pool technical knowledge and to
finance joint research. The proportion of inter-group trade has
been very high. For example, of 91 ships ordered by the Mitsubishi Shipping Company in a given period 67 were built in
Mitsubishi yards, and it is estimated that in recent years one-
third of the goods handled by Mitsubishi Shoji have been on
account of other companies in the group.

On the other hand, Mitsui, the largest *Zaibatsu* before the
dissolution, found the task of the reconstruction more arduous.
The fortnightly meetings of Mitsui's chief executives (*Getsuyokai*)
have exerted a milder influence on the policy of the constituent
firms than is the case with similar meetings of the other *Zaibatsu*.
Whereas several Sumitomo companies collaborated in the task
of finding employment for the Sumitomo mine-workers displaced by rationalization after 1958 and Mitsubishi founded a
construction company for a similar purpose, Mitsui companies
were not easily persuaded to take co-operative action for dealing
with redundancy at the Miike mine. Since the speed and effectiveness of rationalization in Japan depends in no small measure
on success in handling the problem of displaced workers, the
disparity between the *Zaibatsu* in this respect may not be without
its influence on their relative rates of growth and efficiency. To
some extent Mitsui's difficulties can be traced to the individu-
alistic traditions of the house already referred to. Certainly the
executives to whom the control of the successor companies passed
seem to have enjoyed their independence and to have been
reluctant to admit the reimposition of restraints upon their full
liberty of action. But the main reason probably lies in the nature
of Mitsui's chief interests and in the exceptionally devastating
effects of the dissolution, as previously described.

The point may be illustrated by reference to the contrasting
experience of Mitsui and Mitsubishi in the reconstruction of their
trading companies.[13] In this process Mitsubishi was far ahead of
its rival. In July 1954 four of the successor firms of its old trading
company came together; other businesses were quickly absorbed; and by 1956 Mitsubishi Shoji had become the largest

---

[13] *Orient. Econ.*, Jan. 1961, pp. 29–42; Jan. 1962, pp. 39–51; also K. Uchida, 'Trading Firms of Japan' in *B. of Univ. Osaka Prefecture*, 1958, pp. 97–107.

trading company in Japan. Mitsui encountered more serious obstacles in reconstituting MBK. The loss of the colonial trade and the weakness of foreign trade in the early post-war years, fields in which MBK had been very active before the war, had a retarding effect. The rest of its business had been bound up with its close relations with a mass of subsidiary companies in the manufacturing and service industries and with its dealings with numerous small producers. After the war the liquid resources of Mitsui, like those of other merchants, were too exiguous to permit them to finance producers on the pre-war scale and the weakness of the Mitsui Bank meant that adequate help could not be provided from that source. However, the process of reconstruction began slowly in 1952 when two of the successors of MBK amalgamated. In August 1955 Dai Ichi Bussan, another former constituent, merged with two others and later established close links with several previously independent traders, including Katakura, the largest business in the silk trade. Meanwhile, several of the separate companies which resulted from the dissolution of MBK expanded, but it was not until February 1959 that most of the former subsidiaries came together and MBK emerged as the largest trading house in the country.

Even now it no longer enjoys its former predominance. Before the war it was believed to have controlled about 20 per cent of Japan's foreign trade; in 1959–60 the proportion was probably about 10 per cent. Its relations with other Mitsui companies are not very intimate and it handles a relatively small proportion of their transactions. Some of its former affiliated companies, such as Toyo Menka, have followed an independent course. Furthermore, it now has to face several new competitors. A few Osaka textile companies, such as Marubeni-Iida and C. Ito, transformed themselves after the war into general merchants, and their turnover now approaches that of the leaders. In addition, a number of other substantial general merchants have appeared. All these houses have established links with particular industrial companies and with particular banks, e.g. Marubeni-Iida with Hitachi and the Fuji Bank, C. Ito with the Sumitomo and Dai-Ichi Banks and certain Sumitomo industrial companies, and Toyo Menka with the Tokai Bank.

The rise of these new undertakings will probably make it impossible for the trading companies of the two major *Zaibatsu* to recover their former share of Japan's foreign trade—one-third before the war. Yet consolidation has been carried very far in recent years. The numerous small firms which were characteristic of Japan's trading structure in the early post-war period have disappeared and it is probable that the conduct of foreign trade will again be strongly concentrated, even though Mitsui and Mitsubishi have to be content with a less dominating position. This concentration offers advantages to Japan, since capital-goods exports, which have now become prominent, can be handled most efficiently by large firms. From the middle 1950s Mitsubishi has operated a technical service, with headquarters in Calcutta, for South East Asian countries, and Mitsui has for some years administered a Plant Export Council in which several of its constituent firms participate.

After the abolition of the *Honsha*, or top holding companies, power for a time centred on the *Zaibatsu* banks. This came about partly because the shortage of capital left industrial concerns heavily dependent upon banking advances for financing their reconstruction and partly because the banks were for the most part left intact during the dissolution period. The exception, as we have seen, was the Mitsui Bank, which was certainly unable to exert the unifying influence comparable with that of the other *Zaibatsu* banks or like them to take the lead in new enterprises. During the last few years, however, it seems likely that all the *Zaibatsu* banks have lost some of their power in consequence of the development of new industries for the promotion of which *Kombinats* have been constructed. These new ventures have required resources far in excess of the capacity of any single bank, and it has been necessary for each *Kombinat* to resort to several sources of credit. So initiative in starting new ventures seems to have shifted from the banks to the directors of the new industrial complexes and the banks have been left with a more passive role. The development of the securities market is likely to exert a similar influence.

The devices available to the *Zaibatsu* in their efforts to regroup were affected by the provisions of the Fair Trading Laws, which were regarded as an essential buttress of the dissolution policy. The original law prohibited cartels and all kinds of restricted practices normally associated with monopoly; but subsequent amendments weakened its effect. Agreements that exercised an unreasonable restraint on trade remained forbidden, but exceptions were permitted in the case of cartels formed to deal with depressions, to promote rationalization, to prevent dumping, or to foster exports. Some of these permitted cartels, notably those formed to deal with depressions, have been short-lived; but more permanent arrangements have been legalized by a series of special acts which exclude restrictive arrangements in particular industries from the operation of the Fair Trading Laws. Examples are to be found in the legislative provisions for the sealing of surplus cotton spindles and for the prevention of over-fishing by co-operative arrangements, and also in the Export and Import Transactions Law, under which numerous associations have been formed. Although holding companies are still illegal, the restrictions on intercorporate shareholdings and interlocking directorates have been relaxed, and the Fair Trade Commission in recent years has become increasingly well disposed towards mergers. The amendments to the original law and the administrative action that has accompanied them have smoothed the path to the concentration of economic power. Yet the business world is not content and has urged a general legislative retreat on the ground that Japan is suffering from excessive competition. So far these claims have been resisted by liberal opinion and by non-industrial interests. It is anyhow doubtful if the legal obstacles to monopoly have been of major importance. Until the structure of the economy has been further modified and the aggressive entrepreneurial spirit tamed, Japan is not likely to succumb to oligopolistic stagnation.[14]

The *Zaibatsu* of the 1960s differ so markedly from the *Zaibatsu* of former times that some Japanese contend that the use of the old names is misleading. It is not merely that the *Zaibatsu* families have been thrust aside, but also that the highly centralized methods of financial and administrative control which gave the groups their distinctive character have disappeared. What were once well-defined and purposeful entities, it is said, have become amorphous clusters of firms. Yet, although the bonds among the constituents are looser than in the past and the system of interfirm relationships has become more subtle, the identities of the

---

[14] *Orient. Econ.*, Apr. 1962, pp. 193–7; Jan., 1964, pp. 25–29; Fair Trade Commission, *Laws, Orders and Regulations Relating to Foreign Investment in Japan* (Apr. 1963).

several *Zaibatsu* have been preserved. Mitsui, Mitsubishi, and Sumitomo, however, now share economic power with several other great groups, e.g. Hitachi, Yawata, and Tokyo-Shibaura in manufacturing industry, Marubeni-Iida and C. Ito in trade, and the Fuji Bank (the heir of Yasuda) and the rising Tokai Bank in industrial finance. Moreover, the several empires are less clearly marked than in the past. It is often difficult to decide whether a firm that derives substantial financial support from a *Zaibatsu* bank or deals mainly through a *Zaibatsu* trading company is to be regarded as a member of the group. Again there are clearly centrifugal as well as centripetal forces at work within the various *Zaibatsu*. Some executives resist the unifying pressures brought to bear on them, while others welcome every step towards coalescence. Within each group it is possible to find companies that are keen rivals with one another (such as the three successor companies to Mitsubishi Heavy Industries), although they are prepared to co-operate for certain purposes and may offer a common front to outsiders.[15] During the last ten years a struggle has been waged between the disruptive and the unifying forces, and the result has differed from *Zaibatsu* to *Zaibatsu*. Sumitomo has emerged as the most cohesive group, whereas in Mitsui it has been found most difficult to assert the power of the group over the constituents.

The structural changes in Japanese industry, the shift from coal-mining, cotton textiles, and the older branches of engineering to electronics, petrochemicals, and man-made fibres, have presented the *Zaibatsu* with problems of adjustment. Each *Zaibatsu* has been impelled to organize a transference of resources from the older industries in which it was predominant to trades that call both for new technology and also for vast capital investments. These ventures have required a combination of interests within each *Zaibatsu* and also at times a combination of *Zaibatsu* firms with outsiders, as in the new *Kombinats* in the oil and organic-chemical industries and in the development of atomic energy. Thus as a Japanese economist has stated: 'The combination of firms in different industries for new ventures has broken the rigidity of the *Zaibatsu* structure'.

Post-war developments in industrial organization call atten-

---

[15] M. Shinohara, 'Some Causes and Consequences of Economic Growth in Japan', *Malayan Econ. R.*, Apr. 1961, pp. 32–48.

tion to what are apparently inconsistent features of the Japanese economy. On the one hand, there is the strong tendency towards the creation of large, highly diversified industrial groups. On the other hand, there is the vigorous competitive spirit displayed in rivalries not only among the groups but between members of the same group. In spite of the widespread intervention of the government in economic processes, the easing of the prohibitions on cartels and mergers, and the vitality of the old dominant groups, the forces of competition continue to thrive. Prices are still very flexible and contrived rigidities are usually quickly broken. In one sense the presence of the *Zaibatsu* far from curbing this competition helps to stimulate it, for each group feels itself obliged, for reasons of prestige, to obtain a share of every new industry as it appears and to hold its own in all fields with its rivals. So at the beginning of periods of substantial innovation, there is heavy competitive investment in new capital ventures on the part of all the *Zaibatsu*. The appearance of new groups has widened the area of contest.

It has been argued that competition has become excessive for two reasons. First, the efforts on the part of each group to secure a share in every new enterprise sometimes exert detrimental effects on the scale of operations. Secondly, this rivalry leads inevitably to over-investment from time to time and hence to economic instability. The second criticism can be dismissed with the reply that in a rapidly growing economy demand soon overtakes capacity and that instability is a small price to pay for rapid progress. The first criticism has some weight. A failure of certain industries to achieve all the available technical economies of scale has its corollary in the lack of specialization on the part of plants and firms which has already been commented on. In the past a high degree of diversification was probably inevitable because of shortages of capital and of high-grade technical and managerial talent. Until recently, moreover, deficiencies resulting from a lack of specialization were not exposed to competition from foreigners in the home market. Today Japan is well endowed with competent managers and technologists, and although new capital is still scarce in relation to her voracious appetite for it, the channels through which it flows have increased. It is true that there is one factor that has not changed, namely the persistence of the 'lifelong engagement' system among employees. This system, by obliging firms to find jobs for workers displaced from declining trades, has virtually compelled them on occasions to embark on new ventures. Yet although some measure of diversification can be attributed to this cause, the main factors that operated in the post-war years are those already considered.

Great changes may lie ahead. The liberalization of trade has destroyed some of the barriers that formerly sheltered the less efficient forms of productive organization. It has already had the effect of stimulating mergers for the purpose both of securing access to economies of scale and also of presenting a united front to foreign rivals. It may be expected, therefore, that response to this new pressure will bring more intense specialization on the part of plants and perhaps of companies. Whether it will have the same effect on the interests of the *Zaibatsu* is more doubtful.

On the whole, it can be said that the *Zaibatsu*, in a modified and in some respects more complicated form, have returned successfully to the economic scene, but without regaining completely their former domination over the economy. Their empires are less closely knit than in the past and as agents of the State's economic policy they have to share their functions with other groups which are also bound together by loose and subtle ties. The *Zaibatsu* have always been suspect in socialist and radical circles and if the forces of the left were strengthened, their power, and of course the power of other large groups might be vigorously assailed. Yet, in a sense, they are less vulnerable than in the past simply because their organization has become amorphous. They no longer possess a head to strike off and their limbs have an independent life.

Attempts have recently been made by the Economic Planning Agency and the Fair Trade Commission to measure the extent to which various types of production are concentrated in a few firms, and comparisons have been drawn with other countries in this respect.[16] The industries in which concentration ratios are high are for the most part the same in Japan as in Western countries, although (so far as it is possible to make valid comparisons) it appears that in such industries the degree of concentration is usually lower in Japan than in the United States or the United

[16] *Econ. Survey, 1962–3*, pp. 251–5; and *Orient. Econ.*, July 1964, pp. 493–500.

Kingdom.[17] This may be explained, at any rate in part, by the highly diversified character of Japan's great industrial groups, in other words, by the lack of specialization among enterprises. It may be expected that as Japan strives to raise her scales of production to match those of her competitors, her concentration ratios will increase. This has already occurred in a number of industries within the last few years, but generally the tendency has so far been in the opposite direction. The rapid growth in demand has drawn many newcomers into lines of production previously dominated by a small number of firms, or has led to a disproportionate increase in the output of producers of medium size. In these cases concentration ratios have, of course, declined.

These statistical enquiries are of limited value in solving the problems of major economic interest. They afford little help in estimating the power of the great concerns to influence economic policy, for the statistics apply to individual companies rather than to groups, and they cover shares in the output of particular products rather than shares in the aggregate industrial production. The Fair Trade Commission has pointed out that industries with high concentration ratios are usually those where the price structure is found to be the most rigid; but over the greater part of Japanese industry price-rigidity seems to prevail only in the short period, since in the rapidly expanding and changing economy, monopoly positions are easily eroded. Moreover, in Japan as elsewhere, the same type of industrial structure is consistent with sharp contrasts both in the distribution of strategic power and in market behaviour.

[17] The concentration ratios refer to the proportion of output or employment in the hands of the three largest (or the five largest) firms.

XI
Labour in a Changing Economy

CONDITIONS OF EMPLOYMENT BEFORE 1945

ON several occasions in the course of their history the Japanese
have been obliged to modify their institutions through pressure
from without. They have long been accustomed to seek foreign
models and deliberately to naturalize foreign techniques and
institutions. Yet up to 1945 they were able to reserve for themselves freedom of choice and to discriminate in their borrowings
from abroad. As a result of defeat and Occupation, however, the
economic and social system was for some years exposed to reforms introduced by foreigners. Japan lay almost helpless before
the policy, idealistic or vindictive, of the conquerors. We have
already indicated that at the outset the chief aim of SCAP was to
democratize Japanese institutions, with the object of destroying
any seeds of militarism left behind after the plant itself had been
uprooted, and that in the economic sphere this policy found its
chief expression in the Land Reform, the dissolution of the
Zaibatsu, and the encouragement of labour organization. By the
ruin of the conservative landlords and the founding of a land-
owning peasantry, by the break-up of great aggregates of economic power and the wide diffusion of economic initiative, and
by the overthrow of industrial paternalism and the creation of
vigorous trade unions, it was hoped to bring into being an environment in which liberal political institutions could flourish.

The country was in a mood to welcome many of these changes,
and there were Japanese who could be enlisted in the application
of the policy. But Japanese society differed profoundly in its
traditions and structure from that of the Western countries
where those institutions had originated. More than this, although
SCAP could enforce a revolution in certain social arrangements,
it could not change the country's underlying economic conditions, particularly the relative factor supplies available to Japanese enterprise in the post-war world. Capital was even scarcer
than before the war; large-scale entrepreneurship was still
confined to a narrow range of undertakings; access to supplies of

raw materials and foodstuffs was impeded by territorial changes
and the loss of markets; and Japanese technology had fallen
further behind that of the West. At the same time, the over-
population of the countryside and the growth in the population
as a whole meant that at a moment when economic opportunities had been reduced, a great mass of workers was seeking employment. It was evident, moreover, that during the next decade
their numbers would increase at a formidable rate. In such circumstances the new institutions were unlikely to thrive unless
they proved to be malleable to the pressure of economic necessity. It was fortunate, for the success of the innovations, that
SCAP was soon compelled, by a turn in international affairs, to
abandon its preoccupation with reform in favour of a realistic
concern with economic rehabilitation. The change in policy
made it possible for the Japanese the more easily to adapt the
institutional innovations to the needs of their economy. Far from
being a betrayal of liberal and democratic principles, this was in
fact a condition of their survival. By the middle 1950s the economy was operating in a fashion never anticipated by those responsible for the reforms. Yet several of the innovations, though
much modified, had not only survived but had taken root. In
certain branches of her life Japan will continue to bear the
impress of the American reforms. This is particularly true of
industrial relations.

Before the war the system of industrial relations in Japan differed greatly from that in Western countries. The wage system,
when viewed from the standpoint of European or American
practice, presented many peculiar features. Legislative and
administrative measures for the protection of workers and the
establishment of social security were a generation behind those
of Great Britain. Western industrialists damaged by Japanese
competition, and social reformers affronted by the relatively low
standard of life of the Japanese workers, raised charges of 'social
dumping' against Japan and justified discrimination against the
Japanese export trade on those grounds. They usually neglected
to notice that the Japanese workers were far better off than those
of any other Asian country, and they failed to realize that many
of the conditions which they deplored had been commonplaces
in Europe fifty years earlier.

The relative backwardness of Japan in this sphere should not have been surprising. Japanese industrialism made little advance before the beginning of the present century, and even in 1913 the number of workers in factories with 5 or more employees was less than a million. At that time, except in the cotton industry, Japan was only at the beginning of her career as a modern industrial country. Seventeen years later there were still less than 2 million factory operatives out of a total industrial labour force of 4¾ millions.[1] The rapid development of the 1930s raised the number of 'factory' workers to nearly 3 millions and the total industrial labour force (excluding building workers) to nearly 6½ millions in 1937. Yet even then, as these figures suggest, most of the workers were employed in very small workplaces, and a high proportion of those engaged in the manufacturing and service industries, as well as in agriculture, consisted of self-employed or of unpaid family workers. This provided an uncongenial environment for the rise of modern systems of industrial relations.

Nearly all the great increase in the working population after 1900 had been absorbed by manufactures, commerce, and the service trades, but in 1936 agriculture, forestry, and fishing still occupied some 14 millions out of a total working force of 32 millions. In these primary industries income a head compared very unfavourably with that in large-scale manufacturing industry, and the disparity had tended to increase.

There was, therefore, a constant downward pressure, accentuated during the agricultural depression of the 1930s, upon the industrial labour market. A considerable proportion of the urban workers still regarded themselves as only temporarily engaged in industry. The young women who made up the greater part of the labour force in the textile mills were recruited from peasant families and returned to their homes after two or three years' service. Many of the urban male workers were seasonally or temporarily employed in industry. In periods of recession, or when the demand for labour from the manufacturing sector was increasing only slowly, they flowed into the low-paid service industries or back into agriculture. The permanent wage-earning class thus constituted a relatively small proportion of the total working population.

[1] 'Factories' in this context are workplaces with 5 workers and over. In 1930 there were only 1,300,000 workers in manufacturing establishments with 50 or more employees.

O

A corollary of this occupational structure was that, although underemployment or disguised unemployment was characteristic of Japan as of other underdeveloped countries, by the standards of highly industrialized societies the incidence of the wholly unemployed to the total number of wage-earners remained very low. This is not a statistical delusion; it corresponds to a reality which is not difficult to explain. Many of the unpaid family workers were ready to take up wage employment when business was brisk, returning to their former status in times of depression. Women workers formed an important constituent of this group, and it was observed that the 'female participation rate' (i.e. the ratio of women at work to the total number of women of working age) varied widely over short periods. In the second place, the lack of a strongly organized labour market meant that those who could not find employment in the larger firms, or temporary workers discharged from such firms during periods of recession, readily accepted jobs at lower rates of wages in the small-scale manufacturing industries and the service trades. In other words, there was a large field of employment where wages could be forced down to the equilibrium rate. These conditions persisted into the post-war period, although, as we shall see, they have lately been modified.

The Japanese occupational structure may seem strange to those familiar only with industrialized Britain of the twentieth century, where the agricultural labour force has been reduced to only 4 per cent of the whole. But it was characteristic of every country during the period of early industrialization. As long as these conditions existed—and the most highly industrialized societies have passed through them—the growth of trade unions and the rise of modern systems of welfare and industrial relations were bound to encounter serious obstacles. Memories are short, but British critics of Japan at that time might well have recalled that although factory legislation in Great Britain had a long history, it was not until the end of the first decade of this century that a beginning was made with a system of public regulation of wages, that the State did not intervene to limit the hours of work of adult miners until 1908, and that a few years before the First World War the number of trade unionists in Great Britain was only 2½ millions.

In Japan fundamental economic causes were reinforced by

others of a social and political character. Japan had no tradition of political democracy or liberalism, and social relations were governed by concepts of mutual obligation and of loyalty to superiors derived from a so-called 'feudal' past. The very idea of individual rights was a Western importation, and the family group accepted far-reaching obligations for the welfare of its members in return for the deference which it received from them. This was not a soil where militant trade unionism could flourish. Western observers of Japanese industry were sometimes dismayed at the restrictions imposed even by the more beneficent employers upon the lives of their workers, for example, the girls housed in the dormitories of the textile mills. They did not always realize that personal liberty was a luxury to which the Japanese seldom aspired. Again, the unsatisfactory workplaces and long hours that existed in many Japanese manufacturing industries were severely censured by observers who were not conscious that, bad as the conditions might be, they usually represented an improvement over those found in the depressed farming areas from which the workers came. It is significant that the worst conditions were to be found in the very small workplaces which bore the imprint of the pre-industrial society.

Workers' organizations first became of some importance during the years immediately after the First World War. The comparatively liberal attitude of the government during that period and the influence of foreign example helped to foster the growth of trade unions. The establishment of the International Labour Organization also lent some support, for the government was induced to nominate labour delegates from among union leaders. It was at this time that a central organization, the Japan Federation of Labour (*Sodomei*), was founded. But leadership was mainly in the hands of intellectuals who concerned themselves with rival political ideologies rather than with the immediate interests of their members. Consequently, although membership grew from 100,000 in 1923 to 370,000 in 1931, the movement did little to increase the bargaining power of the workers. After the Manchurian incident, it was split asunder by political disunity and declined further when, in the middle 1930s, the government abandoned its policy of toleration. With the outbreak of the Sino-Japanese War in 1937, the right-wing trade unions gave up the right to strike and the left-wing unions were suppressed. Membership declined steeply from the maximum of 420,000 reached in 1936. Finally, in July 1940 the government dissolved all independent labour organizations. This was the end of Japanese trade unionism as a wholly indigenous movement. Its achievement had been insignificant. Membership never attained more than 5 per cent of the total industrial labour force. Only among the seamen and the transport workers had effective organizations existed. The right of collective bargaining had been conceded only in a very few instances, and standard rates of wages embodied in agreements were almost unknown. The unions had never sought to develop friendly society functions which had been so prominent in the activities of British trade unions.

In these circumstances the determination of wages was left largely to individual contracts between employer and worker, and a wide diversity of practice existed. For example, the female employees in the cotton mills were engaged according to the terms of contracts signed with their parents. These contracts provided that for the period of service part of the wages should be sent to the families, part should be paid to the girls as pocket money, and the balance settled when the girls left. The girls were housed and fed by the employers and a small deduction from wages was made for this accommodation. In all branches of industry the workers' remuneration was made up of contractual wages, biannual bonuses, and special payments in money or in kind, but the practice of firms varied widely in regard to the share of each of these constituents in the total payment. Even the wage constituent itself was not to be considered as 'a rate for the job'. In every industry it was made up, in varying proportions, of a basic wage together with payments for length of service, age, personal character, and family responsibilities. These peculiarities of the wage structure will be discussed later in more detail, for they have been carried into the post-war world. Another characteristic of industrial employment in pre-war Japan was the allowance paid on retirement or on dismissal for other than disciplinary reasons. This was a symptom of the paternalism that mitigated the weakness of the wage-earners' bargaining position. It was associated with a reluctance to discharge workers (at any rate those regarded as 'established') in periods of bad trade, a reluctance that was often responsible for the over-staffing of firms, as judged by Western standards.

Government regulation played a very modest part in labour relations and working conditions. The first Factory Act, passed in 1911, was designed to protect women and young persons. Its chief provision, namely the abolition of all-night work for females, did not come into operation until 1929. Even so, many small workplaces (at first those with less than 15 workers and later those with less than 10) were outside its scope. Other measures of protection included limitations on the hours of underground mine-workers, regulations concerning safety and hygiene in factories, certain safeguards for seamen, and workmen's compensation for accidents in building and civil engineering. Shortly after the First World War a National Health Insurance Scheme on the British model was introduced, and in 1936 a law was passed to make the payment of retirement allowances at a certain rate compulsory over a substantial part of industry. On the eve of the Second World War, Japan still lacked unemployment insurance, the public regulation of wages, and official conciliation or arbitration machinery for dealing with industrial disputes. To the large sector of industry composed of small and medium workplaces, the protective legislation either did not apply at all or was unenforceable.[2] With the outbreak of the war it fell into abeyance over the whole of industry.

THE IMPACT OF THE OCCUPATION

When the Occupation began an official apparatus for social welfare and workers' organization for fostering the interests of labour scarcely existed. The authorities addressed themselves at once to filling these institutional gaps, and the measures which they caused to be introduced very soon transformed this part of Japan's economic life. The policy was embodied in three new laws, the Trade Union Act and the Labour Relations Adjustment Act of 1946 and the Labour Standards Act of 1947. The content of these Acts, and their subsequent amendments, must be briefly described.[3] The first of them, which was modelled on the American Wagner Act, gave workers the right to organize, to bargain collectively with their employers, and to take strike action. The only wage-earners to whom these rights were not accorded consisted of certain limited classes of public servants.

---

[2] Cf. I. Ayusawa, 'The Labour Problem in Japan', *Japan Q.*, vol. 1, no. 1, pp. 104–5.
[3] See Min. Lab., *Japan Lab. Code* (1953) and *Japan Lab. YB.* (various issues).

Discriminatory acts by employers against workers who formed
trade unions, and refusal by employers to bargain with union
representatives, were prohibited under penalties. This law, and
also the Labour Relations Adjustment Act, provided for the
establishment of machinery for bargaining. A National Labour
Relations Board and forty-six Prefectural Boards were set up
with powers to mediate and arbitrate in industrial disputes.
These Boards were tripartite in membership, consisting of an
equal number of workers', employers', and public representatives. Finally, the Labour Standards Law attempted to establish
in Japan the employment standards embodied in the conventions
and recommendations of the ILO. Among many detailed provisions, this legislation limited the hours of work of adult males as
well as of women and young persons, and it prescribed conditions
in regard to holidays with pay, employment in mines and dangerous occupations, factory hygiene and safety, apprenticeship and
training, accommodation in factory dormitories, the procedure
for dismissal, and overtime pay, which was to be 25 per cent
above the basic wage. In places where ten or more workers were
employed, the employers were required to draw up 'employment
regulations' by agreement with the trade unions, and these
regulations were to constitute a legal standard with which the
employers had to conform. Heavy penalties were imposed for
breaches of this law, and a system of inspection was devised.
Other enactments dealt with unemployment benefits, industrial
health insurance, and compensation for accidents. A Ministry
of Labour was set up in 1947. So, in two years, the Occupation
authorities with the help of the native bureaucracy conferred
on Japan, hitherto notoriously backward in labour relations, a
labour code in accord with the most advanced standards of
Western nations. It is important to consider whether these innovations were as revolutionary in practice as in law.

The immediate consequences were indeed remarkable. Between the end of the war and December 1946 the number of
trade unionists rose from none to nearly 5 millions. By the end
of 1948 there were nearly 34,000 trade unions with a total
membership of 6,677,000.[4] The unions almost at once achieved
considerable bargaining strength, for not only did they enjoy the

---

[4] Ayusawa, p. 113. For statistical data about Japanese labour see Min. Lab., *Yb.
Lab. Statist.*

favour of the Occupation authorities but they also found that managements, demoralized by war, Occupation, and inflation were in no shape to resist the most extravagant demands. The leaders, many of whom had been imprisoned during the war, were strongly influenced by socialist, syndicalist, or Communist ideas. In a number of instances they wrested management functions from the employers and actually seized control over the plants. Sometimes the breakdown of management left the unions to take charge of the employment, dismissal, and discipline of the workers. At the centre leadership was mostly in the hands of men preoccupied with political aims. The pre-war All-Japan General Federation of Labour (*Sodomei*) was revived and was dominated by the right-wing socialists. A rival organization, the All-Japan Congress of Industrial Labour Organizations (*Sanbetsu*), was formed and this passed under the control of Communists. The majority of the unions were affiliated to one or other of these bodies, but there were some important independent organizations.

This period of extreme militancy was short-lived. SCAP soon took alarm at the monster to which its policies had given birth and in February 1947 it intervened to prohibit a general strike. When the cold war began in 1948 enthusiasm for democratic reform noticeably cooled. The newly won privileges of the Japanese workers were, therefore, curtailed. In July 1948 the rights of collective bargaining and striking were withdrawn from civil servants, and three Commissioners appointed by the Cabinet were authorized to fix terms and conditions of employment in the public service. At the same time workers in public corporations, including those on the national railways, though still allowed to bargain collectively, were prohibited from striking. Compulsory conciliation and arbitration were introduced to deal with disputes that involved these classes of workers. Later the employees of the local authorities and local public enterprises were covered by similar regulations. Henceforth, as a result of these changes, trade unions from a legal standpoint could be classified under three headings: first, those operating in private industry, which came under the Trade Union Law; secondly, those formed of employees in public corporations, which were governed by the Public Corporations and National Enterprise Labour Relations Law (or by a similar law for local enterprises);

and thirdly, civil service trade unions which were governed by
the National (or Local) Public Service Law. In 1962 nearly 70
per cent of the trade union membership was covered by unions
in the first category.[5]

In 1949 and 1950 the labour movement received another setback as a result of the deflation that accompanied the application
of the Dodge Plan. Small firms in particular suffered financially
and many trade unions organized among their employees came
to an end. In the large firms management began to regain its
former bargaining power. At the same time the government tried
to curtail the political activities of the trade unions, and its
emergency powers for dealing with general strikes were strengthened. Then, on the outbreak of the Korean War, Communists
were purged from key positions in industry and government. The
result was that the number of trade unionists fell steeply; in 1951
it was 5,690,000, about a million less than at the peak in 1948.
The number of unions also declined, chiefly through the disappearance of very small organizations. Meanwhile, at the centre of
the movement, considerable changes had taken place. The two
national federations (*Sodomei* and *Sanbetsu*), which had co-
operated together in the late 1940s, dissolved their liaison
council (*Zenroren*). The *Sanbetsu* suffered from internal disagree-
ments, and a new organization, composed of left-wing members of *Sodomei* and certain dissident groups of *Sanbetsu*, combined to form the *Sohyo* (General Council of Trade Unions of
Japan).

After 1951 a slight recovery in the number of trade unions
and of trade unionists began. By 1954 there were over 31,000
trade unions with nearly 6 million members. Yet since the industrial labour force had increased during the previous five years,
the proportion of industrial employees organized in trade unions
was lower in 1954 than in 1948. As industrial growth proceeded
the recovery in membership was accelerated. In 1957 membership rose above its former peak and by June 1964 it amounted to
nearly 9¾ millions. In that year, when the number of 'unit
unions' reached 51,450, about 36 per cent of all wage and salary
earners in non-agricultural occupations were organized.[6]

[5] Japan Inst. of Lab., *Japan Lab. B.*, Mar. 1963, p. 5.
[6] For trade union statistics, see *Yb. Lab. Statist.*, and Japan Inst. of Lab., *Japan Lab. B.* (monthly).

At the centre there was a succession of changes in organization which were related mainly to changes in political aims, especially the attitude taken by rival groups towards the Peace Treaty of 1952 and subsequently to the foreign policy pursued by the Japanese government. The *Sohyo* remained the largest body, but there were dissensions among its members as the political pre-occupations of its leaders increased. In 1953 a split occurred, and some right-wing unions, including those that had formed the more conservative section of *Sodomei*, established a new federation called *Zenro Kaigi* which wished to concentrate on industrial rather than on political aims. Subsequently *Zenro* extended its influence. It was joined in 1959 by a group of unions (*Zenkanko*) formed by workers in government employment and in public corporations who seceded from unions affiliated to *Sohyo*. Politically *Zenro* is now associated with the Democratic-Socialist Party, while *Sohyo* remains a powerful buttress of the left-wing socialists. In April 1962, after much internal dissension, *Zenro* was reorganized into a new federation called *Domei Kaigi*. In the summer of 1963 *Sohyo* accounted for about 45 per cent and *Domei Kaigi* for about 14 per cent of the total trade union membership; the remainder was found in a number of smaller national federations or in independent unions.[7]

During this period the attitude of the government towards the labour movement and industrial welfare underwent a considerable change. In 1952, as soon as Japan was again free to order her own affairs, the labour codes came under fire and a demand arose in certain business quarters for a drastic revision of the legislation of 1946 and 1947.[8] After the middle 1950s the mounting industrial prosperity prevented the attack from developing. But in 1963, with the prospect of more difficult times ahead, the government turned a colder eye on the unions. Measures were considered for the imposition of more stringent rules for union registration, the banning of union membership in the case of government administrative employees, the transference to the Prime Minister's Office of control over the conditions of employment of government employees, and the restriction of the issues subject to collective bargaining. Whether the legal foundations

---

[7] *Japan Lab. B.*, Mar. 1964, p. 6.
[8] Cf. Japan Fed. of Employers' Assocs, *On Present Conditions of the Labour Movement in Japan* (1953), p. 2 and *passim*.

of the unions will actually be assailed in this way remains uncertain, but the fact that these suggestions have been made indicates the extent to which they remain dependent on the government's favour. The national federation of trade unions, in their concentration on political activities, and on the promulgation of wage demands, have hitherto paid little attention to the factors that must ultimately determine their strength, namely the organization of the labour market and of the unions themselves, and only now are they beginning to show serious concern with such matters. Yet in view of the origins of the movement, it is not surprising that it should have been distracted by politics. The power of the State had to be invoked to bring these organizations into existence, and the new trade union movement, in its central organization, was compelled to direct its attention to the task of ensuring that government authority continued to be exerted in a way that favoured its interests.

It is evident that the original principle that informed the Occupation measures was drastically modified in its application. The policy of SCAP had rested on the proposition that the growth of a liberal democracy and the restraint of militant nationalism required the presence of institutions that derived their driving force from the mass of the people. By insisting on the right of collective bargaining SCAP hoped that the decisions on wages and working conditions could be reached in ways that did not necessitate active intervention by the State. But the Occupation authority itself had to intervene to protect the economy from the disruption caused by strikes and to this extent its original intentions were abandoned. Since the economic basis of the unions remained weak, their position during most of the post-war period could easily be shaken by changes in their legal status, and the unions could not afford to lose sight of this danger.

Even in less fundamental ways the conduct of industrial relations continued to reflect the authoritarian origin of the movement. For instance, the tripartite Labour Relations Boards did not become, as had been expected, bodies for assisting in achieving settlements when negotiations between unions and employers had failed. On the contrary, disputes commonly came before these bodies at a very early stage and there have been few important cases which have not required their intervention.

TRADE UNION ORGANIZATION AND THE WAGE SYSTEM

The most interesting questions raised by the post-war development of Japanese labour organization relate, not to the activities
of the central federations, but to the character of the constituent
trade unions themselves and to the part they play in the wage
contract. How does the typical Japanese trade union compare
with its European counterpart? How far has the rise of the unions
affected the structure of wages and the methods of wage determination? These are among the questions with which we shall now
attempt to deal.

In Great Britain most of the trade unions fall into three categories: craft, industrial, or general workers' unions. In Japan
none of these is typical. The national unions that exist in particular industries are all associations of unions formed among workers in particular enterprises, and the 'unit unions', as they are
described in the labour statistics, are mainly of that type. Although each 'enterprise' union is normally composed of workers
in a particular firm, in the case of a multi-plant firm separate
unions are commonly organized for every plant and they are
then linked together in the organization that covers all the workers in the firm, irrespective of the 'industry' in which they are
engaged. For instance, there are separate unions for each of the
numerous plants owned by the Hitachi Engineering Company
and these form parts of an 'enterprise' union called *Hitachi
Soren*. Similarly there are nearly a thousand unions of post-office
workers which together make up the national union. The pattern
is not uniform, and sometimes the 'unit unions' are affiliated to
two or even more national bodies. The separate unions that
cover workers engaged in each of the six mines owned by the
Mitsui Mining Company are indirectly affiliated with *Tanro*
(the Miners' Federation of Japan), but they are also federated
into an enterprise-wide association, known as *Sankoren*. The
national organization of the textile workers is divided into
branches corresponding to the divisions of the textile industry
itself (cotton, wool, rayon), but each unit union draws its members from particular enterprises or plants, and in the case of
multi-plant firms they form enterprise-wide federations which
may, of course, cover several branches of the textile industry. The
'enterprise' unions are the real loci of power.[9] They naturally

[9] 'Enterprise union' is a translation of *Kigyo Betsu Kumiai*.

vary widely in size and strength, but in nearly all cases they are the bodies really responsible for the most important negotiations with employers. Even where the basic wage is settled at the national or regional level, negotiations regarding fringe benefits and bonuses, which make up a high proportion of total earnings, are conducted at the enterprise level.

The national or regional bodies to which the unions are affiliated are in most industries merely loose federations concerned primarily with giving mutual aid and with serving the political aims of the movement. It is true that *Sohyo* and *Zenro* try to formulate policies for their affiliated unions, and every year, in the 'Spring Offensive', they announce demands for the workers as a whole and select the unions or groups of unions which are to act as the spearpoints of the attack. Their action may have some effect on the temper of the unions, but the central federations, like the national associations of 'enterprise' unions in individual industries, seem able to exercise comparatively little authority over their constituents, each of which plays for its own hand and reaches such accommodation with the employers as seems practicable. While the large 'enterprise' unions employ a considerable number of full-time paid officers, the national bodies have small staffs and receive only a modest share of the dues collected from members. Yet, although this is the general pattern, there are important exceptions. Where the boundaries of an enterprise coincide with those of an industry (as in the national railways), bargaining at the centre does in fact occur, and since the unions in public enterprise are among the strongest and most militant in Japan, the exception is of greater significance than is always realized by Western students. Unions in public enterprise have not infrequently taken the lead in the annual 'Spring Offensive'.[10] Industrial bargaining machinery has also been set up for shipping and coal-mining.

The headquarters of the 'enterprise' unions, and the premises of their local branches, are usually to be found at the plants themselves. In the early post-war period the firms often provided buildings and furniture for the use of the unions, and it is still common for union dues to be collected by the employers in the form of deductions from their workers' wages. It not infrequently

---

[10] The important role played by unions of workers in public enterprises may help to explain the political preoccupations of the central federations.

happens that the more successful trade union organizers are taken on as personnel officers by the firms with which they formerly conducted negotiations. In these circumstances it might have been expected that the leaders would be amenable to pressure from the management, and it may be forgiven if Western observers have sometimes detected little difference between these unions and the 'company unions' of the United States. This, however, would be to misinterpret the facts. It has already been shown that in the early post-war period the unions, far from being subservient to management, often dominated it; indeed, members of the salaried staff and even of the higher management sometimes joined the unions. The financial assistance given by the firm was then deemed to be in accordance with the policy of the government and the Occupation authorities. By the middle 1950s management had regained its traditional functions, but the unions remained, in general, effective and independent bargaining bodies.

The explanation of this paradoxical situation is to be sought partly in the social traditions and the economic structure of Japan, and partly in the circumstances in which unions came to be formed. Paternalism, or rather authoritarianism, was always a characteristic of Japanese industrial relations, and the introduction of Western institutions has not destroyed, though it has weakened, older habits of loyalty to superiors and obligations to inferiors. If did not therefore seem extraordinary to the Japanese that when the government prescribed a policy of encouraging trade unionism, firms should readily follow this lead. The organizers of the new unions for their part were faced with the task of creating unions from among workers unfamiliar with any of the forms of labour organization which had grown up gradually in the West. Employees regarded their interests not as coincident with those of fellow workers in the same craft or industry but as common only to those employed by the same firm, and the lack of labour mobility between firms strengthened their disposition to take such a view. The structure of Japanese industry itself was congenial to this type of organization. In the large-scale industries production was concentrated in a relatively small number of great enterprises with a wide diversity of interests while in the numerous small and medium-sized firms personal relationships between workers and employers were very close. Many of the workers in both classes of industry were immigrants from agriculture and had little conception of the common interests of industrial wage-earners as a whole.

These features of Japanese industrial relations exerted a strong influence over bargaining methods, and the structure of wages. At the outset SCAP urged the formation of joint councils of workers and managers, and the National Labour Relations Board, established by the Labour Relations Adjustment Law, recommended that councils of this kind should be set up as institutions for collective bargaining within each firm. These joint councils became very common, and they continued to play an important part in industrial relations. In this way negotiations between employers and workers, whether through these councils or through less formal machinery, became located at the level of the enterprise. In the large firms discussions are conducted between professional union negotiators and the personnel officers of the company. The decisions reached at the centre apply to the workers in all the establishments owned by the same firm. A corollary of this centralization is that there has been no growth of works committees nor of the shop-stewards movement. All disputes are handled at the headquarters of the enterprise.

Western observers are inclined to view the 'enterprise' union as a *pis aller*, a symptom of Japan's economic immaturity. This condescension is unjustified. When production takes place under such varying conditions as are found in many Japanese industries, the 'enterprise' union is the only obvious method of organization. Further, for a society that is intent upon rapid economic development rather than upon establishing uniform conditions of welfare among its working population, it has considerable merits. It may even have lessons for ourselves. The Japanese system at least enables the trade unions to avoid the jurisdictional and demarcation disputes familiar in British industry, and there are shrewd students of industrial relations who are persuaded of the advantages of decentralizing labour negotiations in this country.

In many old-fashioned British industries elaborate voluntary procedures for handling disputes were worked out long ago. These often involve agreements to refer outstanding questions to conciliation boards presided over by an impartial outsider, and even in the last resort to outside arbitration. In Japan such procedures are entirely lacking, except where the law has enforced their adoption, for the Japanese, both employers and employed, appear to be hostile to the intervention of outsiders. This is rather surprising in view of the important place that intermediaries occupy in other branches of social life. To some extent the nature of the issues that are the subject of negotiations may explain this reluctance. Collective bargaining, as introduced since the war, has not been concerned with the establishment of principles of employment, nor with the determination of the 'rate for the job'. Its main purpose has been to interpret, in the context of a particular enterprise, rights already conferred by law and to ensure that these are accorded. Under this head the formulation of rules of employment for the enterprise, as required by the Labour Standards Law, has been a leading activity of collective bargaining. A secondary purpose is to modify or enlarge benefits traditionally given by particular employers.[11]

Even before the war a distinction was drawn by Japanese firms between the permanent and the temporary labour force. The first group enjoyed the full benefits of a paternalistic system, including considerable security of employment. The temporary workers, on the other hand, were not regarded as being members of the enterprise. This distinction has been preserved in the post-war period. Unions have been concerned almost exclusively with the welfare of the permanent or established labour force in each enterprise. In this way they hoped to secure benefits for their members (namely the established workers) which management would be reluctant to accord to every employee. The success of the unions in this aim has naturally induced the managements to increase the number of their temporary employees, and these have been the chief victims of post-war instability. It follows that while there are few 'closed shops' in Japanese industrial establishments, 'union shops', that is to say, shops in which all *permanent* workers are obliged to become union members, are common.

The complications of the traditional Japanese wage system have been maintained in the new era. Before the war, apart from the basic wage which was related to the nature of the job performed, the following components of monthly earnings were distinguished: age allowance, education allowance, length-of-service allowance, attendance allowance, family allowance, housing

[11] S. B. Levine, *Industrial Relations in Post-War Japan* (1958), chs. v and vi.

allowance, transport allowance, cost-of-living allowance, incentives payments, and several others. In addition, workers normally received bonuses at *O-bon*[12] and New Year, and they were entitled to allowances on retirement or dismissal for reasons of bad trade. The proportion of each constituent in the total earnings varied from firm to firm, from worker to worker, and from time to time. The rise of trade unions and the establishment of collective bargaining have not disturbed this system. If anything, the complications have increased. The inflation of the early post-war years led to a rise in cost-of-living allowances, and so to a decrease in the proportions of earnings provided by the basic wage. The trend persisted, despite the relative stability of prices, throughout the 1950s. An inquiry by the Ministry of Labour showed that over the period 1954 to 1961 the ratio of special cash payments a year (mainly of biannual bonuses) to contractual average monthly earnings rose from year to year. Between 1958 and 1962 the ratio varied consistently with the size of the establishment, as the following figures show. The fact that in the year of recession, 1962, the ratio fell in the large and medium establishments but increased in the smaller establishments, is a symptom of the change in the labour market presently to be examined.

Ratio of Special Cash Payments a Year to Contractual Average Monthly Earnings
(Manufacturing Industry)

Size of establishment (No. of workers)	1958	1961	1962
500 or more . . .	2·9	3·6	3·5
100–499 . . .	2·2	3·2	3·0
30–99 . . .	1·4	1·9	2·0
5–29 . . .	0·8	1·4	1·5

Source: Min. Lab.

The trade unions have accepted this wage structure. In their negotiations they have, of course, been intimately concerned with actual earnings. In particular, during the years of inflation they tried to ensure that wages kept in line with increases in the cost of living. They aimed at ensuring that the family needs of the

[12] The summer festival.

workers would be given weight in wage determination. Yet while they might try to influence the relative importance of the several constituents in the wage, they have made no serious attempt to alter the system itself. In some firms they have bargained with the employers for increases in the aggregate sum paid in wages to the employees as a whole, and they have then shared out this sum among the several groups in their membership. The impact of 'enterprise' trade unionism on the traditional wage system is responsible for some of the peculiarities in the nature of the collective bargaining. Wage negotiations are not usually set going by periodical presentation of claims for increases in standard rates, as happens in the West, but they are directed in turn to each of the numerous constituents of the total wage and so form an almost continuous series.[13]

The Japanese have had their share of labour troubles during the post-war period. The number of man-days lost through strikes or lock-outs has fluctuated widely from year to year. It reached a maximum of 15 millions in 1952, when there were prolonged stoppages in the coal-mining and the electricity industries. In the years of deflation 1954–5 there was a fall to between 3 and 4 millions, but later there was an upward tendency and since 1957 the number has ranged between 5 and 6 millions a year.[14] This is a high figure by European standards. Most of the strikes have been short, partly because of the lack of large strike funds but mainly because of the readiness of 'enterprise' unions to reach compromises with their employers even in cases where the strikes began as national or industrial disputes. The chief exception is to be found in the coal-mining industry where there have been several long and bitterly fought struggles that have involved the whole of the industry.

The future is uncertain. The Japanese trade union movement depended in the early post-war period on strong and comprehensive laws introduced by the Occupation authorities. But its economic basis long remained weak, for many of the conditions that frustrated development in the pre-war days persisted, namely, the multiplicity of small establishments and the in-

---

[13] Japan Fed. of Employers' Assocs, *Analysis of Personnel Practices in the Principal Industries of Japan* (1953), *passim*; and All-Japan Cotton Spinners' Assoc., *Labour Situation of the Cotton Spinning Industry in Japan* (1955), pp. 10–22.

[14] *Yb. Lab. Statist. & Research, 1961*, pp. 380–90.

P

creasing supply of unorganized labour in search of employment. The decentralization of authority was extreme, and effective action on an industrial or national scale difficult to organize. It may be expected, however, that as labour becomes scarcer and competition for jobs from the unorganized sector less keen, the unions will gain an accession of strength. They are now advocating the adoption of a system of national wage bargaining and the establishment of a legal minimum wage for all workers. A Minimum Wage Law was indeed passed in 1959 and by 1962 a minimum wage had been fixed for some 2 million workers.[15] But this minimum has been very low and the unions are dissatisfied with the procedure. The central federations have now announced their policy to be the raising of wages to the European level, but how far they succeeded will depend on continued economic prosperity as well as on their own bargaining power in industrial disputes and their influence over government policy. It seems probable that if the unions are to deploy their power effectively they will have to make fundamental changes in organization and procedure. It will be ironical if at a time when the present trade union organization is under attack in Great Britain and other Western countries and when many critics advocate a decentralization of bargaining procedure, the Japanese trade union movement should incline towards the European model. If the Japanese were persuaded by the weakening of competitive forces in the labour market to consider the introduction of a national wages or national incomes policy, the new trend would doubtless be considerably strengthened.

THE CHARACTER OF THE LABOUR MARKET

It has already become apparent that the system of industrial relations has been profoundly influenced by certain peculiarities in the labour market, and these must now be examined in some detail. The outstanding characteristic of that market, in British eyes, is the extent of wage differentials. The wages of particular classes of workers vary widely from firm to firm even when the establishments are broadly comparable in size and equipment.

---

[15] Most of the minimum wages so far fixed under the new law have been settled by agreement between unions and employers, and only in one case, coal-mining, has the minimum been fixed by government edict (*Japan Lab. B.*, Feb. 1963, pp. 4–5).

Within particular industries they also differ according to location, and within firms according to the age and length of service of employees. Over industry as a whole the contrasts are very sharp indeed, for the diversity of technical methods and the conditions of labour supply combine to produce wide disparities between the wages paid by firms in different size-groups.

First, let us consider the differences based on age and years of service. These are very large. For example, the Ministry of Labour's *Survey of the Wage Structure* showed that in 1960 male employees in the iron and steel rolling mills received (as contracted monthly earnings exclusive of bonuses and special payments) 15,000 yen at the age of 20, 20,000 yen at the age of 25, and 44,000 yen at 45. Machine-tool operatives (male) at the age of 45 received about twice the wages of those aged 25. The relationship shown in these examples is fairly typical and it may be asserted, without much exaggeration, that wages vary with age rather than with function.[16]

In the second place there are the wage disparities among firms of different sizes; these are the chief symptom of what is known as the 'dual economy'. The disparities can be attributed only in part to differences in the age composition of the labour force. It is true that small firms tend to employ a disproportionately large number both of young workers and of workers beyond the prime of life. But even when comparisons are made between workers of the same age and experience, the differences remain; for example, in 1960 rolling mill workers of the same age in firms employing from 10 to 29 persons received only two-thirds of the wages of those in firms employing 1,000 persons and over.[17]

[16] A large firm of motor-component manufacturers provided the following data about its structure of wages in 1963:

Average Monthly Contractual Wages in Yen

Age	Males	Females
15–22	13,000	12,000
25	20,400	16,300
30	27,000	20,000

The biannual bonuses amounted to the equivalent of five months' salary for all groups of workers.

[17] Data supplied by Min. Lab.

Since the origin and extent of these differences have been mis-understood the problem must be considered and analysed.

The wage disparities between firms of different sizes are a comparatively recent phenomenon. At the beginning of the century—at a time when large-scale enterprises were few—they were very small and it was only after the First World War that they became at all conspicuous. Since then they have fluctuated with changes in economic conditions. During the Second World War, when all types of labour were scarce and wages were sub-jected to official control, the differences narrowed, and there was little change in the immediate post-war period because of the slow recovery in the large-scale industries. After 1950 they widened again and by the middle 1950s they were probably greater than before the war. In 1957 average wages in very small firms (4–9 employees) were probably only about 30 per cent of those in firms with a thousand employees and over, and even medium-sized firms (200–499 persons) paid wages that were only 65 per cent of those in the largest size-group. Subsequently the trend was reversed. The change was especially noticeable in 1962 when wages in the small and medium establishments rose much faster than those in large establishments; for ex-ample, the increases gained in the 5–29 group were 25 per cent over the previous year, compared with only 6 or 7 per cent in establishments with 500 employees or more. The dis-parities are still very wide compared with those in Western countries, but they are narrower than they were in the middle 1950s.

A sample survey by the Ministry of Labour in April 1962 showed that disparities in wages among industries were also diminishing. For example, the rate of wage increases in the well-paid industries over the previous year (in finance, insurance, electric power, and other public utilities) was much smaller than that in the hitherto badly paid industries, such as food and textile manufacture. Women textile workers, who used to be very low on the wage ladder, have moved up, partly because of the greater opportunities for employment provided by other industries, notably the manufacture of light electrical apparatus. Between April 1961 and April 1962 the average wage in food manufacture rose by 18·9 per cent and in textiles by 23·6 per cent. In finance and insurance the average increase amounted to only 11·4 per cent and in gas, water, and electricity to only 9·3 per cent.[18]

The existence of the differentials and the changes in their magnitude over time can be attributed partly to the nature of the labour market and partly to the distribution of capital among various types of firms. When the development of large-scale manufacturing industries began, firms were faced with a shortage of adequately-trained labour, for workers in the existing small-scale industries were not necessarily of the type required and there was still some reluctance to enter factory employment. The earlier attempts to overcome this shortage were unsuccessful, and by the inter-war period employers had come to the conclusion that the most effective means was to offer employment on good conditions to school-leavers who would submit to training and to factory discipline. They not only paid relatively high wages but they also provided many fringe benefits and gave an informal undertaking that the job, once secured, would be permanent. This was the origin of what came to be known as the 'life-long engagement' system under which workers received an implied guarantee against dismissal, and wages rose with seniority and length of employment. The 'life-long engagement' system has sometimes been attributed to the transference into modern industrialism of social traditions that governed the relations of master and apprentice, but while it would be rash to conclude that vestigial attitudes had no influence on the evolution of the new system, the facts do not bear out the view that these were its primary cause.[19] Indeed, in the early Japanese factories, few traces of it are to be found, except among the staff workers. For many years the rate of labour turnover was extremely high in all classes of industry and indeed, as we have seen, in the textile factories (in which the majority of the industrial workers up to the 1930s were employed) the average working life of the girl operatives was very short. It was the labour requirements of the expanding large-scale industries rather than ancient social tradition that brought about a wide extension of the system.

The result was the appearance of a dichotomy in the labour market. In the large firms the labour force was recruited almost

---

[18] In 1958 34 per cent of all wage-earners had a monthly wage of less than 10,000 yen; in 1962 the proportion was only 12·5 per cent.

[19] Cf. K. Taira, 'The Characteristics of Japanese Labour Markets', *Economic Development and Cultural Change*, Jan. 1962.

entirely from carefully selected school-leavers, who, in the case of males, normally remained for the whole of their working life with the firm that originally engaged them. On the other hand, the labour force in the small and medium establishments, both in manufacturing industry and in the service trades, was supplied from the army of immigrants from the countryside, including school-leavers who could not get jobs in the large firms. Offers of permanent work for the bulk of the employees in such establishments could not be effective, since the mortality rate of such businesses was high.[20] Persons discharged from these establishments could not find work in the large factories, except perhaps as temporary workers to whom the privileges of the permanent class did not apply, and they therefore competed for jobs in the same sector of the labour market. The small firms were more vulnerable to recessions than large firms, and they at all times faced a more highly competitive market for their goods. Such of them as acted for sub-contractors for the big firms were weak bargainers *vis-à-vis* their customers. Their prices, therefore, were highly flexible and in the circumstances of an abundant labour supply the competitive pressure was easily communicated to wages.

It is not difficult to explain why the dichotomy became more pronounced after the Second World War. The change in the structure of industry was associated with the growth in the demand for new types of skill, and the employers in large-scale industries were forced to strengthen the inducements needed to attract school-leavers of ability and to retain the workers once they had been trained, especially as the industrial sector was growing very fast. At the same time the new trade unions deployed their main strength in improving conditions in the large establishments and in preventing any influx of cheap labour into them from the unorganized market. When temporary workers (*rinji-ko*) were engaged by the large employers, they did not as a rule share in the benefits of collective bargaining and the unions remained indifferent to their lot. One may conclude then that the disparities in wages for plants of different sizes are due, first, to the existence of two distinct labour markets in Japan, separated by institutional arrangements which preclude mobility between them, and secondly, to the more highly competitive

[20] EPA, *Employment Structure and Business Fluctuations*, July 1959, p. 17.

conditions that prevail in the product-markets of the small firms as compared with those of the large firms.

The above account does not, however, provide a complete explanation. Disparities in wages in the two sectors of the economy are matched by corresponding disparities in labour productivity. The latter are associated mainly with differences in the quantity of capital a head. When Japan was launched on her career as an industrial State, capital was very scarce while labour was plentiful. It was rational, therefore, for her to select, wherever technical conditions made this possible, industries and processes which made use of labour-intensive methods. But there were certain industries in which the advantages of highly capitalistic methods were overwhelming, and these industries had to be conducted on a large scale if at all. Most of them were built up either by the State or by a few business groups to which the State granted privileges of various kinds. For many years the large establishments so created remained as exceptions in an economy still composed of multitudes of small producers, and the great firms that controlled them acquired a special position in the economy through their financial activities and their almost exclusive command over investment resources. The concentration continued even after the Second World War despite the appearance of new centres of business initiative. Without it there would have been difficulty in introducing the new technologies which made heavy demands on capital. But the result was that new investment was mainly directed into large-scale enterprises and that the disparity in labour productivity between the two sectors of the Japanese economy was increased.

These differences in productivity and in the quality and constitution of the labour force between the large-scale and the small-scale sector go far towards explaining the wage disparities. But they do not of themselves entirely account for the ability of the large firms to offer life-long employment at rates of wages that rise steadily with length of service and age in circumstances in which the employers are faced by market uncertainties. For this the reason is to be found in the cushions which enable the firms to soften the impact of economic change or, in other words, in practices which enable them to adjust their costs to market fluctuations. These cushions have already been referred to. The first consists of the fringe of casual or temporary workers who can be abruptly dismissed in times of bad trade,[21] and the second of the practice of paying a proportion of the wages in the form of special allowances, biannual bonuses, and fringe benefits which can be raised or lowered as prosperity waxes or wanes. Finally, there is the widespread use of sub-contractors (inside or outside the employer's workplace), who recruit workers from the un-organized market and give no guarantee of permanent employment or stable wages. Almost every large firm, especially in the engineering and metal industries, is surrounded by a ring of tied sub-contractors from which it obtains components on terms reflecting its superior bargaining power. These sub-contractors are, in a sense, the successors of the labour 'bosses' who were responsible for providing the employers with labour in the early days of the factory-system.[22] It is significant that in recent years the sub-contractors of the great Yawata Steel Works, itself a high-wage employer, have paid wages which amounted to only half those of the parent concern.

The change in wage trends after 1956 was the direct consequence of the appearance of new conditions in the labour market. The extremely rapid industrial growth not merely called for a great expansion in employment in large-scale manufacturing, but it also affected the small-scale sector, immediately by increasing the demands made on sub-contractors, and indirectly by raising the purchasing power of consumers for the goods and services which small-scale industry supplied. At the same time the stream of new recruits from the countryside, once considered an inexhaustible reservoir of labour, began to approach its limit. Workers in small enterprises no longer found themselves faced with an over-stocked labour market, and those who required their services were forced to bid up wages. The labour statistics illustrate these general statements. They demonstrate the steep fall in the agricultural labour force because of the great migration to industry and also the decline in the number of unpaid family

[21] According to one estimate casual workers (i.e. those employed on a day-to-day basis) and temporary workers (i.e. those employed for more than 30 days but without any long-term commitment) accounted in the late 1950s for more than a fifth of the wage-earners in the metal, machinery, electrical engineering, and transport industries. For manufacturing industry as a whole the proportion was probably about 12–15 per cent.

[22] This was not peculiar to Japan. In the early days of the factory system in England sub-contractors and butties were prominent features of many British industries.

workers and of the self-employed as they were drawn into wage employments. Between 1956 and 1961 the annual average decline in the number of self-employed amounted to 110,000 and that of unpaid family workers to 400,000. Figures relating to school-leavers are even more illuminating. In 1956 only 16 per cent of middle-school leavers who entered industry found jobs in firms with 500 workers or over, compared with 20 per cent in the 100–499 group, and 64 per cent in the 99 and under group; in 1962 the proportions were 31, 32, and 37 per cent respectively. For high-school leavers the trend was very similar.[23]

These figures serve to explain how it is that the main benefits of the enlarged demand for labour have been secured by the younger workers. These constitute the most mobile sector of the labour supply and there has been exceptionally keen competition for their services. Since large-scale industry has been taking more of them, the supply left for small and medium firms has been much reduced and employers in those size groups have been forced to raise wages very substantially.

The alteration in the wage structure is clearly a threat to the established systems of wage payment. The practice of linking earnings to seniority rather than function cannot easily be sustained when the supply of the younger and more mobile workers becomes scarce. Young workers, fully conscious of the rising demand for their labour, are beginning to rebel against the established system and the supply of such labour to individual employers has become very elastic. If industrial growth continues at a high rate the challenge will become more vigorous, and when after 1965 the absolute number of new recruits falls (as is likely to happen because of the decline in the post-war birth-rate), the old system may wither away. Some of the leading firms have already decided that the time for change has come, and they have undertaken analyses of the jobs in their factories as a prelude to instituting a modern system of wages.[24] Its establishment, however, is being delayed by opposition from the trade unions which, in general, look with disfavour on the principle of payment by results.

Other features of the labour market are also likely to be affected. If labour becomes very scarce it will hardly be possible to maintain the distinction between permanent and temporary

[23] Data from EPA.   [24] *Orient. Econ.*, July 1964, p. 519.

workers, and the employer may then lose a valuable cushion in periods of recession. Should this happen (and already many temporaries have been offered permanent jobs) the 'life-long engagement' system itself may be undermined. This change is all the more likely to occur if the pressure of international competition should require extensive structural changes in industry, for then employers would seek at all costs to increase their freedom of manœuvre. Some of them are already attempting to modify the 'life-long engagement' system despite the opposition of the trade unions, and it is not unlikely, therefore, that many of the characteristic features of the Japanese labour market will disappear in the course of the next decade. Japan in these respects will then present a less sharp contrast with other industrial countries and her labour problem will assume a form familiar in the West. The change will presumably be not unwelcome to the government, whose long-term policy is ostensibly the removal of the extreme inequalities of income in the different sectors of the economy. But it can scarcely be accomplished without disturbing social conventions that are deeply cherished; and this may give rise to conflict. On the other hand, social conventions in Japan as in other progressive countries yield readily to economic forces; and some practices, such as the 'life-long engagement' system, which have often been regarded as rooted in tradition, are found on examination to have received a wide application only in recent times.

A more difficult problem is concerned with the effect of the change on costs. Japanese wages have hitherto been very plastic, that is to say, readily responsive to changes in economic conditions. For the post-war period this is demonstrated by the check to the rise in money wages that occurred in the years of recession, 1954–5 and 1957–8. On the other hand, the recession of 1962 did not prevent a sharp rise in money wages, and it may be that that year was in some sense a turning-point in Japan's economic career. If her wages should become rigid downwards, as they are in the West, this would indeed transform the conditions under which her economy operates.

EDUCATION AND TRAINING

It has been explained that one of the factors that made possible the rapid growth of Japanese industry was the large annual flow of new recruits to the labour force. But this is obviously not a sufficient condition for industrial growth, for vast supplies of underemployed labour have existed in many countries that have failed completely to organize industrial development. Many other causes must also have been at work. Even if we consider only the supply of *manual* workers it is evident that quality as well as quantity is vital, and this consideration is of even greater moment in the case of managerial and technical personnel. Now there can be little doubt that the quality of Japanese labour from the early days of modernization has been high. Skill in diverse crafts was widely diffused even in feudal times, and the habit of industrial by-employment was common among the peasantry for centuries. Further, when modernization began, the new branches of industry and commerce could call on many people who had been trained in administration in the service both of government and of large business houses. Here was a valuable legacy from the past. The early Meiji governments realized that success in national building would depend on the quality of their people, and it is a commonplace that the educational system which they established made a vital contribution to economic development.[25]

After the Second World War the educational system was re-constituted under American guidance, and although many of the changes were bitterly criticized by Japanese educationists, one important result was the extension of the period of compulsory schooling. From 1947 a period of nine years' education became obligatory, six years in a primary school and three years in a lower secondary school. In addition, more provision was made for higher education in upper secondary schools (a three-year course), technical and other colleges, and universities. Even in 1950, before these changes had exerted much effect upon the educational equipment of the people, one-third of employed persons had received nine years or more of schooling and a tenth had received higher education, that is, twelve years or more. For males the proportion with a higher education was 13 per cent.[26] In the 1950s annual expenditure on education came to nearly 6 per cent of GNP;[27] in 1959–60 it amounted to 21 per cent of

[25] Cf. M. Shinohara, *Growth and Cycles in the Japanese Economy* (1962), pp. 96–98.
[26] Min. Ed., *Education in Japan* (1961), p. 27.
[27] For the UK the corresponding ratio was under 5 per cent.

public expenditure, local and central. At that time there were 600,000 undergraduates at universities and in addition, 80,000 students in junior colleges, where the duration of the course was two or three years. Educationally Japan has been well supplied with men of trained intelligence to tackle the complex tasks of a modern State. She has had an *élite* equipped to discharge administrative and executive functions in government, industry, and the professions, and a people literate, knowledgeable, and adaptable to new tasks.

From the middle of the Meiji era technical and commercial schools provided a flow of technicians and business executives as well as workers trained in manual or clerical skills. In addition, the old apprenticeship system still played a part in fitting craftsmen for the traditional trades, and before the end of the Meiji era a few of the large-scale enterprises introduced their own methods of training within the plant, usually a combination of classroom work with instruction in the shop. The Hitachi Company, which systematized its methods of recruiting and training skilled workers in 1910, was one of the pioneers. Other large firms followed its example and there was a considerable advance during the 1930s, when there was a rising demand for skilled labour from the metal and engineering industries. The government began actively to encourage this intra-works training in 1940, and after the Second World War systematic training within the plant became fairly common in medium firms as well as in large. All this was apart from the general education, or the instruction in domestic arts, provided for many years by employers in the textile industries for their female workers, whose factory life was short.

The importance of systematic vocational training became increasingly obvious during the later 1950s with the growth of industries that made high demands on technical competence. Moreover, it was evident by this time that the supply of workers available for training could no longer be regarded as inexhaustible and that future development would depend to an even greater extent than in the past on the quality of labour. Hence in 1958 the Vocational Training Law was passed which was intended to provide new facilities in technical training and to systematize arrangements already in existence. Public vocational training centres were set up all over the country both for skilled workers and foremen. The government also encouraged intra-firm training and provided textbooks and training facilities for instructors. Subsidies were given to co-operative vocational training schemes set up by small enterprises. These arrangements were co-ordinated with the education provided by technical schools, and formal tests of skill conducted by the Ministry of Labour were introduced for forty trades. The number of persons taking such tests rose from 31,000 in 1959 to 99,000 in 1961 and is expected to reach 150,000 a year by the end of this decade. The government's present programme provides for the training of about $1\frac{1}{2}$ million new workers by 1970 and at re-training about the same number of persons already skilled, in addition to over 400,000 foremen. This represents about one-third of the total number of workers at present employed in the industries covered.[28]

The training under this scheme is thorough. For example, a machine-tool operative, during a year at a public vocational centre, will receive about 450 hours of class work and 1,350 hours of workshop practice. For training within industry the scheme provides for a three-year course of 1,800 hours a year, divided between class work and workshop practice. Some of the class work is provided in factory schools and some in technical schools. These schemes are in active operation not only in large firms but in medium-sized firms also.

The leading firms are actively promoting the training of engineers and managers. One firm, for example, recruits trainees from the technical high schools at the age of 18, gives them two years of systematic training in the shops, and then sends them to technical colleges for a year. Those who show exceptional promise in specialized work are sent for a time to the appropriate department of a university where they sometimes act as research assistants. Another firm is accustomed to choose fifty of the best entrants each year for a specialized three-year course. Like many others it arranges for some of its technicians to spend several years abroad with the firm with which it has established technical links. Nor is it only technical training that is being encouraged. For many years observers of Japanese industry have been impressed by the high proportion of managers and directors

[28] Min. Lab., *Present Situation of Vocational Training in Japan* (1961), and personal inquiries at the Vocational Training Bureau, Min. Lab.

who have been trained in specialized institutions, such as the former Higher Commercial Schools or the Economics and Commerce Departments of the universities. Since 1955, when the Japan Industrial Training Association was organized by the Japanese Federation of Employers' Associations, a system of specialized managerial training has been introduced. In 1962 there were some 180 associations engaged in fostering management at different levels by study and training.[29] A typical example is the Japan Productivity Centre which has organized various studies in this field for the benefit of small as well as of large firms. It has sent study teams overseas and has brought foreign consultants to Japan. The Japanese have thus prepared themselves for the economic problems that lie ahead. In their business affairs they place little reliance on the inspired amateur whom even the British are beginning to distrust.

Education and training received much emphasis in the Income Doubling Plan. This proposed a large annual increase in the number of university graduates in science and engineering and also of technical-high-school graduates, the former from 29,000 in 1958 to 45,000 in 1970 and the latter from 95,000 to 180,000. The corollary of this increase in trained personnel is an expansion of expenditure on scientific and industrial research, which is to grow from 0·9 per cent of GNP in 1958 to 2 per cent in 1970.[30] A policy of providing secondary education for all was also adumbrated in the plan. This will result in raising the number of entrants to senior high schools as a proportion of junior-high-school graduates from 60 per cent in 1958 to 72 per cent in 1970.[31]

---

[29] Internat. Management Assoc. of Japan, *Materials on Management and Economy of Japan* (November 1962).

[30] Japan's expenditure on scientific and industrial research was 1·5 per cent of GNP in the early 1960s. This is a rather higher percentage than in European countries but much lower than that in Great Britain or the United States. About two-thirds of this research has been financed by industry.

[31] EPA, *New Long-Range Econ. Plan, 1961–70*, pp. 52–55; and S. Okita, *Economic Planning in Japan* (Seminar on Economic Planning, 1962), pp. 51–53.

XII

The Problem of Foreign Trade

DURING the 1930s Japan became one of the great trading nations of the world, and on the eve of the Second World War her exports were exceeded in value only by those of the United States, the United Kingdom, and Germany. At the same time she had become a great sea carrier. Her mercantile marine was the third largest in the world, and her sales of shipping services to foreigners brought in receipts sufficient to pay for nearly one-tenth of her imports. Her exports had grown sharply during a period when international trade as a whole was stagnating. Between 1929 and 1937 the volume of her exports to foreign countries rose by 83 per cent and the volume of her imports from them by 30 per cent.[1] The extreme dependence of her economy upon trade was a commonplace of economic discussion. In 1938 the ratio of imports to the national income was well over 20 per cent.[2]

Japans' trade was widely distributed, but two great regions predominated both as markets and as sources of supply. They were the Far East (the Japanese colonies and China) and the United States. In the period 1934–6 the former took 39 per cent of her exports and provided 36 per cent of her imports; the shares of the latter were 17 and 25 per cent respectively. The other most important market and source of supply consisted of the countries of South East Asia. These took 19 per cent of the exports and supplied 16 per cent of the imports.[3] Japan's trade with these several regions fell into a clearly marked pattern. She sold raw silk, canned fish, tea, and pottery to the United States, machinery and other capital goods to Manchuria and North China, and manufactured textiles and cheap miscellaneous consumption goods to a wide range of countries, especially to continental Asia and the South Seas.

Most of her imports consisted of primary products. She

---

[1] League of Nations, *Review of World Trade, 1937*, p. 41. Trade with Japanese colonies is excluded.

[2] S. Okita, *The Rehabilitation of Japan's Economy and Asia* (1956), p. 8; see also EPA *Econ. Survey, 1955–6*, p. 37.

[3] Ibid. p. 11; and *Fuji Bank B.*, Sept. 1956, pp. 15–35.

obtained her food imports (except wheat) from regions under her own control, rice from Korea and Formosa, sugar from Formosa, and soya beans from Manchuria. Eastern and Southern Asia supplied cotton, rubber, vegetable oil, mineral oil, and ores and metals, and North America raw cotton, mineral oil, wheat, steel scrap, and engineering goods, including motor vehicles and certain types of machinery. During the 1930s there had been significant changes in the importance of these regions. North America had declined relatively as a customer because of the fall in the value of raw silk exports. The Far East had become much more important to Japan's trade as a result of her heavy investment in that area and of the privileges conferred on her traders in areas that had passed under her political control.

The export trade became more highly diversified during the 1930s and in this it reflected the changes which had taken place in Japanese industry. In 1929 nearly 70 per cent of the trade of Japan Proper *with foreign countries* consisted of textiles, and her exports of metals and metal manufactures made up only 4 per cent. By 1936 the share of the latter group had risen to 14 per cent, and miscellaneous exports had also become more important. Yet textiles still provided well over half the total exports and Japan's specialization in this field, though diminished, had by no means disappeared.[4] Among the textiles themselves specialization on raw silk and cotton, though lessened by the expansion of wool, rayon, and knitted-goods exports, was still conspicuous. These two commodities were responsible for about two-thirds of the value of all textile exports.

Japan's achievement in foreign trade was a tribute to the resourcefulness of her merchants and manufacturers and to the resilience of her economy. The damaging restrictions imposed by foreign countries on imports of her manufactured goods and the chronic depression in her former chief export trade, raw silk, had failed to check her commercial progress. She had won trade from others in a period of general stagnation and she had created new demands by her ability to supply cheap manufactures to the impoverished Asian peoples. It is a curious commentary on the political sense of mankind that during this period Japan's com-

---

[4] In 1934–6 52 per cent of the export trade of Japan Proper (*including* exports to her colonies) consisted of textiles and 15 per cent of metals, metal goods, and machinery.

mercial expansion and her territorial aggression were treated by many critics as moral equivalents, as though the sale to Asians of cheap goods that they were anxious to buy was as mischievous as the imposition on them of a political domination which they abhorred.

War and defeat completely destroyed this great commerce and recovery was very slow. Japan's trading organizations were dismembered, and her exporters were even deprived of offices and branches abroad from which to operate. From 1945 to 1949 the low level of industrial production excluded the possibility of exporting more than a meagre quantity of goods; the quantum index of exports (1934–6=100) was only 8 in 1948, 16 in 1949, and 30 in 1950. At the same time the destruction of the mercantite marine meant that Japan's enterprise in the carrying trade was suspended. Imports recovered hardly more rapidly than exports. In 1949 the quantum index of imports was only 28. Since Japan's terms of trade had worsened and since she now had a heavy deficit on her invisible trade, a high proportion of these imports had to be financed by United States' aid. During the period from 1945 to 1950, the amount of aid was equivalent to 57 per cent of the value of imports.[5] In the early post-war years most of these imports consisted of grain required to prevent starvation and raw materials for restarting industry.

At the beginning of the Occupation control over foreign trade was in the hands of SCAP which after December 1945 delegated certain administrative functions to a Board of Trade established by the Japanese government for the purpose. In April 1947 four official trade corporations were set up and until the end of 1949 these handled most of the overseas transactions, although after the summer of 1947 foreign trading concerns were permitted a limited operation. During these years transactions were conducted at rates of exchange that varied from commodity to commodity.

A tentative approach to normal methods of overseas commerce was made during 1949 with the institution of a single exchange rate and the transference of exchange dealings from SCAP to a Foreign Exchange Control Board appointed by the Japanese government. The Board of Trade was at the same time

---

[5] Between 1945 and 1951, when aid ceased, the amount provided was $2,054 million. Data from EPA and Min. Fin.

Q

absorbed into the Ministry of International Trade and Industry. Early in 1950 controls over private trading were simplified and relaxed and the government's trade corporations were abolished. During that year also a number of bilateral trade agreements were signed with several countries; one of them, for example, provided for the exchange of Burmese rice for Japanese cotton goods.

The outbreak of the Korean War in June 1950 transformed the trading situation. In 1951 the dollar value of Japan's exports was 165 per cent greater than in 1949. At the same time she began to earn large amounts of foreign exchange by her sales of goods and services to the United Nations forces in the Far East. In 1951 the ratio of 'special procurement' expenditure to exports was 44 per cent and in 1952, when it reached its peak, 65 per cent.[6] Japan was fortunate that this procurement expenditure began just as American aid was coming to an end. The new orders called for an enlarged supply of raw materials and so imports also rose steeply.

The increased foreign demands led to a sharp rise in Japanese prices and, as already shown, the internal price level was maintained even after the war boom had collapsed and prices abroad had declined. The result was that the export expansion was checked, although 'special procurement' remained high. In 1953 the dollar value of the exports was less than in 1951; in volume they were still only about two-fifths of the 1934-6 quantity. On the other hand, the (dollar) value of imports continued to rise, for Japan proceeded to use the credits earned during the boom (and subsequently from procurement) to finance imports needed to re-equip industry and to raise levels of consumption. In 1953 the quantum index of imports reached 83.

The stagnation of the export trade and the disequilibrium in the balance of payments, however, called for drastic remedial measures. In addition to the deflationary policy introduced at the end of 1953, the Japanese government now began to make use of various devices to offset the disparity between the home price level and that of the outside world. Among these was the 'link system', which had for its model a method introduced in the early days of the Sino-Japanese War.[7] Firms were granted

[6] Min. Fin., *General Survey of the Japan. Econ.*, Attached Tables, p. 72.
[7] Cf. *Orient. Econ.*, May 1954, p. 245.

import licences for particular commodities on condition that they exported specified manufactured goods. Since the import trade was controlled and the domestic prices of imported goods high, goods brought in under this system could be sold in Japan at prices well above those at which they were purchased. So an importer who obtained a licence could make a substantial profit on the deal, and this enabled him to subsidize the export which he had to undertake as a condition of acquiring it. Arrangements of this kind covered not only imports of raw cotton against exports of cotton textiles, but even imports of textile raw materials, sugar, petroleum, and bananas against exports of machinery, ships, and silk. Further, tax discrimination was exercised in favour of certain export industries, and by strict control over foreign-exchange transactions the government was able to regulate the nature and amount of imports.

Devices such as these, together with the narrowing of the gap between Japanese and international prices during 1954, brought about a marked growth in the value of exports and a decline in the value of imports. In the next year exports rose by nearly 24 per cent. Subsequently both the value and volume of foreign trade oscillated widely with alternations of boom and slump in the economy. The fluctuations in imports were particularly violent. They increased very fast during periods of activity in the domestic market only to be cut back sharply on the occasion of each successive balance-of-payments crisis. For example, imports rose from $3,230 million in 1956 to $4,284 million in 1957 and then fell to $3,033 million in 1958. Despite these cyclical fluctuations, however, the secular trend was steeply upwards, and in 1963 exports were 4·3 times those of 1952 (in value) and imports 3·3 times.[8]

The high rate of growth after a long period of hesitancy was noteworthy, but by comparison with what was achieved in production, the results were not impressive. Industrial production in 1963 was over four-and-a-half times that of 1934–6, while the national income in real terms had probably trebled. Yet it was not until 1959 that the quantum of exports exceeded the pre-war level, and although it grew very fast in the next four years, in 1963 it was still less than double. Thus Japan's performance as an exporter in the post-war period taken as a whole,

[8] Figures of trade from Bank of Japan, *Econ. Statist.*; and *Japan Statist. Yb.*

(though not, of course, in the last decade) was inferior to Britain's. Even the very rapid advance of recent years left Japan until 1963 with a smaller proportion of world exports than before the war. In 1937 her share was 4 per cent, in 1954 2·1 per cent, and in 1960–1 3·6 per cent.[9]

The delay in the recovery of trade and its comparatively modest expansion compared with pre-war quantities call for an explanation. Up to 1950 the revival was retarded by the necessity for devoting resources to internal reconstruction. Then in the early 1950s the renewal of inflation was accompanied by a boom in domestic trade which checked exporting activities. The heavy 'special procurement' expenditure at this time was one of the chief factors in generating the boom, and the trade situation is liable to be seriously misunderstood if the effect of that expenditure is incorrectly evaluated. Further examination is therefore necessary. The ratio of foreign income earned by 'special procurement' to total foreign earnings for the period 1951–5 ranged from 21 per cent (1955) to 38 per cent(1952), and over that period as a whole income from procurement was sufficient to pay for about 30 per cent of commodity imports. Before the export recovery of 1955, this degree of dependence gave rise to misgivings among the Japanese. They regarded 'special procurement' as a precarious source of income, while the financial dependence upon the United States which it involved meant that the pursuance of an autonomous foreign policy was out of the question. Yet, to abstract from politics and to consider only the economic aspects of the problem, the sale of goods and services to Americans in Japan was equivalent to a dollar export. Moreover, the commodity export trade and procurement expenditure were not independent variables. Despite the existence of underemployment, there were many scarce factors in the Japanese economy— capital equipment and certain kinds of technical skill. Consequently exports were smaller and imports larger than they would have been if the Americans had spent less in Japan. In other words, in the absence of that expenditure, which had its influence on the internal price level, Japanese goods at the time would have been more competitive in world markets.

The decrease in the expenditure after 1953 certainly enforced price adjustments on the economy, and a sudden termination of

[9] IMF, *International Financial Statist*. Trade among Communist countries excluded.

it would have produced a serious strain. Yet, in fact, the income earned in this way proved to be no more precarious than that gained from the commodity export trade and it fell much less steeply during the 1950s than had been expected. Finally, it appears that the resilience of the post-war economy was under-estimated and the difficulties of adjustment to a reduction in 'special procurement' expenditure were much exaggerated. After 1953 Japan achieved an outstanding success in bringing her prices into line with world prices and in raising exports. The experience suggests, moreover, that the price elasticity of demand for her exports was much greater than was commonly supposed at that time.[10]

The above argument seems to justify the opinion that the delay in rebuilding an export trade on the pre-war scale was not so disquieting as the authorities sometimes claimed. Yet even if all allowance is made for the displacement of exports by 'special procurement', it must be conceded that the recovery in this sector of the economy was slow. Nor should this have caused sur-prise. Japan's exporters in the post-war world found themselves in the presence of several new unfavourable factors. Some of these, such as the dissolution of the great *Zaibatsu* trading com-panies, which had been potent instruments of the export drive before the war, had only a temporary influence, since by the late 1950s the companies had been reconstructed. Other causes of damage were more enduring. There was a marked shrinkage in the area in which Japanese traders had formerly enjoyed special privileges. The dissolution of Japan's empire and the loss of her special position in Manchuria and North China had damaging consequences for her overseas trade, and the restrictions imposed for political reasons on dealings with Communist China aggra-vated difficulties caused by the break-up of what was formerly a highly integrated economic unit centred upon Japan Proper. Throughout this great region (China and the former colonies),

[10] It is certainly significant that the fall of 4 per cent in Japan's export prices be-tween 1954 and 1955 was accompanied by a rise in the volume of her exports of 24 per cent. In the US exports rose by 10 per cent and prices by 1 per cent, in the UK the increases were 8 and 2 per cent respectively, and in Germany 15 and 2 per cent. Japan was the only country (except Switzerland) in which export prices went down and it was her exports that made by far the greatest advance (IMF, *Ann. Rep.*, *1956*, p. 15). Over the period 1953–61 Japan's export prices fell by 9 per cent, while the volume of her exports rose by 290 per cent.

which in 1934–6 took over two-fifths of Japan's exports and supplied more than a third of her imports, trade has been narrowly
confined. In 1956, the best year of the 1950s, only 8 per cent of
the export trade and 5 per cent of the import trade was with these
countries; in 1963 the proportions were 6 and 3 per cent respectively.

Other adverse influences on Japanese trade came from technical change and industrial developments overseas. As has already been shown, the substitution of synthetic yarns for raw
silk brought about the loss of one of her main exports. The rise
of the cotton industry in former customer-countries, notably
India, had a similar effect. Thus political, territorial, technical,
and economic changes all threw obstacles in the path of Japan's
trade recovery.

She responded to the pressure of adversity in various ways, by
import-saving devices, by attempts to find new markets and
sources of supply to replace those she lost, and by resorting to
forms of production which reduced her dependence upon foreign
trade. Throughout the period she was assisted by the flourishing
condition of international trade as a whole. The strong demand
for capital goods by underdeveloped as well as by advanced
countries, and the steep rise in incomes in the Western world
enabled Japan to break into new markets, while technical innovations which she borrowed from the West and adapted to her
own needs made it possible for her to dispense with certain raw-
material imports without retarding her industrial progress.

As in the case of other industrial countries the most buoyant
exports consisted of goods in the metal and machinery groups.
In the late 1930s such goods already occupied a prominent place
in the country's industrial production, but their importance in
the export trade was small. In 1934–6 only 15 per cent of the
total exports were in this class and most of them went to privileged
markets, especially Manchuria. Between 1953 and 1956 the
proportion ranged between 28 and 33 per cent and in the years
1959–63 between 35 and 44 per cent. Chemicals in this latter
period accounted for between 5 and 6 per cent. Thus in recent
years nearly half the exports have been made up of types of
products which comprise the bulk of the exports of advanced
Western nations. The contrast between the importance of these
goods in Japan's industrial production and their lowly place in

her exports which was so characteristic of the pre-war years has disappeared.

In the development of some of these new trades Japan during the middle 1950s was favoured by accidental and temporary circumstances. For instance, the inability of Western producers to meet the demand for steel which the investment boom created brought orders for Japanese steel at that time despite its high price. Similarly, the shortage of ships, especially tankers, and the congestion in the European yards, were responsible in part for the boom in Japanese shipbuilding. But these factors cannot explain the continued buoyancy of exports. The truth is that by the time the temporary stimuli were spent, Japan had raised her efficiency in these industries to the point at which she was fully competitive with producers overseas. Indeed the rise in her technical efficiency after 1956 was the main cause of her mounting success in a wide range of exports, especially in light engineering goods, electronic apparatus, and various instruments. These include products of which foreign sales have greatly exceeded sales in the home market.[11]

The increase in the importance of the above classes of goods was accompanied by a decline in textiles. Indeed, up to the middle 1950s, it was this decline rather than the absolute growth in the metal and machinery group that was responsible for the structural change. After 1955 textile exports increased rapidly, especially during the next five years. But since exports of other products grew much faster, the share of textiles continued to fall. In the middle 1930s it has amounted to 52 per cent of the total; between 1953 and 1956 it ranged between 35 and 40 per cent; and by 1962–3 it had fallen to only 24 per cent. This still represents a high degree of specialization compared with other countries, and Japan's difficulties with her exports have in part arisen out of it.

The changes in the export trade affected the composition of imports. The importance of textile materials has naturally declined, while that of fuel (especially oil), ores, and scrap metal has much increased. In 1960–3 these growing imports together made up nearly one-third of the total. The rise in the population

[11] In 1960 the ratio of exports to production (in value)was 71 per cent for radio receiving sets, 65 per cent for optical instruments, and 60 per cent for sewing machines.

and the relatively high price of food during the early post-war period brought about a considerable increase in the share of foodstuffs, and in 1955 they represented a quarter of total imports. By the late 1950s, the expansion of agricultural production and the fall in world food prices reduced the proportion to about 15 per cent. In 1961–3 they amounted to 13·7 per cent. The import of machinery grew faster than that of any other class of commodity during the period of exceptionally heavy industrial investment after 1956.

The transformation in the structure of foreign trade was attended by equally great changes in the importance of the different regions as customers and suppliers. The outstanding difference between pre-war and post-war conditions is the decline of Asia and the rise of the United States. The decline of Asia can be accounted for entirely by loss of trade with North East Asia. The United States's position as a customer has much improved, and the share of total exports taken by that country in the middle 1950s ranged between 17 and 22 per cent and in the period 1960–3 between 26 and 29 per cent. Whereas before the war exports to the United States consisted mainly of raw silk, tea, fish, pottery, and manufactured textiles, they now also include metals and a wide variety of highly finished manufactured goods, such as electrical apparatus and other light engineering goods, optical and other instruments, and pharmaceuticals. As a supplier the United States has taken the lead over all others. In the middle 1930s she provided about one-quarter of total imports; during the post-war period her share has usually been about one-third. In the years just after the war America was the most obvious, and even the only, alternative source of supply for the raw materials and foodstuffs which Japan had formerly obtained from her near neighbours, and in regard to certain goods this is still largely true. The special economic relations between Japan and the United States (and between particular Japanese firms and American firms) also helped to explain the predominance of American products in the Japanese market. This applies especially to machinery.

South East Asia,[12] the other main area of Japan's pre-war trading enterprise, has also come to occupy a more important

[12] The Indian subcontinent, Ceylon, Burma, Malaya, Indonesia, British Borneo, Hong Kong, the Philippines, Thailand, and Indo-China.

place both as a market and as a source of supply. The economic and political instability of the area, however, has been a source of anxiety to the Japanese, and exports to the region as a whole and to its constituent countries have fluctuated violently from year to year. Europe, South America, and Africa have also grown in importance. In short, Japan has found compensation for the loss of her great markets in East Asia by extending her trade over the rest of the world.

The exports in the last decade have conformed to a fairly well-defined pattern and one may distinguish between the types of goods sold in high-income countries and those sold to the rest of the world. The former, as one might expect, have been for the most part highly finished labour-intensive goods (clothing, textiles, light electrical goods, instruments, ships, pottery, and food products), while the latter have consisted of capital-intensive goods (heavy electrical and other machinery, chemical fertilizers, and cement).[13] As trade with the rich countries has grown faster than that with the poor countries, and as this trend is likely to continue, Japan is naturally much concerned to maintain and improve her access to that group of markets. For this reason the recent rise in the cost of labour is regarded with some disquiet, since it threatens what have hitherto been regarded as the most promising types of exports. To this problem we shall presently return.

The geographical redistribution of trade since the war cannot be explained solely in economic terms, for politics and strategy have been very influential. Deference to American policy removed the possibility of any considerable growth of trade with China, while Japan's political and strategic links with the United States have helped to foster the expansion of trade with that country. By reason of the 'special procurement' expenditure Japan has been well supplied with dollars. Dealings with the sterling area, however, for much of the post-war period were covered by agreements between the United Kingdom and Japan regarding reciprocal trade and payments. At times in the early 1950s Japan was short of sterling, although at other times she accumulated sterling in excess of her needs and was precluded

[13] K. Miyata, 'Trade Liberalization and Japan's Economy', *Kwansai Kakuin Univ. Annual Studies*, Nov. 1962, pp. 161–2; S. Fujii, 'Structure of Japan's Export Trade and its problems', *Pakistan Development R.*, Winter 1962, pp. 616–19.

by the agreements from exchanging the balance into dollars. In the 'open account' countries Japan's trade has been governed by bilateral bargains, and to some of these countries, including Indonesia, she has in effect sold exports on long-term credits which have sometimes become frozen.

This division of trade into distinct and separate currency areas has been a contributory cause of the violent fluctuations in the dealings with certain markets, and it can be hoped that a complete return to multilateral trade and the abandonment of exchange controls will do much to remove this source of instability. Trade with certain Asian countries has been affected by reparations agreements (according to which Japan has undertaken to supply goods to a certain value over a long period), by her participation in international arrangements for giving aid to underdeveloped countries, and by Japanese investment overseas. Finally, the total volume of trade as well as its geographical distribution has been intimately affected by the devices employed by Japan for regulating imports and exports as well as by foreign discrimination against Japanese goods.

Japan's own import controls have certainly constituted an important factor in keeping down the ratio of foreign trade to the gross national product. It may surprise those who have accepted uncritically the proposition that Japan is exceptionally dependent upon international trade to learn that that ratio since the war has been extremely low. Whereas in 1934–6 the ratio was 23 per cent for both imports and exports, in 1955 it had fallen to 11 per cent for exports and 14 per cent for imports. Even the rapid growth of overseas trade in subsequent years failed to raise the proportion significantly; in 1959–61 the ratio for exports ranged between 11 and 13 per cent and that for imports between 14 and 16 per cent.[14]

This change was brought about in part by the modifications in the structure of production already described. The sector of the industry in which the greatest expansion has occurred, namely the engineering industries, is one in which the ratio of imported raw-material costs to labour and capital costs is low. The reverse relationship is, of course, true for the textile industries, which have declined. Another important cause is the substitution of home-produced materials for imports in several of the leading

[14] EPA, *Econ. Survey, 1955–6*, pp. 37–38; and *Econ. Statist.* (1962), p. 5.

branches of manufacture. Of this the changes in the textile industries provide an illuminating example. A steep reduction in the imports of raw materials required for this group of industries has been achieved through the rise in the importance of the rayon and synthetic-fibre trades and the absolute decline in cotton-goods production, and also through the substitution, in the manufacture of rayon pulp, of domestically-grown latifoliate trees for imported acerose trees. Similarly, in the manufacture of nitrate fertilizers, the former imports of soya-bean cake from Manchuria have been replaced by ammonium sulphate produced from domestic resources. In certain other branches of industry that have grown since the war, expansion has been possible without a proportionate increase in imports of raw materials. For example, in the manufacture of pig-iron, technical improvements have made it possible to use domestic supplies of iron sand and sulphuric-acid dross to a far greater extent than in pre-war days.[15] Finally, Japan's dependence upon overseas supplies of food has fallen, and she has benefited by the movement of the terms of trade in her favour. Here is a marked contrast with the 1930s, when the steep rise in exports was accompanied by a considerable worsening in the terms of trade.

In the early 1960s a new phase in the development of Japan's overseas trade began. The change had its origin partly in movements in her own economy and partly in trends in the economic policy of other countries. The domestic changes were derived from the fall in the supplies of surplus labour and the consequent rise in industrial wages. This rise suggests that Japan's long-held superiority in many lines of highly finished labour-intensive products will not be so easy to maintain and that she must rely henceforth on other classes of exports. But this is still a matter for the future. By 1963 the structure of exports and the pattern of markets established after the war had not been threatened, and exports as a whole still remained buoyant. The impact of the import policy of other countries on Japan has had a more immediate effect. Japan, though a member of IMF, has been allowed to employ various exchange controls under Article 14 on the ground of her difficulties with the balance of payments. Similarly, though a member of GATT, she continued to use various devices for fostering exports and restricting imports, just as many other

[15] EPA, *Econ. Survey, 1955–6*, pp. 37–38; Okita, *Rehabilitation*, pp. 8–9.

member-countries exercised the right of discriminating against Japanese goods. By the late 1950s, however, world opinion had turned towards trade- and exchange-liberalization. In Europe the EEC and the EFTA had been formed. These international tendencies were strengthened in the next decade, especially after President Kennedy had initiated discussions for world-wide tariff reductions. Japan was obliged to adapt her commercial policy to these movements of opinion. As a great trading Power she could not remain isolated from current trends, and she found herself under increasing pressure from her trading partners and from international bodies. In February 1963 the IMF called upon her to adhere to the obligations described under Article 8, that is to say, to abandon exchange controls in connexion with current transactions. At the same time she was required to change to Article 11 status under GATT. This meant that she must abandon quantitative restrictions on imports and certain measures for stimulating exports.[16]

Japan felt bound to acquiesce. The process of trade liberalization began in 1959. During the next four years a very high proportion of imports (94 per cent by value according to Japanese estimates) was freed from quantitative controls, while restrictions upon foreign-exchange dealings were progressively relaxed. Meanwhile Japan signed a number of commercial treaties with Powers that formerly discriminated against her trade (including the United Kingdom), and most of the chief trading countries have now ceased to invoke Article 35 of GATT which enabled them to impose quota restrictions upon imports from Japan. She has also been admitted as a member of OECD, and this presumably foreshadows a further reduction in trade and exchange controls. By the autumn of 1965 only a small number of articles is likely to be covered by Japan's import restrictions and the process of liberalization will be, in appearance at any rate, almost complete.

Appearances, however, may be misleading. While Japan has shown little hesitation in freeing the great bulk of her imports, which consists of materials and fuel, she has a different attitude towards the goods still controlled. These comprise certain foodstuffs and a few finished manufactured goods such as motor cars, heavy electrical machinery, machine tools, and heavy chemicals.

[16] *Orient. Econ.*, Jan. 1963, p. 8; July 1963, pp. 386–93.

In these classes of product Japan's costs are still rather high and she fears that liberalization may endanger some large and important industries. She is, therefore, reluctant to complete the process of liberalization until these industries have had time to raise their efficiency. Meanwhile the government is prepared to provide financial help, particularly through the Export-Import Bank, to enable producers to defend themselves against competition in both home and foreign markets by offering extended credit. More generally, the abandonment of quantitative controls has been accompanied by a steady rise in import duties during the last three or four years, but this increase will become difficult to defend if the policy of world-wide tariff reductions at present under negotiation is pressed home.[17]

If Japanese businessmen are unenthusiastic about a thoroughgoing policy of trade liberalization, it should be remembered that their country's remarkable economic growth since the war has taken place under a régime of tightly regulated foreign trade. One reason why Japan was able to keep her rate of economic growth at a very high level was that she knew that her powerful import and financial controls enabled her to restore equilibrium in the balance of payments very quickly whenever it was disturbed. She is well aware that certain large industries are likely to be at considerable risk if unprotected, and she realizes that many of the import-saving devices which have resulted in a low ratio of imports to GNP are likely to be denied to her. This would not matter if she could be sure that her exports would benefit to an equivalent extent by liberalization. She observes with disquiet, however, that several countries, themselves advocates of liberalization, have insisted upon replacing formal restrictions upon Japanese goods by 'understandings', negotiated between themselves and the Japanese government, by which the latter has undertaken 'voluntarily' to curtail the quantity of exports to particular markets. In the case of the United States these 'voluntary' restrictions, it is claimed, cover about two-fifths of Japan's exports to that country.[18]

The next decade may, therefore, present Japan with very

[17] Japan cannot be considered a high-tariff country. In 1962 about half the goods subject to tariff were in the 15–20 per cent range, and the ratio of customs revenue to dutiable imports was about 18 per cent. A high proportion of her imports are raw materials and most of these are duty free.

[18] *Orient. Econ.*, June 1963, p. 325.

different trading problems from those she has so far encountered. The Income Doubling Plan has recognized this. It postulates that during the 1960s exports must grow faster than production; they are required to increase at the rate of 9·3 per cent a year compared with 7·2 per cent for GNP. By 1970–1 they should amount to 5·6 per cent of world exports (compared with 3·6 per cent in 1960–1). This is an ambitious export programme and the prospects must be examined.

During the last ten years the exports that have grown most rapidly have been those for which the income elasticity of demand has been high, and the best markets have been found in countries where incomes have risen most substantially.[19] These trends may well persist. But there are misgivings about whether Japan can maintain her competitive superiority in the classes of goods sold in those markets. This doubt arises because, as already shown, the most rapidly growing exports have consisted mainly of labour-intensive goods, including those that require technical expertise and adroit organization as well as manipulative skill. Many of these are turned out by small and medium firms and the rise in labour costs may threaten the future of this section of the export trade. Consequently, official circles consider that Japan must strive to improve her efficiency in the manufacture of goods produced by capital-intensive industries, expecially those employing mass-production methods and advanced techniques. Her relative advantages in international trade have not hitherto lain in industries such as these, but policy is now being directed towards their encouragement with the object of rendering them competitive with foreign producers both in the overseas and the home markets.

What does this mean in terms of actual products? Japan cannot hope that textiles will provide a major contribution to the expansion of her exports. She will probably continue to enjoy superiority in such goods as cameras, sewing machines, ships, pottery, radios, and certain made-up textiles, and her exports of these goods to high-income countries will grow. But it may be difficult to maintain the rate of expansion of recent years and she may have to rely increasingly upon chemicals, heavy-engineering goods, and the products of advanced technology, where she

[19] Although Japan's exports to the non-industrialized countries are still larger than those to industrial countries, they have been growing less rapidly.

will encounter keen competition from Western countries. Ten years ago, when Japan was regarded as a marginal supplier of these goods, the prospects seemed dim. But since then her remarkable advance in manufacturing efficiency has greatly extended the range of opportunity. Even so, it will be less easy for Japan to build up large markets for these goods in the high-income countries than it was for her to sell light manufactured products to them. The recognition of this problem has turned attention towards the possibilities of increased trade with the less developed countries of the world. Japan is obviously well fitted for participating in the economic growth of Asian countries and she would gain immensely from any acceleration in their rate of development. Her reparations settlements with her former victims, her contributions to various programmes of economic aid, and her considerable investments in and long-term credits to Asian countries have all been undertaken with an eye to future trade, especially in capital equipment. Since she can supply technical experts to assist in development projects more cheaply than the Western countries, she should be well placed for benefiting from the orders likely to ensue. Yet so far the rate of economic development in Asia has been disappointing, and it may be that Japan will continue to find more ample opportunities in the West than in those countries which are sometimes regarded as her natural markets.

In this connexion the Japanese have been inclined to stress the consequences of their failure to re-establish satisfactory commercial relations with China. Critics of Japan's America-inspired foreign policy have held that the chief obstacle to the resumption of trade between these countries consists of the embargo that has existed since the Korean War on the export of many classes of goods to China. It is not easy to test the validity of this argument. No one can deny that Japan's economy in the early post-war years was seriously damaged by the loss of China as a market and source of supply, although the significance of the loss is sometimes exaggerated. Before the war, when Japanese traders enjoyed special privileges, especially in Manchuria and the North, China took only 18 per cent of the total exports and supplied 12 per cent of the total imports. Admittedly, the economic importance of China to Japan was greater than these figures suggest. The growth of certain industries in Japan was bound up with complementary developments in China. Japanese weaving sheds used cheap yarn produced in Japanese-controlled spinning mills in Shanghai. The Japanese steel industry drew coking coal, ores, and various semi-products from North China and Manchuria. Exports of Korean rice to Japan depended upon exports of Manchurian millet to Korea. Commercial dealings with China were obviously of very substantial value, if not of such over-whelming importance as is sometimes suggested. Yet the part that China then played in Japan's economic life largely depended upon Japan's political domination of North East Asia. The post-war fragmentation of that area has destroyed the former system of economic relationships. Neither China nor Korea now looks for economic leadership to the Japanese, and China during most of the post-war period turned to the Russians rather than to the Japanese or the Western world for technical experts and for capital. Her quarrel with Russia, however, has now forced her to look elsewhere for the equipment which she needs for her own industrialization, and in the presence of this opportunity Japan may not always be willing to acquiesce in the maintenance of an embargo. Even were it abolished, only a moderate expansion of reciprocal trade could be expected in the immediate future, but in the long run the opportunities, though clouded by political uncertainties, are substantial. Japan is naturally attracted by these prospects because of the kind of exports likely to be re-quired. As a commentator has said: 'Future structural changes in Japan's economy will necessitate the expansion of markets for heavy and chemical products and this may in turn require closer trading relations with neighbouring countries, including China.'[20]

In conclusion we must examine the reconstruction of the mercantile marine. During the 1930s the growth in Japan's shipping industry was as rapid as that of her foreign trade, and at the beginning of the Pacific War the mercantile fleet had a gross tonnage of over 6 millions. By the end of the war this great asset had been almost destroyed. In 1945 the tonnage left afloat was only 1,344,000, and most of it consisted either of obsolete ships or of ships built to an inferior wartime standard. Hardly any of them were capable of operating efficiently in the ocean-carrying trade. In the years that followed, recovery was impeded

[20] S. Okita, *Sino-Japanese Trade and Japan's Economic Growth* (1962), p. 11.

not only by the disorganization of the shipbuilding industry, but also by restrictions placed by SCAP on the operations both of the ship-owners and of the shipbuilders. These restrictions were gradually relaxed, but it was not until 1950 that Japan was completely free to plan the reconstruction of her mercantile marine. At that time she still possessed only 1,700,000 gross tons and very few ocean-going ships.[21] Freedom from restrictions coincided with the recovery of industrial capacity. So, from then onwards, the shipping industry, assisted by low-interest loans from the government and the banks, rapidly expanded. By the end of 1954 the size of the fleet reached 3·3 million tons, but the recovery still left it about 12 per cent smaller than in 1941. During the late 1950s growth was accelerated. In 1960 the previous maximum was overtaken, and in 1964 the tonnage rose to 9·1 million. An official plan provides for increasing the fleet to 16 million tons by 1968. As in the recent past, government financial help in carrying out this programme will greatly benefit ship-builders as well as ship-owners.

Japan's shipping policy, as revealed in the type of vessels built during this period, was closely related to one of her major post-war problems. Economic growth required that she should be able to import raw materials cheaply, but the post-war changes in the distribution of her trade had increased the average length of the sea haul. She had become particularly dependent upon imports of oil and ore from distant countries. Hence she supplied herself with a large fleet of tankers and bulk-ore carriers and these together now make up about a third of her mercantile marine (in gross tonnage). In the interests of economical haulage, her ship-owners were anxious to acquire vessels of large size and high speed, and in recent years they have succeeded in reducing operating costs by mechanization and even automation.

While the recovery of the mercantile marine carried with it the growth in the size of shipping firms, it was also attended by a proliferation in their number. Even in 1961 ownership was by no means highly concentrated; fifteen companies, each with 1,000 gross tons and over, owned just over half the total, and the rest

[21] H. Yamamoto, 'The Recovery Method of the Japanese Shipping Industry in the Post-War World', *Kobe Econ. & Business R.*, pp. 89–97; Orient. Econ., *Japan Econ. Yb., 1954*, p. 89; Min. Internat. Trade & Ind., *Foreign Trade of Japan, 1950*, pp. 31–34.

R

was divided among numerous smaller firms. This structure was chiefly attributable to the fact that government assistance in the reconstruction of shipping was widely distributed in the early post-war period. During recent years, however, Japan has become conscious of the need to consolidate interests in all trades likely to suffer the impact of the more vigorous international competition that lies ahead. As a result of official pressure, six of the leading companies agreed at the beginning of 1964 to merge into three groups. Two of these three groups will fall within the ambit of the old *Zaibatsu*, namely the Osaka Shosen Kaisha–Mitsui Shipping Group and the NYK[22]–Mitsubishi Shipping Group. The former can claim to be one of the largest shipping companies in the world. It is intended that within the next few years the bulk of the tonnage will be controlled by five large groups.[23]

Throughout the 1950s foreign ships, including foreign ships chartered by Japanese, carried a much higher proportion of Japan's imports and exports than before the war. Even in the early 1960s, when Japan had a larger fleet than in the 1930s, when she had restored many of her former liner services, and when she was again carrying goods between foreign ports, she had a net debit in her shipping account with the outside world. This was in contrast with the position before the war when she had earned a substantial credit from her shipping services. Several factors were responsible for this change. Many cargoes, including the much diminished cross-freight business, have been lost because of the policy of discrimination in favour of their own ships by foreign countries, especially the United States. Payments in foreign ports have been very large because Japanese ships take on the bulk of their fuel oil abroad. So the growth in the mercantile marine, though substantial, has not kept pace with the development in the rest of the economy and the growing deficit in the invisible trade account can be ascribed chiefly to this fact.[24]

---

[22] Nippon Yusen Kaisha Shipowners.   [23] *Orient. Econ.*, Oct. 1963.
[24] F. Kawata, 'A Study of Japan's Invisible Trade', *Kobe, Econ. & Business R.*, 1962, pp. 43–60. See also Statist. App., Table 21.

XIII

Summary: Achievements and Prospects

IN previous chapters we have described and explained the processes by which Japan, having successfully overcome the difficulties caused by her immense material losses and the post-war disorganization of her economy, came within a few years to rank with the leading industrial countries of the world. Her 'recovery' may be said to have been accomplished by the middle 1950s. By then she had restored financial stability, rebuilt in large part her industrial and commercial organization, increased manufacturing output to twice that of the middle 1930s, and raised income a head above the pre-war level. An achievement of this magnitude was remarkable when viewed against the adversities with which the post-war world had afflicted her. Her traditionally intimate economic relations with North East Asia had been destroyed by territorial changes and political upheaval. Her former specialization in textiles proved to be ill suited to the demands of post-war markets. Her technology had been cut off from the sources of invention just when they were gushing copiously in the outside world. Meanwhile, her old centres of initiative had been dissolved, and resources for re-equipment were scarcer than ever at a moment when they were most urgently required.

There can be little wonder that the outlook was considered bleak. The rehabilitation of the economy called for qualities of resilience and energy which the Japanese, in their exhaustion and despair at the end of the war, seemed unlikely to command. Foreign opinion about Japan's capacity to find a successful issue from her troubles was for some years deeply pessimistic, largely because attention in the outside world was focused on the persistent weakness of the export trade. Up to 1955 the Japanese themselves shared this opinion. At that time they still spoke of themselves as 'marginal suppliers' of manufactures for international trade, and they feared that such recovery as had occurred was insecurely based on American 'special procurement' and on temporary shortages of capacity in competitor-countries.

The contrast in temper between that period and the early

1960s is striking. Pessimism and diffidence have given place to an easy self-confidence, The present mood can find ample justification. Since 1950 Japan has achieved a rate of growth which is the marvel and envy of the rest of the world.[1] She cannot claim to have enjoyed 'stable growth', but at least she has been skilful in coping with the recurrent balance-of-payments crises which her rapid development has provoked, and she has so far avoided serious inflation.

In manufacturing industry, where her major successes have been won, she has found a new dimension. Her accomplishment is demonstrated not merely by the growth of industrial output as a whole but also in the wide extension of her range of products. Trades that went unremarked during the pre-war decade now rank among her largest industries, and several entirely new branches of manufacture have grown to great size. Many of her leading industries still rest on her resources of skilled and assiduous labour, but the most notable developments of the last seven or eight years have occurred in industries that depend on advanced technology. The result is that her industrial activities are now centred upon the production of metal, engineering, and chemical goods, including the latest innovations among them, and Japan has joined the company of the half a dozen countries which are responsible for the bulk of these products. Among the leaders her position has constantly improved. For instance, in the non-Communist world she has lately come to occupy the second place in steel production; she is the largest producer of ships and of some kinds of electrical apparatus; she is second only to the United States as a manufacturer of synthetic fibres. In the generation of electric power and the production of finished textiles, machinery (including machine tools), motor vehicles, plastics, and certain kinds of chemicals, she holds rank with the four or five largest producing countries.

It has been claimed that in the recovery of the economy during its initial stages Japan owed a heavy debt to fortune. No one can deny that the Korean War and the sustained 'special procurement' demand gave an immense stimulus to industry, especially

---

[1] Between 1950 and 1960 the annual rate of growth of GNP (in real terms) is estimated to have been 9·5 per cent for Japan, 7·6 per cent for West Germany, 5·9 per cent for Italy, 4·3 per cent for France, 3·3 per cent for the US, and 2·7 per cent for the UK (UN, *Yb. of National Accounts Statist., 1962*).

to the heavy trades, and that they presented Japan with exceptionally favourable opportunities for acquiring foreign exchange
essential for reconstruction. Indeed, the American demand for
Japan's goods and services that was called into being by the
political situation in the Far East may be said to have offset the
damaging effects of the loss of trade with North East Asia, itself
the consequence of the same train of events. Then in the middle
1950s, a further stimulus was administered by the world investment boom, and as this was accompanied by a large demand for
ships, especially tankers, it brought expansion to a sector of
industry in which Japan's competitive position had hitherto been
undistinguished. Finally, at the end of 1956, the Suez crisis for a
short period conferred considerable advantages on Japan in her
competition with Western producers in Asian markets.

Fortune has certainly shown Japan her engaging and amiable
aspect. Yet even in the early post-war period her favours would
have availed little without good management, and for the accelerated development of the last seven or eight years other ex-
planations must be sought. They have been discussed in earlier
chapters, and at this point the factors mainly responsible need
only be listed. They are:

1. The closing of the technical gap by the import of new technology.
2. An exceptionally high rate of investment buttressed by a very
   high rate of saving, both institutional and personal.
3. The direction of investment into uses which yielded quick
   returns and the absence of wasteful investment in armaments.
4. The large reserve army of workers at the beginning of the
   period of growth and the successful transference of huge numbers from low-productivity to high-productivity occupations.
5. The reconstruction of the *Zaibatsu* and the creation of other
   business groups capable of organizing development.
6. A monetary system and policy which were successful both in
   providing industries with the finance needed for expansion
   and also in cutting back credit quickly whenever the economy
   became 'overheated'.
7. A taxation system which kept clear of measures likely to curb
   industrial investment and damage personal incentives.
8. The effective use of official controls over foreign trade and
   payments.

The outside world may wonder whether the convergence of so many factors favourable to growth is likely to persist, and this question must certainly be examined. Before embarking on such speculation, however, some other comments on Japan's economic experience are necessary. First, it should be emphasized that Japan today possesses one of the most highly competitive economies in the world. This characteristic is revealed most obviously by the conduct of small and medium-sized firms in manufacturing industry and distribution, but it is also present among large-scale enterprises. Indeed, the fierce rivalry among oligopolists has undoubtedly been responsible for much of the breathless innovation and lavish investment in new equipment during the last few years. The progress of Japan, the flexibility of her costs and prices, and her quick adaptation to economic change owe much to these conditions. Yet keen competition and the boisterous struggles of free enterprise are not there associated with *laissez-faire*. On the contrary the government in regulating, guiding, and directing the economy, during the post-war period as in the past, has made an essential contribution to the achievement. The public sector itself is small by modern standards. Many industries which in the majority of Western countries are under State ownership, in Japan are in private hands. Nevertheless, the government has made constant use of a number of powerful instruments in shaping the economy, e.g. the official banks which direct capital resources into the preferred fields, fiscal devices, foreign trade controls, and 'indicative planning'.

This combination of free enterprise and government control imposed at key points in the economy has been a familiar feature of Japan since early Meiji. Throughout the modern era up to the Second World War responsibility for development and innovation had been shared between the State and the *Zaibatsu*. During the war economic authority became more highly centralized in the government, and the eclipse of the *Zaibatsu* after 1945 and the circumstances of the Occupation confirmed this concentration. For a time private entrepreneurial initiative seemed to have lost direction and purpose. After 1952, however, the broad pattern of leadership in industry and commerce was redrawn. While the government, aided by a highly competent bureaucracy, steadily gained assurance and skill in its administration of economic policy, some of the economic empires of the past were reorganized and other powerful centres of initiative arose. In this way the forms of economic direction were restored and its efficiency augmented.

Responsibility for reconstruction was, of course, shared with the Americans. For over six years after the end of the war the Occupation authorities were in control of policy, and even after 1952 the United States government exerted a powerful influence upon it. In certain respects, the effect of the intervention, at any rate in the early post-war period, may have been to retard recovery; but on balance there can be no doubt that the American association with Japan's affairs during the Occupation period conferred signal benefits upon her. Without the aid so abundantly provided between 1945 and 1951, Japan would almost certainly have sunk deeper into economic chaos. The same conclusion applies to the subsequent period when, although her trading enterprise was handicapped by limitations imposed by the United States on her dealings with China, she enjoyed the advantage of a vast dollar expenditure at a critical stage of her reconstruction. Then in 1960 the flow of private American capital began.

Of the reforms introduced by the Americans, and of their continuing influence on the economy, it is more difficult to make a just appraisal. SCAP has been accused of impercipience in its effort to impose American ideals on a society where they were little esteemed, and of obtuse benevolence in trying by administrative measures to remove blemishes in social arrangements which were the manifestations of deep-rooted economic disabilities. Yet whatever may have been the immediate effect of the reforms in thwarting recovery and provoking social tensions, the enduring consequences were by no means deleterious. The reforms which were out of tune with Japan's purposes could not, and did not, long survive the end of the Occupation. This does not mean that any of the social and economic institutions or relationships were restored to precisely their old form. The American impress was nowhere completely obliterated, nor did the Japanese themselves wish that it should be. But we have shown how in several spheres of national life (notably in industrial and financial organization) the reforms soon yielded to the policy of the 'reverse course'. On the other hand, not all of them were equally fragile. Some were acceptable to the Japanese and could readily

be assimilated, even though they might not have been undertaken on native initiative. The Land Reform can be quoted as
an outstanding example. It is true that the conditions of tenure
that it created are now proving detrimental to agricultural progress. But in the early post-war years the Reform certainly made
some contribution to efficiency besides exerting a stabilizing
social influence at a critical time. Again, many of the innovations
in labour relations have survived intact. Here the result was to
bring into existence, by edict, a code of industrial relations and a
trade union movement which might otherwise have taken many
years to evolve.

The initiative came from without, but even during the
Occupation success in formulating and administering the reforms depended closely on the co-operation of the Japanese
authorities and individuals. Where this co-operation was accorded, the reforms endured. Where there was opposition, they
were fugitive. As in earlier times the Japanese showed themselves
ready to tread new paths once they were convinced that the
route led towards national well-being, as they conceived it. They
certainly did not offer a sullen resistance to the zeal of the reformers merely because the latter were foreigners in occupation
of Japanese territory.

The Occupation period during which the foundations of future
growth were laid can now be viewed in perspective. Even the
most censorious foreign commentator must pay tribute to the
generosity of the Americans in providing resources for rebuilding
Japan's economy, and to their enthusiasm, if not their tact, in
reshaping her institutions. And when Americans themselves are
reflecting glumly on the great stream of dollar aid which mal-
administration or corruption, in one recipient country after
another, has allowed to run to waste, they can perhaps find some
solace in recalling one Asian protégé who has used their bene-
factions to good effect. For their part in these transactions the
Japanese also deserve credit. They showed a sure political
instinct in their readiness to co-operate in the institutional
innovations imposed by the victors. A people less oppor-
tunist in temper and less adroitly governed might well
have rejected the chance of testing the merits of what the
Americans had devised for them. Since on balance the innovations were instrumental in promoting both economic and social

progress, the Japanese were rewarded for their inspired empiricism.

No one acquainted with their history is likely to be surprised at their acquiescence on this occasion. The Japanese have never hesitated to use foreign models when they have been devising institutional constructions apt for some new national purpose. They have always welcomed novelties and have then proceeded to adapt them to their needs. This process can be seen at work throughout the post-war period. On the other hand, identities with the past are more numerous than is sometimes supposed. We have observed these in our examination of financial organization and monetary policy. It was shown in Chapter IV that throughout the modern era Japan has been inclined to follow a boldly expansionist policy. The result was that for long periods she found herself on the verge of inflation, with her balance of payments frequently precarious. But the situation was never allowed to get out of hand, at any rate up to the outbreak of the Second World War. Short periods of ruthless deflation punctuated the general expansionist tendency.

The post-war period reproduced these experiences. We have described how the violent inflation of the late 1940s was brought to an abrupt end by the Dodge deflation. This measure was, of course, imposed by the Occupation. But the Japanese authorities themselves were responsible for the successful policies of 1954 and 1958. On both these occasions the deflationary measures prepared the way for the forward surge in production that followed. The more limited success that attended similar measures in 1962 may foreshadow a time when different methods of monetary control will have to be employed. It is ironical that at a moment when Europeans are ready to do obeisance to Japan's skill in handling her monetary problems, the Japanese (or at least the financial authorities) profess themselves increasingly dissatisfied with their own methods and are inclining towards what in this country are regarded as the conventional instruments of monetary policy.

The dissatisfaction has its roots in the fundamental changes to which the economy has been subjected. The success of the existing policy has depended in large measure on two conditions, first the flexibility of Japan's costs in response to financial pressure, and secondly the powerful official controls over foreign transactions. The first of these conditions is threatened by the growing shortage of labour and the approximation of employment conditions in large-scale and small-scale industry. The second can hardly survive the policy of liberalizing trade. The consequences of the change may be momentous. Japan has not hitherto felt nervous at times of extraordinarily rapid growth because she has had at hand effective weapons for dealing with a crisis. Should these weapons become blunted the whole policy of rapid economic growth might have to be reconsidered, especially as it may not be easy for Japan to operate the conventional measures of continuous monetary control if the existing measures of spasmodic control should fail her.

Yet the problem itself is largely the consequence of her success in carrying development to the point at which the barriers between the two parts of the dual economy have crumbled. Up to the middle 1950s Japan inhabited two worlds. To the Asian she appeared as a modern state masquerading as undeveloped; to the Westerner, and to many Japanese themselves, it was the vestigial remains of a pre-industrial society that were most prominent. Peasant agriculture, though far more efficient than elsewhere in Asia and yielding higher financial returns than before the war, was still over-stocked with labour. The same was true of the great mass of very small units in manufacturing industry and the service trades where (though by no means universally) productivity, incomes, and conditions of work compared unfavourably with those of large modern establishments. In manufacturing industry these contrasts are fast disappearing, with consequences already described. In other sectors also the dichotomy is becoming less and less obvious. It was once usual to contrast the efficient and up-to-date railway and shipping services with the ill-developed system of motor transport, handicapped as it was (and still is) by the primitive roads. The proposed heavy investment in both urban and trunk roads may well remove this contrast by the end of the present decade. In distribution the most casual observer was impressed by the co-existence in the great cities of the huge departmental stores and the multitude of family shops with a minute turnover. The distributive trade as a whole is now on the eve of a transformation brought about by the introduction of supermarkets, and many of the small shops are likely to disappear in the years ahead. Again, the premises occupied by large industrial, financial, and commercial concerns are indistinguishable from their counterparts in the West, and the most recently built are impressively well-equipped. Yet throughout the country the standard of housing accommodation remains exceedingly low.[2] This contrast may persist for many years, but the present Income Doubling Plan, which looks forward to a substantial increase in housing investment, should gradually make it less glaring. Thus throughout all branches of the economy there is a trend towards uniformity.

In the past Japanese economists were much preoccupied with the problem of 'disguised unemployment' or 'underemployment' in the small-scale sectors of industry, agriculture, and the service trades. This condition had been associated with the insufficiency and biased distribution of capital in a society in which the labour supply was rapidly increasing. Throughout the modern era a high proportion of new fixed investment was directed into a narrow range of industries, mainly those concerned with capital and intermediate goods, where for technical reasons factor-proportions were rigid. The result was that agriculture and most of the consumption-goods industries and service trades, where factor proportions were elastic, attracted comparatively little investment, and they were left to absorb, in low-productivity occupations, a large share of the increasing labour supply.[3] Such a distribution of capital was probably justified in a period when rapid development depended on the establishment of basic industries, especially those concerned with power and transport. It has been argued, however, that in the early 1950s an excessively high proportion of the new investment was directed by the government and its financial agencies towards a few large-scale undertakings. The productivity of Japanese industry as a whole might have benefited if the smaller establishments had been able to obtain improved equipment and to gain readier access to new techniques. However this may be, it is evident that as soon as the demands by large-scale industry for labour became of such a magnitude as to absorb the bulk of the recruits to the labour market and also to draw off the surplus workers from

---

[2] The Japanese point out that people who are comfortable at work but uncomfortable at home have every inclination to 'keep at it'!

[3] Cf. K. Ohkawa, 'Economic Growth and Agriculture', *Ann. Hitotsubashi Acad.*, Oct. 1956, pp. 56–60.

agriculture, the problem of underemployment was on the way to solution. Once the small firms were forced to pay rates of wages as high as those in the large firms, they could survive only by modernizing their methods and so raising their productivity. The same forces at work in agriculture have led to a substitution of capital for labour to an extent unimaginable only a few years ago. It is true that Japan by the standards of industrial Western countries still retains a high proportion of its occupied population in the primary industries and in small-scale industry and trade. For some years to come she will have reserves to draw upon (more particularly, reserves of female labour), and they will help to sustain her rate of growth. But the time when massive and apparently inexhaustible reserves were available has gone.

With this discussion as a background, we can now return to the question posed earlier in this chapter. Are the factors which produced the rapid development of the last decade likely to operate during the rest of the 1960s as powerfully as in the past? The short answer is that the effect of some of these factors is weakening and that further success depends upon the solution of hitherto familiar problems. Let us consider the list of factors on page 249 from this point of view.

First, the great technological advance through the assimilation of foreign inventions and processes is virtually complete and Japan must henceforth rely increasingly, though not, of course, exclusively, on her own innovations. Secondly, so far as investment is concerned, we have seen that its direction is now changing. Whereas in the 1950s most of it went into industrial equipment, in the present decade a high proportion is being turned into the infrastructure. The latter kind of investment will add much to the efficiency of the economy[4] as well as to social amenity, but most of it will not yield returns as quickly as investment in industrial machinery. Up to the present it has been possible to maintain a high rate of investment without the risk of inflation because of the high rate of savings. With the recently awakened desire of the people to acquire such goods as refrigerators, television sets, and motor vehicles, which are now heavily adver-

---

[4] For example, investment in improved means of transport will not only reduce the direct costs of distribution but will also lead to economies by making it possible for manufacturers and merchants to hold smaller stocks; hitherto the investment in stocks has been very high.

tised in the home market, the propensity to save may possibly decline to an extent that more than counter-balances the rise in personal incomes.[5] The combination of an increased propensity to consume together with a reduction in the rate of investment in industrial plant may affect the rate of growth during the next few years. On the other hand, some Japanese economists are of the opinion that during the present decade a high rate of growth can be sustained only by a great expansion of expenditure on consumers' capital goods, since otherwise the volume of effective demand will be inadequate. They may be right. But if such expenditure must be relied on increasingly as the agent of rapid growth, then the adverse effect on savings may release the danger of inflation.[6] Of this the rapid rise in prices during the last two years may be a symptom. In other words, the rate of growth that can be contemplated without excessive risk may be lower than in the immediate past.

We have already emphasized certain significant changes in the third factor (the supply of underemployed workers available for transference to high-productivity occupations). The transformation in the labour market lies, indeed, at the foundation of the new order that is now emerging. The labour shortage is likely to affect profits and private investment by closing the gap between the growth of productivity and the rise of wages that was a prominent feature of the 1950s.[7] The narrowing wage-differentials foreshadow the demise of the dual economy. The decline in wage plasticity may well reduce economic resilience and complicate the process of correcting disequilibrium. Hitherto, as we have seen, inflation has been effectively controlled by restraints on demand. If the problem of 'cost-push' should present itself for solution, Japan may not be so well equipped to deal with it. When wage settlements are local and particular, and when earnings differ widely for the same occupation, the introduction of a national wages or incomes policy encounters peculiar difficulties. For these and other reasons, the new conditions in the labour market are likely to provoke a resolute attack on some of the most cherished features of Japanese industrial rela-

[5] Within recent years a slight decline in saving habits has in fact been detected (EPA, *Econ. Survey, 1963–4*, pp. 274–7).
[6] The monetary authorities will probably find greater difficulty in controlling this type of expenditure than they have hitherto found in controlling investment.
[7] See Stat. App., Table 19, p. 278.

tions, namely, the 'lifelong engagement' system and the method of payment by seniority. Such an attack (and already it is being mounted), might have serious social repercussions. It is also probable that many of the self-employed (e.g. farmers, small manufacturers, and shopkeepers) who find difficulty in adapting themselves to economic change may react vigorously against it. Pressure from these quarters might well retard the redistribution of labour unless the government were ready to provide compensation payments or subsidies to assist migration to other occupations. A solution of this problem may become more difficult because of other changes which are now only just beyond the horizon of Japan's experience. The age of automation is now treading on the heels of the full-employment era with social consequences that may be as momentous for Japan as for other countries. It is, however, a matter of speculation whether automation in the course of the next decade will reverse the present trends in the labour market to the detriment of all those not already installed in the comfortable security of the great concerns.

Finally, we must refer to the controls until recently exercised over foreign trade and payments. The controls made it easier for the Japanese authorities to drive their economy ahead in the knowledge that powerful weapons were in their hands for dealing with any disequilibrium in the balance of payments that might accompany very rapid growth. Now, with the controls abandoned, the authorities must watch any oscillations in the balance of payments with apprehension, and they must adopt a more cautious attitude towards the 'overheating' of the economy. Their anxiety will not be relieved by the growing deficit in the balance of invisible payments. Another aspect of liberalization deserves comment. The control over imports meant that certain new industries, despite fierce inter-firm rivalries, were not exposed to foreign competition. Hence their methods of production and forms of organization have sometimes been inefficient from an international standpoint. One of the chief defects has been the lack of plant specialization. The liberalization of trade is now enforcing reorganization on the most vulnerable industries, and it is reasonable to suppose that the problem will soon be solved. Rationalization may sometimes be impeded by inter-group rivalries, but in some industries these are being overcome by the growth of *Kombinats*.

It is clear that in many respects Japan has entered upon a new phase in her economic development. While it seems that she will easily achieve the goals set by the Income Doubling Plan, some of the factors which contributed most powerfully to growth are weakening or are changing their form, and certain industrial and social relationships intimately associated with Japanese enterprise are now being modified. The revolution in agriculture, the disappearance of the dual economy, the change in the nature of investment and personal expenditure, the liberalization of trade, the new financial and monetary problems, all these are calling into being a new kind of economy. The time is in sight when some of the most familiar contrasts between Japan and the West will have faded, and as the changes described gather strength Japan is likely to meet with difficulties of choice in the field of social as well as of economic policy similar to those that have long perplexed Western countries.

Neither her recent successes nor her capacity for dealing with the problems that lie ahead can be assessed solely in economic terms. The proximate forces responsible for the high felicity of her economic achievement are not difficult to identify and to analyse. But observers of the process of development are tempted to extend their curiosity towards the deeper springs of this unique accomplishment. It may perhaps be rewarding to refer briefly to the social and political conditions that made possible the emergence of Japan as a modern State in early Meiji, and underlay her subsequent achievement, and then to consider how far those conditions have persisted into the present era. The causes of the early development may be summarized as, first, a political and social system that presented opportunities for the exercise of leadership to persons (private individuals or bureaucrats) whose interests lay in promoting economic change; secondly, an inheritance of organizing capacity and skill; and finally, institutional arrangements conducive to the rapid accumulation of capital. The society that satisfied these conditions was hierarchical, drawing its leaders mainly from a privileged class constantly invigorated by the entry of men of talent from outside its ranks. When, by a conjunction of political and social changes, the leaders were enlisted on the side of modernization and economic development, they found in the mass of the people, long trained in obedience to authority, a ready instrument to their hand.

There was a fine legacy of skill in textiles and metal manufactures, and certain family businesses had a long experience of large-scale organization. The capital accumulation required for development was a function of the unequal distribution of income characteristic of that type of society and of the propensity of the wealthy to apply their savings to industrial and commercial development. The taxation system which succeeded the old feudal arrangements was very regressive, pressing lightly on high personal and corporate incomes and harshly on the peasants. These conditions persisted with comparatively little modification up to the Second World War.

The war, the inflation, and the post-war reforms destroyed powerful sections of the oligarchy, chiefly the military cliques and the rural landlords. These formed, however, the most conservative or reactionary element in society, elements which in Japanese opinion were largely responsible for the catastrophe of 1945. The dismissal of the chief 'architects of ruin' still left power highly concentrated and, in spite of the growth of parliamentary institutions, the leadership of the official and business oligarchies has not yet been seriously disturbed. Labour organizations have arisen and their economic foundations, once weak, have been strengthened by the changes in the labour market. But the political side of the movement has not yet acquired the power that it has long enjoyed in Britain and other European countries. On the other hand the mood of the people has changed. They now breathe the air of freedom. They are less pliable than in the past and more concerned with enjoying the amenities of life which prosperity has presented to them. The release of energy by the social and political reforms immediately after the Second World War probably deserves a high place among the causes of growth.

It will be generally conceded that the progress that began in the Meiji era cannot be explained solely in terms of economic calculation. As in all great movements in human affairs, in the material no less than in other aspects of national life, an element of grandeur was present, a touch of the idealism which, as Alfred Marshall said, 'can generally be detected at the root of any great outburst of practical energy'. In Japan it was patriotic fervour that supplied the impulse to achievement and at the same time made it possible for her to undergo massive material changes without the disruption of social unity. In the end this sentiment was polluted and drove the country to a disastrous indulgence in military aggression. Present-day Japanese have been deeply affected by this experience and have displayed new powers of self-criticism. Yet self-criticism is more likely to chill the ardour of ambition than to inspire practical endeavour. It cannot furnish a clue to the enterprise and self-confident leadership of recent years. Where, then, is an explanation to be found? Japanese writers, teachers, and politicians lament that their country has failed to discover a new source of inspiration or a strong unifying purpose. One may suggest to them that a certain ideological scepticism is to be expected of the victims of an age of faith, and it may be that material progress itself has proved to be a sufficiently absorbing pursuit. Perhaps the explanation is that the challenge presented to Japan after her defeat was of a kind that called forth the full energies of her people and concentrated them on economic achievement. The disaster that had overtaken her former policy was so complete that she was impelled to set out on a new course undistracted by regrets for past ambitions. She may have been fortunate in being left with only a single rational choice in 1945, the acceptance of temporary political subordination and co-operation with her victors in economic rehabilitation. Once she had crossed that threshold she seems to have allowed no regret for the past to haunt her journey into the new world. In this she may be contrasted with Britain, where to a large extent the challenge presented to the nation by post-war problems went unremarked in the confusion of voices, where economically progressive courses received conventional deference rather than the assent of conviction, and where the imperialist past, though outgrown, was still remembered with pleasure.

It cannot be claimed that Japan has entirely escaped internal conflict. She has suffered from numerous and occasionally prolonged industrial disputes. There have been a few occasions of civic disorder. Political stability, although never so far seriously threatened, is not invulnerable to the struggles of factions over Japan's foreign policy in regard to the United States and China, or to the propaganda of new right-wing parties such as that supported by the *Soka Gakkai*, a movement representing those who have failed to share in the benefits of recent progress. As elsewhere, the war interposed a screen between old ways and the

S

new, between the conventions of the middle-aged and the aspira-
tions of the young, and this screen has become more opaque with
the years. In academic circles Marxist ideas have enjoyed a
vogue and the Communist Party, though small, has been asser-
tive. The history of modern Japan suggests, however, that the
ready acceptance of intellectual and political fashions does not
necessarily have much effect on conduct among a people who are
inclined to esteem administrative efficiency more highly than
political principles. Nevertheless it would be rash to predict that
extremist movements on the left or the right would not enlist
considerable support in the event of any deterioration in economic conditions or of a rebuff from outside. But so far, despite
the crumbling of many institutions and conventions once regarded as part of the essential fabric of Japanese life, social unity
has been maintained unimpaired.

Japan today moves with assurance among the most progressive
nations of the world. But the problems which are now emerging
out of the revolutionary economic changes of the last decade are
different in kind from those which have previously confronted
her. Their solution will make heavy demands on her resources of
administrative ingenuity, political wisdom, and social tact. The
problems, economic and political, are for the most part those
with which advanced industrial societies have long been familiar.
Japan has taken her place with them and now shares their per-
plexities. It is yet another question to ask how far the transformation in her economic life will permit the survival of the more
graceful qualities of the old Japan—the fine manners, the eti-
quette that relieves the acerbities of personal relations in a
materialistic society, the aesthetic traditions, the strong sense of
reciprocal obligation among individuals that corresponds to the
recognition of public duty in the West. To such a question, which
is similar to that posed in all countries during periods of rapid
economic progress, no easy answer can be found. There are
Japanese who turn a cold eye on the past and view ancestral
institutions and conventions with indifference or distaste. But
others have been able to combine a liberal and modern outlook
with respect for aesthetic and social traditions. One can at least
hope that their influence will prevail.

Statistical Appendix[1]

TABLE 1

Population, 1930–64*

('*000 persons*)

1930	.	.	.	.	63,900
1935	.	.	.	.	68,700
1940	.	.	.	.	71,400†
1945‡	.	.	.	.	72,200§
1950‡	.	.	.	.	83,200‖
1955	.	.	.	.	89,300‖
1960	.	.	.	.	93,400‖
1964	.	.	.	.	97,200

* The figures are for October in each of the Census years, with the exception of the figure for 1963 which is an estimate. They cover the population, civilian and military, of the four main islands and the small outlying islands.

† Excl. overseas military personnel estimated at over 1 m.

‡ Of the increase of 10,800,000 between 1945 and 1950, the repatriation of Japanese from overseas accounted for over 5 m. (repatriates 6,250,000 less 1,190,000 emigrants—chiefly Koreans and Chinese—from Japan).

§ Excl. overseas military personnel estimated at 3 m.

‖ Excl. Allied military and civilian personnel and their dependants.

TABLE 2

Industrial Distribution of Occupied Population, 1961

('*000 persons*)

Agriculture & forestry	.	.	.	.	13,530
Manufacturing	.	.	.	.	10,160
Mining	.	.	.	.	460
Fishing	.	.	.	.	560
Building & construction	.	.	.	.	2,550
Transport, communications, public utilities	.	2,540
Wholesale & retail trade, finance, etc.	.	.	8,420
Government	.	.	.	.	1,340
Other service industries	.	.	.	5,600
Other industries	.	.	.	.	20
					45,180

Source: Based on Labour Force Survey, the results of which are shown in *Japan. Statist. Yb., 1962*, p. 46. The classification is according to the main occupation and the figures cover persons of 15 years and over. The numbers in agriculture are subject to wide seasonal fluctuations.

[1] The figures in these tables are for calendar years except when there is a specific reference to fiscal years; e.g. F.Y. 1961 covers period from April 1961 to March 1962.

TABLE 3

Number of Farm Households

('000)

Year	Total	Full-time	Part-time I	Part-time II	Estimated number of persons engaged in agriculture and forestry
1935 (Dec.)	5,611	4,164	1,447		14,160
1940 (Dec.)	5,480	3,771	1,709		13,650
1946 (Apr.)	5,698	3,056	1,667	974	—
1950 (Feb.)	6,176	3,086	1,753	1,337	16,530
1955 (Feb.)	6,043	2,106	2,274	1,663	16,040
1960 (Dec.)	5,980	1,854	1,854	2,272	13,910
1962 (Dec.)	5,880	1,529	1,940	2,411	13,110
1963	—	—	—	—	12,400

Source: Ministry of Agriculture & Forestry, *Abstract of Statistics* (annual) and *Japan. Statist. Yb.* Households classified as 'Part-time I' are those for which agriculture is the main occupation, whereas households classified as 'Part-time II' are those for which agriculture is a subsidiary occupation. Estimates of the numbers engaged in agriculture differ widely from one another according to the definition adopted and the period of year to which the estimate applies. In 1960–1 36 per cent of the numbers engaged in agriculture consisted of working proprietors, 60 per cent of unpaid family workers, and 4 per cent of paid employees. Women made up 53 per cent of the total number. The pre-war figures for employment are for December and the post-war figures are averages for the year.

TABLE 4
Indices of Agricultural & Fishery Production
(1933–5 = 100)

Year	Agri-culture general	Rice	Vege-tables	Livestock & products	Fruit	Cocoons	Fisheries
1936	105	112	109	81	96	92	111
1937	111	111	113	107	107	95	105
1938	107	110	108	113	109	84	105
1945	60	65	89	24	63	25	83
1946	77	102	104	30	48	20	53
1947	75	98	96	22	62	16	84
1948	86	104	87	62	89	19	104
1949	93	104	124	87	92	18	86
1950	99	107	131	119	109	24	109
1951	99	100	136	133	93	28	132
1952	111	110	139	154	176	31	171
1953	97	96	123	162	139	28	171

(1950–2 = 100)

Year	Agri-culture general	Rice	Vege-tables	Livestock & products	Fruit	Cocoons	Fisheries
1953	93	86	93	127	97	101	110
1954	103	96	95	149	121	109	120
1955	125	125	111	173	122	124	137
1956	117	110	110	178	168	118	138
1957	122	115	116	189	182	130	161
1958	127	121	115	216	189	128	163
1959	131	126	121	224	203	121	174
1960	133	130	133	247	255	122	182
1961	135	125	131	317	234	126	206
1962	137	131	140	348	234	119	207

Source: Ministry of Agriculture & Forestry, *Abstract of Statistics.*

TABLE 5

(a) Indices of Industrial Production (1934–6 = 100)

Year	Public utilities	Industrial production		
		Total	Mining	Manu-facturing
1937	119	130	118	131
1938	130	142	126	144
1939	137	148	131	149
1940	140	149	143	149
1945	88	60	73	59
1946	109	31	52	29
1947	124	37	67	35
1948	138	55	80	53
1949	155	71	92	69
1950	168	84	97	82
1951	185	114	111	115
1952	201	126	114	128
1953	221	155	123	160
1954	243	167	117	174
1955	263	181	118	189
1956	295	219	130	231

Source: Economic Counsel (Planning) Board, *Japanese Economic Statistics*, Section I, *Industrial Production.* Composite indices weighted by value added in base period.

(b) Indices of Industrial Production (1960 = 100)

Year	All industries	Utilities	Mining	Manu-facturing	Capital goods	Non-durable consumer goods
1935	28·7	22·4	64·8	27·9	12·7	49·3
1937	37·7	26·7	77·9	37·2	22·0	57·8
1940	44·9	31·2	93·3	44·3	36·7	54·0
1946	9·1	26·0	32·7	7·4	6·5	13·9
1950	23·0	38·8	63·6	20·4	15·4	30·2
1952	33·7	44·7	75·5	31·1	25·1	43·5
1953	40·7	48·0	80·9	38·5	31·6	56·6
1954	44·1	51·1	77·9	42·2	35·0	62·1
1955	47·4	54·6	78·3	45·7	34·3	69·0
1956	58·4	62·8	86·5	56·4	49·4	75·5
1957	67·9	70·0	95·4	66·9	68·0	83·0
1958	67·0	74·2	92·5	65·7	61·7	85·9
1959	80·3	85·1	91·6	79·6	72·3	91·8
1960	100·0	100·0	100·0	100·0	100·0	100·0
1961	119·3	116·2	107·0	119·9	130·0	109·0
1962	129·3	123·9	109·4	130·1	143·6	121·5
1963	141·7	138·0	107·6	143·3	153·9	130·8

Source: Ministry of International Trade & Industry. Weights are added values of 1960.

TABLE 6

Indices of Production of Certain Manufactured Goods (1960 = 100)

Year	Ferrous metals	Machin-ery	Ceram-ics	Chemi-cals	Petroleum & coal products	Rubber products	Textiles	Food
1935	19·5	9·0	33·8	22·9	11·8	26·6	70·0	57·5
1937	25·3	15·3	36·7	31·0	15·8	30·4	85·3	64·3
1946	4·3	5·0	9·0	6·0	2·6	6·5	9·1	17·8
1950	22·9	11·9	26·2	20·8	11·1	26·0	26·4	33·5
1955	43·8	28·5	51·2	49·5	39·7	40·5	62·0	77·4
1959	76·3	72·6	79·5	83·2	78·3	80·0	84·8	94·8
1960	100·0	100·0	100·0	100·0	100·0	100·0	100·0	100·0
1961	126·1	129·0	114·4	113·8	120·1	114·0	107·9	108·2
1962	125·5	145·0	126·9	130·0	135·0	126·4	113·5	117·2
1963	140·4	157·2	135·9	151·2	159·8	135·8	122·5	126·0

Source: Ministry of International Trade & Industry.

TABLE 7

Output of Certain Industrial Products

Year	Coal (m. metric tons)	Electricity ('000 m. kwh.)	Steel ingots & castings (m. metric tons	Cement (m. metric tons)	Ships ('000 gross tons)	Radio receiving (m. units)
1937	45	30	5·8	6·1	446	·4
1945	23	22	2·1	1·2	646	·1
1949	38	41	3·1	3·3	140	·6
1950	38	46	4·8	4·5	348	·3
1951	43	48	6·5	6·5	434	·4
1952	43	52	7·0	7·1	608	·9
1953	47	57	7·7	8·8	557	1·4
1954	43	60	7·7	10·7	414	1·4
1955	42	65	9·4	10·6	829	1·8
1956	47	74	11·1	13·0	1,736	3·0
1957	52	81	12·6	15·2	2,432	3·6
1958	50	85	12·1	15·0	2,067	4·9
1959	47	99	16·6	17·3	1,723	10·0
1960	51	115	22·1	22·5	1,725	12·9
1961	54	132	28·3	24·6	1,799	13·7
1962	54	140	27·5	28·8	2,189	14·6
1963	52	160	31·5	29·9	2,367	17·1

Source: Ministry of International Trade & Industry, and *Lloyd's Register of Shipping.*
The figures for ships are for launchings of steel vessels of 100 gross tons and over.
In and after 1954 the figures for radio sets exclude electric gramophones equipped
with radio receivers. The figures for electricity relate to fiscal years.

TABLE 8

Textile Yarn & Fibre Production

(*million lb*)

Year	Pure cotton yarn	Rayon filament	Spun-rayon yarn	Synthetic fibre & yarn	Wool yarn	Raw silk
1935	1,424	224	4	—	133	96
1937	1,586	336	81	—	148	97
1945	43	6	7	—	14	13
1947	266	16	14	—	26	15
1950	518	103	87	1	72	24
1951	712	138	150	7	113	24
1952	748	142	207	8	151	34
1953	861	163	250	13	187	33
1954	932	185	323	21	169	34
1955	827	195	411	35	185	38
1956	1,033	227	515	63	232	41
1957	1,120	268	547	93	256	42
1958	923	186	357	102	205	44
1959	1,010	256	378	178	256	42
1960	1,119	314	475	261	295	40
1961	1,218	311	447	338	317	41
1962	1,023	301	409	403	326	44
1963	1,002	293	405	528	335	40

Source: Toyo Spinning Co., Inst. for Econ. Research, *Statistical Digest of Japanese Textile Industry.*

TABLE 9

Textile Fabrics Production

(million sq. yds)

Year	Cotton	Rayon filament	Spun rayon	Wool	Silk and spun silk
1935	4,112	731	14	323	341
1937	4,826	1,304	263	280	439
1945	55	6	24	6	50
1947	662	46	32	21	38
1950	1,519	397	211	75	97
1951	2,179	487	323	115	118
1952	2,238	497	462	151	194
1953	2,810	595	504	168	170
1954	3,184	660	651	154	183
1955	3,018	774	896	186	209
1956	3,480	921	1,112	220	213
1957	3,841	925	1,358	246	241
1958	3,165	785	1,089	268	216
1959	3,297	871	1,132	324	265
1960	3,853	921	1,265	385	250
1961	4,047	950	1,174	401	195
1962	3,688	789	1,005	398	203
1963	3,515	743	1,027	424	169

Source: As for Table 8. The production of synthetic fabrics (excluding mixtures) in 1963 was estimated at 986 m. sq. yds.

TABLE 10

Changes in the Structure of Manufacturing Industry

(a) *Distribution of employment among various industries*
(*as percentage of total*)

	1930	1937	1954	1959
Textiles	54·6	36·8	21·9	18·5
Metal & metal products	5·5	11·1	12·1	13·3
Machinery & vehicles	10·4	20·9	20·5	24·9
Chemicals	7·4	11·2	13·2	12·2
Food	8·6	6·5	10·8	10·2
Wood products	3·7	3·8	8·6	7·7
Ceramics	3·9	4·2	5·3	5·1
Printing & publishing	3·4	2·4	4·4	4·1
Others	2·4	3·1	3·2	4·0
	100·0	100·0	100·0	100·0

(b) *Distribution of output by gross value*
(*as percentage of total*)

	1930	1937	1954	1959
Textiles	38·0	27·3	17·9	13·4
Metal & metal products	9·6	22·8	16·1	18·4
Machinery & vehicles	10·6	14·3	16·6	23·7
Chemicals	15·3	17·8	18·7	18·4
Food	16·1	9·0	17·2	13·2
Wood products	2·8	2·4	4·9	4·5
Ceramics	2·9	2·7	3·7	3·4
Printing & publishing	3·2	1·7	3·3	2·7
Others	1·5	2·0	1·6	2·3
	100·0	100·0	100·0	100·0

Source: Ministry of International Trade & Industry, *Fifty Years of Industrial Statistics* (Mar. 1963), pp. 18–19. The tables cover workplaces employing 5 or more persons in private industry.

TABLE 11

(*a*) *Size Distribution of Establishments in Manufacturing Industry in 1939*

(*Percentage of workers in each size-group*)

Size of Unit	
Under 5 persons	22·7
5–29 ,,	23·5
30–199 ,,	19·2
Over 200 ,,	34·6
	100·0

Source: E. P. Reubens, 'Small-Scale Industry in Japan', *Q.J. Econ.*, Aug. 1947.

(*b*) *Size Distribution of Establishments in Manufacturing Industry in 1955 and 1960*

(*Percentage of workers and production in each size-group*)

Size of Unit	1955		1960	
	Employment	Output	Employment	Output
3 workers & under	10·0	3·1	6·9	1·9
4–29	31·5	19·1	27·1	14·7
30–99	18·6	17·0	20·5	16·1
100–299	12·9	16·9	15·1	16·5
300–999	12·4	20·4	13·6	20·5
1,000 & over	14·6	23·5	16·8	30·3
	100·0	100·0	100·0	100·0

Source: EPA, *Econ. Survey, 1961–2*, p. 337. The figures of output apply to the value of deliveries.

TABLE 12

Foreign Trade

(a) *Index of volume of trade* (*1934–6 = 100*)

Year	Exports	Imports
1948	8	18
1949	16	28
1950	30	33
1951	31	48
1952	38	61
1953	41	83
1954	55	86
1955	72	90
1956	86	114
1957	95	143
1958	99	117
1959	117	148
1960	132	183
1961	141	240
1962	169	235
1963	190	276

Source: Ministry of Finance.

(b) *Value of Foreign Trade*
(*$ million*)

	Exports (*f.o.b.*)	Imports (*c.i.f.*)
Sept.–Dec.		
1945–6	103	306
1947	174	526
1948	258	684
1949	510	905
1950	820	974
1951	1,355	1,995
1952	1,273	2,028
1953	1,275	2,410
1954	1,629	2,399
1955	2,011	2,471
1956	2,501	3,230
1957	2,858	4,284
1958	2,877	3,033
1959	3,456	3,599
1960	4,055	4,491
1961	4,236	5,810
1962	4,916	5,637
1963	5,448	6,737

Source: Ministry of Finance.

TABLE 13

The Structure of the Export Trade

(*in percentages of total value*)

	1934–6	1954	1956	1959	1963
Textiles & products	52·0	40·3	34·8	29·8	22·8
Raw silk	11·1	2·9	1·7	1·3	0·9
Cotton fabrics	16·5	15·5	10·7	8·4	5·6
Clothing	—	3·4	4·9	6·0	3·9
Metals & metal products	8·2	15·3	13·6	11·6	17·3
Machinery & vehicles	7·2	12·4	19·3	23·4	27·1
Textile machinery	0·4	2·8	1·5	1·0	1·0
Sewing machines	—	1·9	1·4	1·5	1·0
Ships	—	3·5	10·4	10·6	6·2
Food & drink	9·5	8·3	7·2	7·6	5·3
Chemicals	4·3	4·8	4·3	4·8	5·8
Ceramics	2·9	3·9	4·1	1·7	1·3
Toys	0·9	1·9	2·2	2·2	1·6
Other goods	15·0	13·1	14·5	18·9	18·8
	100·0	100·0	100·0	100·0	100·0

TABLE 14

The Structure of the Import Trade

(*in percentages of total value*)

	1934–6	1954	1956	1959	1963
Food	23·3	27·3	17·3	13·8	16·1
Textile materials	31·8	26·6	24·7	18·2	13·1
Petroleum & coal	4·9	11·1	12·8	15·5	18·0
Iron ore & steel scrap	3·2	4·6	10·2	13·8	8·0
Machinery	4·7	7·4	5·0	9·8	11·9
Others	32·1	23·0	30·0	32·9	32·9
	100·0	100·0	100·0	100·0	100·0

Source: Ministry of Finance.

TABLE 15

(*a*) *Changes in Export Markets*
(*in percentages of total exports*)

	1934–6	1954	1956	1959	1963
United States	17	17	22	30	28
China (mainland)	18	1	2	—	1
Korea & Formosa	21	8	6	4	5
South East Asia	19	30	26	22	22
Europe (incl. USSR)	8	9	10	11	16
Other countries	17	34	34	33	28
	100	100	100	100	100

(*b*) *Changes in Sources of Imports*
(*in percentages of total imports*)

	1934–6	1954	1956	1959	1963
United States	25	35	33	31	31
China (mainland)	12	2	3	1	1
Korea & Formosa	24	3	2	2	2
South East Asia	16	19	19	16	15
Europe (incl. USSR)	10	8	7	10	13
Other countries	15	33	36	40	38
	100	100	100	100	100

Source: Ministry of Finance.

TABLE 16

Textile Exports

	1934–6 (ann. av.)	1954	1956	1963
Raw silk (m. lb)	68·9	10·2	10·0	8·4
Cotton yarn (m. lb)	52·9	29·5	27·3	32·2
Silk fabrics (m. sq. yds)	84·8	25·9	47·9	49·2
Cotton fabrics (m. sq. yds)	2,944·5	1,278·1	1,262·0	1,205·5
Wool fabrics (m. sq. yds)	39·5	12·1	22·3	44·2
Rayon filament fabrics (m. sq. yds)	502·5	264·0	438·1	233·3
Spun-rayon fabrics (m. sq. yds)	16·8*	302·6	695·2	450·5

* 1937.

Source: Toyo Spinning Co., Inst. for Econ. Research, *Statist. Digest of Japanese Cotton Industry*, and Ministry of Finance. Synthetic fibre exports in 1963 were 224m. sq. yds.

TABLE 17

Transport

(a) *Mercantile Marine*
('*000 gross tons*)

1935	3,759
1939	5,729
1941	6,094
1945	1,344
1950	1,711
1955	3,395
1959	5,853
1960	6,478
1961	7,313
1962	8,478
1964	9,125

Source: Statistical Yearbook of Japanese Empire (pre-war) and *Japan Statist. Yb.* (post-war). The figures for 1935, 1939, and 1964 are for March, the rest are December. Figures cover registration of steel ships of 100 gross tons and over in Japan Proper. In August 1945 it is estimated that only 557,000 gross tons were operable (see Cohen, *Japan's Economy*, p. 267).

(b) *Motor Vehicles Registered*
('*000*)

End of fiscal year	Trucks & buses	Private cars standard size	Motor-cycles, 3-wheelers, & scooters
1936	123	52	18
1953	559	124	430
1955	728	157	582
1958	1,081	269	998
1959	1,224	331	1,278
1960	1,379	440	1,679
1961	1,609	602	2,141
1964	1,856	789	2,398

Source: Automobile Bureau of Ministry of Communications.

Table 18

Prices, Wages, and Consumption

(a) *Wholesale Price Index*

($1934-6=1$)

Average for year		Average for year	
1946	16	1955	343
1947	48	1956	358
1948	128	1957	369
1949	209	1958	345
1950	247	1959	348
1951	343	1960	352
1952	349	1961	356
1953	352	1962	350
1954	349	1963	356

Source: Bank of Japan, *Econ. Statist.*

(b) *Consumer Price Index (All Cities)*

($1960=100$)

Average for year		Average for year	
1949	73	1957	96
1950	68	1958	96
1951	79	1959	97
1952	83	1960	100
1953	88	1961	105
1954	94	1962	113
1955	93	1963	121
1956	93		

Source: As above.

(c) *Real Wage Index, Manufacturing Industry*

($1955=100$)

Average for year		Average for year	
1952	92	1958	112
1953	96	1959	120
1954	95	1960	125
1955	100	1961	132
1956	109	1962	136
1957	109	1963	140

Source: Employment Statistics Section, Ministry of Labour. The index covers all cash earnings and applies to workers in establishments with 30 or more regular employees.

(*d*) *Index of Family Consumption*
(1934–$6 = 100$)

Average for year	Urban	Rural
1952	80	118
1953	94	125
1954	100	129
1955	107	130
1956	112	134
1957	117	135
1958	124	138
1959	131	144
1960	137	154
1961	146	166
1962	155	177
1963	163	188

Source: EPA.

TABLE 19

Movements of Wages & Productivity in Manufacturing Industry
(*Percentage increases over previous year*)

Year	Nominal wages	Physical productivity
1955	3·9	—
1956	9·3	12·6
1957	3·3	5·7
1958	2·4	6·0
1959	7·3	9·1
1960	7·9	8·7 (12·9)
1961	11·8	8·3 (10·2)
1962	10·0	2·9 (2·8)
1963	10·8	— (8·5)

Source: The Ministry of Labour's productivity index, which is the basis of the figures in the third column above, is derived by dividing the production index of the Ministry of International Trade and Industry by the Ministry of Labour's employment index of workers employed by establishments normally employing 30 or more workers. The figures for wages cover gross amounts of cash payments and are from the Ministry of Labour's *Monthly Labour Statistics*. The figures are averages for each year, except for 1963 where they apply to the first five months. The figures in brackets are estimates made by the Japan Productivity Centre. According to the EPA, *Econ. Statist. of Jap.*, Sept. 1962, pp. 8–9, the productivity index in 1961 was 159.0 and the wage index 150·2 (base year 1955 in each case).

TABLE 20

Foreign Income from American Aid & 'Special Procurement'

($ *million*)

Year	Aid	Special procurement	Value of imports
Sept.–Dec. 1945–6	193	—	306
1947	404	—	526
1948	461	—	684
1949	535	—	905
1950	361	149	974
1951	164	592	1,995
1952	—	824	2,028
1953	—	809	2,410
1954	—	596	2,399
1955	—	557	2,471
1956	—	595	3,230
1957	—	549	4,284
1958	—	476	3,033
1959	—	464	3,599
1960	—	539	4,491
1961	—	449	5,810
1962	—	376	5,637
1963	—	347	6,736

Source: Bank of Japan, *Foreign Exchange Statistics*, and EPA. 'Special procurement' includes Allied military expenditure in dollars and pounds, yen purchases for Joint Defence Account, expenditure of Allied soldiers and civilians in Japan, and payments in respect of certain off-shore procurement contracts.

TABLE 21

Invisible Trade : Current Balance

(a) Receipts

Fiscal year	U.S. security forces	Transport	Interest, dividends, commissions	Overseas travel	Other items	Total
1957	398	124	42	23	73	660
1958	374	93	34	29	78	608
1959	349	114	58	38	92	651
1960	402	97	78	47	99	723
1961	373	138	100	59	134	804
1962	363	137	110	59	157	826

(b) Payments

Fiscal year	Transport	Interest, dividends, commissions	Royalties	Overseas travel	Other items	Total	Balance
1957	271	72	36	17	119	515	+145
1958	206	76	46	18	131	477	+131
1959	288	95	60	25	145	613	+ 38
1960	321	118	94	51	213	796	− 73
1961	377	176	111	59	220	943	−139
1962	351	236	113	61	290	1,051	−225

Source : EPA, *Econ. Survey, 1961–2,* p. 59; *1962–3,* p. 332.

T*

TABLE 22

Gold and Foreign Exchange Reserves

($ *million*)

1952 Mar.	930	1958 Dec.	861
1953 ,,	913	1959 ,,	1,322
1954 ,,	637	1960 ,,	1,824
1955 ,,	738	1961 ,,	1,486
1956 Dec.	941	1962 ,,	1,841
1957 ,,	524	1963 ,,	1,878

Source: Ministry of Finance. The figures cover gold and *convertible* foreign currency held by the Government and the Bank of Japan. They are not comparable with the figures of foreign-exchange reserves quoted in ch. IV; those reserves included inconvertible as well as convertible currencies.

TABLE 23

Changes in the National Income ($1934-6 = 100$)

Fiscal year	Real national income	Real income a head
1946	57	52
1947	60	53
1948	71	61
1949	82	69
1950	97	80
1951	107	87
1952	117	94
1953	124	98
1954	128	100
1955	142	110
1956	156	119
1957	167	126
1958	176	131
1959	204	151
1960	234	172
1961	264	192
1962	277	201
1963	311	224

Source: EPA, *Econ. Statist.*, Sept. 1962; and *Japan Statist. Tb.*

TABLE 24

Estimates of Rates of (Real) Economic Growth
(*Percentage increase on previous year's GNP*)

Fiscal year	Per cent	Fiscal year	Per cent
1947	10·0	1956	9·0
1948	16·4	1957	7·9
1949	3·9	1958	3·2
1950	12·2	1959	17·9
1951	13·5	1960	13·2
1952	10·5	1961	14·0
1953	6·7	1962	5·9
1954	3·3	1963	12·3
1955	10·3		

Source: Economic Planning Agency.

TABLE 25

Ratio of Gross Domestic Investment to Gross National Expenditure
(*percentage*)

Fiscal year	Total	Producers' equipment	Govt fixed investment	Changes in stocks	Private housing
1946	22·2	7·8	5·5	6·7	2·2
1947	26·4	7·2	7·9	9·9	1·7
1948	28·2	7·9	6·9	11·5	1·8
1949	24·6	8·5	6·9	8·2	1·0
1950	25·5	9·9	6·2	7·9	1·5
1951	30·6	11·2	6·5	11·6	1·3
1952	27·4	11·6	7·2	7·1	1·6
1953	27·9	11·3	8·9	5·9	1·8
1954	23·4	10·2	8·1	3·3	1·8
1955	25·3	9·4	7·1	7·1	1·7
1956	31·8	14·8	7·1	7·8	2·1
1957	31·8	16·8	8·1	4·7	2·2
1958	27·2	15·9	8·8	0·3	2·3
1959	35·0	17·3	8·6	7·0	2·2
1960	38·2	20·9	8·9	6·0	2·3
1961	42·6	22·9	9·7	7·5	2·5
1962	37·1	19·8	11·5	3·0	2·8

Source: Econ. Statist., Sept. 1962, p. 3, and *Japanese Econ. Statist.*, Mar. 1963, p. 59.

TABLE 26

Main Features of the Income Doubling Plan

(values at 1958 prices)

	Average Fiscal year 1956–8	Estimates Fiscal year 1970
Population (m.)	91·1	102·2
Population aged 15 & over (m.)	62·2	79·0
Population at work (m.)	41·5	48·7
Gross National Product ('000 m. yen)	9,743	26,000
National income a head (yen)	87,736	208,600
Gross capital formation ('000 m. yen)	2,947	8,283
Industrial production index	100	432
Agriculture, forestry, & fishery production index	100	144
Exports (US $ m.)	2,701	9,320
Imports (US $ m.)	3,126	9,891
Energy demand (in coal equivalents—'000 tons)	131,815 (1959)	320,760

Postscript to Table

In the first three years of the Income Doubling Plan (F.Y. 1961–3) the average annual real growth-rate was 10·7 per cent, compared with 9 per cent as predicted for those years by the Plan and with 7·2 per cent as predicted for the whole decade. In 1964 a Medium-Range Economic Plan covering the five fiscal years 1964–8 was drawn up, with estimates of growth-rates revised in the light of experience and current expectations. The average annual (real) growth-rate for this period was put at 8·1 per cent. If this is achieved, then by 1968 GNP will have exceeded the original estimate for 1970 (27,900 million yen at 1958 prices compared with 26,000 million yen). Exports are required to increase at an annual rate of 11·8 per cent (9·3 per cent in the original Plan).

Select Bibliography

I. JAPANESE OFFICIAL OR SEMI-OFFICIAL PUBLICATIONS[1]

Bank of Japan. *Economic Statistics Monthly.*
—— *Economic Statistics of Japan.* Annual.
—— *Outline of Financial System in Japan.* 1953.
—— *Recommendations of the Committee on Financial System: Research concerning the System of the Bank of Japan and Explanation.* 1960.
—— *Excessive Dependence of Commercial Banks on Central Bank Loans in Japanese Economic Development,* by T. Yoshino. 1960.
—— *Money and Banking in Japan.* Mar., 1961.
—— *The Bank of Japan: its Function and Organization.* Mar. 1962.
—— *A Short History of the Bank of Japan.* 1962.
—— Foreign Capital Research Society. *Japanese Industry.* 1953, 1954.
—— —— *Statistical Data and Principal Cases of Foreign Capital Investment in Japan.* 1953–6.
Economic Planning Agency.[2] *Economic Planning in Japan,* by S. Okita. 1961.
—— *Economic Survey of Japan.* Annual.
—— *Japanese Economic Statistics.* Monthly.
—— *Economic Statistics of Japan.* Sept. 1962.
—— *New Long-Range Economic Plan of Japan, 1958–62.* 1957.
—— *New Long-Range Economic Plan of Japan, 1961–70.* 1961.
—— *Outline of Regional Development Programmes in Japan.* July 1961.
—— —— Economic Research Institute. *An Analysis of Deposits, Loans and Liquidity of Japanese Banks.* July 1962.
—— —— *Economic Growth and Agriculture.* Apr. 1962.
—— —— *Employment Structure and Business Fluctuations.* July 1959.
Economic Stabilization Board. *Annual Report for Japan to Food and Agriculture Organization.* 1951.
Fair Trade Commission. *Laws, Orders and Regulations relating to Foreign Investment in Japan.* Apr. 1963.
Holding Company Liquidation Commission. *Final Report on Zaibatsu Dissolution.* July 1951.
—— *Laws, Rules and Regulations concerning the Reconstruction and Democratization of the Japanese Economy.* 1949.
—— *Report on Restrictive Practices to the United Nations.* n.d.

---

[1] Published in Tokyo.
[2] This body has been known under different names: the Economic Stabilization Board before 1953, the Economic Counsel Board, 1953–5, and the Economic Planning Board, 1955–7.

Japan Development Bank. *Activities and Functions*. 1960.
—— *Annual Financial Statements*.
—— *Annual Reports*.
—— *Japan Development Bank Law and Articles of Incorporation*. 1962.
—— *Prospectus for External Loan Bond Issue*. New York, Jan. 1963.
Japan External Trade Organization. *Foreign Trade of Japan*. Annual.
Ministry of Agriculture and Forestry. *Abstract of Statistics on Agriculture, Forestry and Fisheries*. Annual.
—— *Annual Report on the State of Agriculture*.
—— *International Comparisons of Productivity in Agriculture*. Paper by K. Ohkawa. 1949.
—— *Japan's Agricultural Basic Law*. 1962.
—— *The Land Reform in Japan*. Paper by Y. Kondo. 1952.
—— National Research Institute of Agriculture. *Summary Report of Researches, 1946–8*. 1951.
—— —— *Summary Report of Researches, 1949*. 1952.
Ministry of Education. *Education in Japan*. 1961.
Ministry of Finance. *General Survey of the Japanese Economy*. 1953.
—— *Monthly Return of Foreign Trade of Japan*.
—— *Quarterly Bulletin of Financial Statistics*.
Ministry of Foreign Affairs. *The Rehabilitation of Japan's Economy and Asia*, by S. Okita. 1956.
Ministry of International Trade and Industry. *Foreign Trade of Japan*. Annual.
—— *A Guide Book on Agricultural Machinery and Implements in Japan*. 1954.
—— *Fifty Years of Industrial Statistics*. Mar. 1963. (Wholly Japanese text.)
Ministry of Labour. *Japan Labour Code*. 1953.
—— *Japan Labour Year Book*.
—— *Labour Conditions in the Japanese Textile Industry*. 1952.
—— *Yearbook of Labour Statistics and Research*.
—— *Monthly Labour Statistics and Research Bulletin*.
—— Vocational Training Bureau. *Present Situation of Vocational Training in Japan*. 1961.
—— *Wage Problems in Japan*. 1962.
Prime Minister's Office. *Japan Statistical Yearbook*. Annual (post-war).
—— *Statistical Year-book of the Japanese Empire*. Annual (pre-war).
Statistical Standards Bureau, Administrative Management Agency. *Supplement to Monthly Statistics of Japan: Explanatory Notes*. Jan. 1963.

2. OTHER PUBLICATIONS

(a) *Economic Development before 1945*
Ackerman, E. A. *Japan's Natural Resources and Their Relation to Japan's Economic Future*. Chicago Univ. Press, 1953.

Allen, G. C. *A Short Economic History of Modern Japan.* London, Allen & Unwin, 1962.
—— *Japanese Industry: its Recent Development and Present Condition.* New York, Institute of Pacific Relations, 1940.
—— and A. G. Donnithorne. *Western Enterprise in Far Eastern Economic Development: China and Japan.* London, Allen & Unwin, 1954.
Cohen, J. B. *Japan's Economy in War and Reconstruction.* Minneapolis, University of Minnesota Press, 1949.
Columbia University, American Assembly Graduate School of Business. *The United States and the Far East.* New York, 1956.
Cowan, C. D., ed. *The Economic Development of China and Japan.* London, Allen & Unwin, 1964.
Farley, M. S. *Aspects of Japan's Labor Problems.* New York, Day, 1950.
Haring, D. G., ed. *Japan's Prospect.* Cambridge, Mass., Harvard University Press, 1946.
Ishii, R. *Population Pressure and Economic Life in Japan.* London, 1937.
Johnston, B. F. *Japanese Food Management in World War II.* California, Stanford Univ. Press, 1953.
Jones, F. C. *Manchuria since 1931.* London, Royal Institute of International Affairs, 1949.
Lockwood, W. W. *The Economic Development of Japan.* Princeton University Press, 1954.
Ohkawa, K. *The Growth Rate of the Japanese Economy Since 1878.* Tokyo, Kinokuniya, 1957.
Rosovsky, H. *Capital Formation in Japan, 1868–1940.* Glencoe, Ill., Free Press, 1958.
Schumpeter, E. B., ed. *The Industrialization of Japan and Manchukuo, 1930–40.* New York, Macmillan, 1941.
Shinohara, M. *Growth and Cycles in the Japanese Economy.* Tokyo, Kinokuniya, 1962.
Taeuber, I. B. *The Population of Japan.* Princeton Univ. Press, 1958.
United States Dept. of Commerce. *Japanese Banking,* by H. M. Bratter. Washington, 1931.
Uyeda, T., and associates. *The Small Industries of Japan.* New York, Institute of Pacific Relations, 1938.

(b) The Japanese Economy after 1945
Abegglen, J. G. *The Japanese Factory.* Glencoe, Ill., Free Press, 1958.
All-Japan Cotton Spinners' Association. *Labour Situation of the Cotton Spinning Industry in Japan.* Osaka, 1955.
—— *Monthly Report of Japanese Cotton Spinning Industry.* Osaka.
Asia Kyokai. *The Smaller Industry in Japan.* Tokyo, 1957.
Ayusawa, I. F. 'The Labour Problem in Japan', *Japan Quarterly* (Tokyo), Oct.–Dec. 1954.

Baba, K. 'Dynamic Analysis of Agricultural Income in Japan', *Hitotsubashi Journal of Economics* (Tokyo), Mar. 1962.

Beika, M. 'The Structure of Industrial Districts in Japan', *Kobe Economic and Business Review*, 1956.

Bisson, T. A. *Zaibatsu Dissolution in Japan.* Berkeley, Univ. of California Press, 1954.

Central Raw Silk Association of Japan. *Raw Silk Statistical Monthly* (Tokyo).

Cohen, J. B. *Japan's Postwar Economy.* Bloomington, Indiana Univ. Press, 1954.

'Consider Japan', *The Economist* (London), 1 and 8 Sept. 1962.

Danno, N., *see* Japan Institute of Pacific Relations.

Dore, R. P. *Land Reform in Japan.* London, Oxford Univ. Press, 1959.

—— 'Beyond the Land Reform', *Pacific Affairs* (Vancouver), Autumn 1963.

Ehrlich, E. E. and F. M. Tamagna. 'Japan', in B. H. Beckhart, ed., *Banking Systems.* New York, 1954.

Fair Trade Institute. *Fair Trade.* Tokyo, Sept. 1956.

Fuji Bank Bulletin (Tokyo). Quarterly.

—— *Banking in Modern Japan.* Tokyo, 1961.

Fujii, S. *Japan's Trade and Her Level of Living.* Tokyo, Science Council of Japan, 1955. (Econ. ser. 6.)

—— 'Structure of Japan's Export Trade and its Problems', *Pakistan Development Review* (Karachi), Winter 1962.

Fujioka, M. 'Appraisal of Japan's Plan to Double Income', *IMF Staff Papers* (Washington), Mar. 1963.

Hadley, E. M. 'Trust-Busting in Japan', *Harvard Business Review*, July 1948.

Hax, K. *Japan, Wirtschaftsmacht des Fernen Osten.* Cologne, Westdeutscher Verlag, 1961.

Horie, S. *Banking System and Bank Liquidity in Japan*; report to International Credit Conference, Rome, Oct. 1951. Tokyo, 1952, mimeo.

Hitotsubashi University. *Annals of Hitotsubashi Academy*, cont. from Oct. 1960 as *Hitotsubashi Journal of Economics* and *Hitotsubashi Journal of Commerce and Management* (Tokyo). Quarterly.

Inaba, N. 'Integration of Enterprises', *Annals of School of Business Administration* (Kobe), 1960.

Industrial Bank of Japan. *Industrial and Financial Statistics.* Tokyo, half-yearly.

—— *List of Principal Japanese Companies.* Tokyo, various dates.

—— *Survey of Japanese Finance and Industry.* Tokyo, quarterly.

—— *Long-Term Credit Banking System of Japan.* Dec. 1957.

Inouye, T. 'Note on the Zaibatsu Combines', *Kobe Economic and Business Review*, 1956.
International Management Association of Japan. *Materials on Management and Economy of Japan*. Tokyo, Nov. 1962, mimeo.
International Labour Office. *Problems of Wage Policy in Asian Countries*. Geneva, 1953.
Japan Chemical Fibres Association. *Rayon and Synthetic Fibres of Japan*. Tokyo, 1963.
Japan Federation of Employers' Associations. *Analysis of Personnel Practices in Principal Industries of Japan*. Tokyo, Apr. 1953.
—— *On the Present Conditions of the Labour Movement in Japan*. Tokyo, 1953.
—— *Outline of the Post-War Trade Union Movement in Japan*. Tokyo, 1951.
Japan FAO Association. *Agriculture in Japan*. Tokyo, 1953.
—— *Agriculture at the Cross-roads*. Tokyo, 1961.
—— *A Strategy for New Agriculture*. Tokyo, 1962.
Japan Institute of Labour. *Japan Labour Bulletin* (Tokyo). Monthly.
Japan Institute of Pacific Relations. Data Papers Presented to 12th Conference of Institute of Pacific Relations, Kyoto, 1954:
Arisawa, H. *Level of Living in Japan*.
Danno, N. *Japanese Agriculture since the Post-War Agrarian Reform*.
Fujibayashi, K. *A Bird's-Eye View of the Labour Movement in Post-War Japan*.
Miyashita, T. *Observations on Trade Relations between Japan and China*.
Morika, Y. *Changes in Standard of Living*.
Ohkawa, K. *Level and Standard of Living in Post-War Japan*.
Okazaki, A. *The Present and Future of Japan's Population*.
Japan Iron and Steel Federation. *The Iron and Steel Industry of Japan*. Tokyo, 1952.
—— *The Iron and Steel Industry: Recent Developments and Labour Conditions*. Tokyo, 1952.
—— *Statistical Year Book*. Tokyo.
Japan Silk Association. *The Raw Silk Industry of Japan*. Tokyo, 1953.
Jiji Press Ltd. *Japan Trade Guide*. Tokyo, 1963, 1964.
Kawata, F. *Japan's Iron and Steel Industry, 1953-4*. Tokyo, Foreign Service, 1954.
—— 'Japan's Trade with South and South East Asian Countries', *Kobe Economic and Business Review*, 1953.
—— 'World Trade and Japan's Export', *Kobe Economic and Business Review*, 1962.
Kishimoto, E. 'A Short History of the Labour Movement in Japan', *Kyoto University Economic Review*, Apr. 1951.
Kondo, Y., see Ministry of Agriculture, p. 285 above.

Kyoto University Economic Review. Quarterly.

Koizumi, A. 'The Overloan Problem', *Hitotsubashi Journal of Commerce and Management*, Nov. 1962.

Levine, S. B. *Industrial Relations in Postwar Japan.* Univ. of Illinois, 1958.

Meade, J. E. 'Japan and the General Agreement on Tariffs and Trade', *Three Banks Review* (London), June 1957.

Mitsubishi Economic Research Institute. *Mitsui, Mitsubishi, Sumitomo.* Tokyo, 1955.

—— *Survey of Economic Conditions in Japan.* Tokyo, monthly.

Miyata, K. 'The Position of Japan in the Asian Economy', *Kobe University International Review*, 1953.

—— 'Trade Liberalisation and Japan's Economy', *Kwansai Gakuin University Annual Series.* Kobe, Nov. 1962.

Nose, M. 'A Research into Wage Income in Post-War Japan', *Kobe Economic and Business Review*, 1953.

Ogura, T., ed. *Agricultural Development in Modern Japan.* Tokyo, Japan FAO Association, 1963.

Ohkawa, K. 'Economic Growth and Agriculture', *Annals of the Hitotsubashi Academy*, Oct. 1956. (*See also* under Japan Inst. of Pacific Relations.)

Okazaki, A., *see under* Japan Institute of Pacific Relations.

Okita, S. *Japan's Trade with Asia.* Reprinted from *Contemporary Japan*, xxii/10–12. Tokyo, 1954.

—— *Economic Growth of Postwar Japan.* Tokyo, Institute of Asian Economic Affairs, 1962.

—— 'Sino-Japanese Trade and Japan's Economic Growth', in E. F. Szczepanik, ed., *Economic and Social Problems of the Far East.* Hong Kong, 1961.

Oriental Economist. Tokyo, monthly.

Oriental Economist. *Japan Economic Year Book.* Tokyo.

Ozaki, C. *Farm Household Economy Survey in Japan : Agriculture, Forestry and Fisheries.* Productivity Conference. Tokyo, 1958.

Pacific Affairs. Vancouver, quarterly.

Reubens, E. P. 'Small Scale Industry in Japan', *Quarterly Journal of Economics* (Cambridge, Mass.), Aug. 1947.

Schiffer, H. F. *The Modern Japanese Banking System.* New York, Univ. Publishers Inc., 1962.

Seki, K. *The Cotton Industry of Japan.* Tokyo, Japan Society for the Promotion of Science, 1956.

Shibata, G. 'The Present Status of Japan's Shipping', *Kobe Economic and Business Review*, 1956.

Shindo, T. *Labour in the Japanese Cotton Industry.* Tokyo, Japan Society for the Promotion of Science, 1961.

Shinohara, M. 'Factors in Japan's Economic Growth', *Hitotsubashi Journal of Economics*, Feb. 1964.
—— 'Relative Production Levels of Industrial Countries and their Growth Potentials', *Weltwirtschaftliches Archiv*, lxxvi/1, 1961.
—— 'Some Causes and Consequences of Economic Growth in Japan', *Malayan Economic Review*, Apr. 1961.
—— *Survey of Japanese Literature on the Small Industry*. Tokyo, Hitotsubashu Univ., 1964.
Shiomi, S. *Japan's Finance and Taxation, 1940–56*. New York, Columbia Univ. Press, 1957.
Shionoya, T. *Problems Surrounding the Revision of the Bank of Japan Law*. Nagoya, Beckhart Foundation, 1962.
Society for Economic Cooperation in Asia. *The Major Industry and its Technique in Japan*. Tokyo, 1954.
—— *The Smaller Industry in Japan*. Tokyo, 1954.
Sumitomo Bank Review (Osaka). Quarterly.
Taira, K. 'The Character of the Japanese Labour Markets', *Economic Development and Cultural Change* (Chicago), Jan. 1962.
—— 'The Dynamics of Industrial Relations in Early Japanese Development', *Labour Law Journal* (Chicago), July 1962.
—— 'The Inter-Sectoral Wage Differential in Japan, 1881–1959', *Journal of Farm Economics*, May 1962.
Tokyo Foreign Service. *Japan's Iron and Steel Industry*. Tokyo, annual.
Toyo Spinning Company, Inst. for Economic Research. *Cotton Industry Wages in Japan*. Osaka, 1955.
—— *Statistical Digest of Japanese Textile Industry*. Osaka.
Tsuru, S. *Essays on Japanese Economy*. Tokyo, Kinokuniya, 1958.
—— 'Business Cycles in Post-War Japan', in International Economic Association, *The Business Cycle in the Post-War World*, ed. by E. Lundberg. London, Macmillan, 1955.
Uchida, K. 'Japan's Foreign Trade after the War', *Bulletin of University of Osaka Prefecture*, 1957.
—— 'Trading Firms of Japan', *Bulletin of University of Osaka Prefecture*, 1958.
Unemura, M. 'An Analysis of Employment Structure in Japan', *Hitotsubashi Journal of Economics*, Mar. 1962.
—— 'Structure of Commerce in Japan', *Bulletin of University of Osaka Prefecture*, 1962.
United Nations: *Monthly Bulletin of Statistics* (New York).
—— Economic Commission for Asia and the Far East. *Economic Survey of Asia and the Far East*. Bangkok, annual.
White, H. *Japanese Aid*. London, Overseas Development Institute, 1964.
Yamamoto, H. 'Can the Anti-Monopoly Legislation Preserve Competition?', *Bulletin of University of Osaka Prefecture*, 1957.

290Select Bibliography

—— 'The Recovery Method of the Japanese Shipping Industry in the Post-War World', *Kobe Economic and Business Review*, 1954.

Yamanaka, T., ed. *Small Business in Japan*. Tokyo, Japan Times, 1960.

Yawata Iron and Steel Company. *Guide to Japan's Iron and Steel Industry*. Tokyo, 1953.

ADDENDA

Bienfait, J. *La Sidérurgie japonaise*. Lausanne, Centre de Recherches Européenes, 1965.

OECD. *Japan*. Paris, July 1964.

Sakurabayashi, M. and E. Nagasawa. 'Inter-Firm Wage Differentials in Postwar Japan', *Monumenta Nipponica* (Tokyo), vol. xviii, 1963.

Small Business Finance Corporation. *Outline Description*. Sept. 1964.

Index